Exploring IBM Technology and Products

Other titles of interest from Maximum Press

Building Intranets with Lotus Notes & Domino: Krantz, 1-885068-10-7

Marketing on the Internet, Second Edition: Mathiesen, 1-885068-09-3

Exploring IBM Client/Server Computing: Bolthouse, 1-885068-04-2

Real World Client/Server: Krantz, 0-9633214-7-1

Dr. Livingstone's Online Shopping Safari Guidebook: Fiore, 1-885068-07-7

Exploring IBM Personal Computers, Ninth Edition: Hoskins, Wilson, 1-885068-12-3

Exploring IBM RS/6000 Computers, Seventh Edition: Hoskins, Pinkerton, 1-885068-14-X

Exploring IBM AS/400 Computers, Seventh Edition: Hoskins, Dimmick, 1-885068-13-1

Exploring the IBM AS/400 Advanced 36, Second Edition: Hoskins, Dimmick; 1-885068-11-5

Exploring IBM's New Age Mainframes: 1-885068-05-0, Young

Exploring the PowerPC Revolution! Second Edition: Hoskins, 1-885068-02-6

Exploring IBM Print on Demand Technology: Wallace, 1-885068-06-9

What About ProductManager? Curtis, 0-9633214-4-7

For more information, visit our World Wide Web site at:
http://www.maxpress.com
or e-mail us at *moreinfo@maxpress.com*

Exploring IBM Technology and Products

Edited by Jim Hoskins

MAXIMUM PRESS
605 Silverthorn Road
Gulf Breeze, FL 32561
(850) 934-0819
www.maxpress.com
moreinfo@maxpress.com

Publisher: Jim Hoskins
Manager of Finance/Administration: Donna Tryon
Production Manager: ReNae Grant
Cover Design: Lauren Smith Designs
Compositor: PageCrafters Inc.
Copy Editor: Janis Paris
Proofreader: Julie Cameron
Indexer: Janis Paris
Printer: Malloy Lithographing

This publication is designed to provide accurate and authoritative information in regard to the subject matter covered. It is sold with the understanding that the publisher is not engaged in rendering professional services. If legal, accounting, medical, psychological, or any other expert assistance is required, the services of a competent professional person should be sought. ADAPTED FROM A DECLARATION OF PRINCIPLES OF A JOINT COMMITTEE OF THE AMERICAN BAR ASSOCIATION AND PUBLISHERS.

Copyright 1998 by Maximum Press.

All rights reserved. Published simultaneously in Canada.

Reproduction or translation of any part of this work beyond that permitted by Section 107 or 108 of the 1976 United States Copyright Act without the permission of the copyright owner is unlawful. Requests for permission or further information should be addressed to the Permissions Department, Maximum Press.

Recognizing the importance of preserving what has been written, it is a policy of Maximum Press to have books of enduring value published in the United States printed on acid-free paper, and we exert our best efforts to that end.

Library of Congress Cataloging-in-Publication Data

    Hoskins, Jim.

        Exploring IBM technology and products / Jim Hoskins and others.

        p. cm.

        Includes index.

        ISBN 1-885068-29-8 (pbk.)

        1. IBM computers. 2. Computer networks. I. Title.

    QA76.8.I1015H66 1998

    004--dc21   97-45261

                                  CIP

Acknowledgements

Hats off to David Bolthouse, Doug Davies, Roger Dimmick, Cheryl Endres, Jim Fletcher, Dave Pinkerton, Bill Wilson, and John Young for their contributions to this work.

Disclaimer

The purchase of computer software or hardware is an important and costly business decision. While the author and publisher of this book have made reasonable efforts to ensure the accuracy and timeliness of the information contained herein, the author and publisher assume no liability with respect to loss or damage caused or alleged to be caused by reliance on any information contained herein and disclaim any and all warranties, expressed or implied, as to the accuracy or reliability of said information.

This book is not intended to replace the manufacturer's product documentation or personnel in determining the specifications and capabilities of the products mentioned in this book. The manufacturer's product documentation should always be consulted, as the specifications and capabilities of computer hardware and software products are subject to frequent modification. The reader is solely responsible for the choice of computer hardware and software. All configurations and applications of computer hardware and software should be reviewed with the manufacturer's representatives prior to choosing or using any computer hardware and software.

Trademarks

The words contained in this text which are believed to be trademarked, service marked, or otherwise to hold proprietary rights have been designated as such by use of initial capitalization. No attempt has been made to designate as trademarked or service marked any personal computer words or terms in which proprietary rights might exist. Inclusion, exclusion, or definition of a word or term is not intended to affect, or to express judgement upon, the validity of legal status of any proprietary right which may be claimed for a specific word or term.

Table of Contents

Introduction xii
    What This Book Is xii
    What This Book Is Not xiii
    How to Use This Book xiii
    Your "Members Only" Web Site xiv

Chapter 1: Network Computing Basics   1

What Is the Internet? 1
    Where Did the Internet Come From? 2
    It's About Content 5
    What About Online Services? 5
    What Are People Doing Right Now? 6
IBM's Network Computing Vision 10
    Why Does IBM Like the Internet So Much? 10
    Where Do Intranets Fit In? 15
IBM's E-Business Strategy 17
    Internet Commerce 19
        Marketing 20
        Sales 21
        Customer Services 22
        Net.Commerce 23
    Intranets and Extranets 23
        Message and Information Sharing 26
        Authoring and Publishing 27
        Collaboration 28
        Introducing Lotus Notes/Domino 29
    Content Management 30
        Legacy System Enablement 32
        Business Extension 33
        Business Process Transformation 33
Vassos' 17 Stages 34
The Foundation Supporting IBM's E-Business Strategy 36

    Network Computing Framework 37
    Java, the Key to Independence 39
    Server Hardware 41
    IBM Global Network 42
    Security 42
A Story of Three Businesses 43
    Small Business—Ned Connolly's Auto Parts 44
    Medium Business—Blue Sky Musical Instruments 45
    Large Business—Stonefield Audio/Video 46

Chapter 2:
IBM Personal Computers   49

A Glance Backwards 49
Meet the Family 52
Hardware Architecture 57
    Microprocessors and Memory 57
        Microprocessor Basics 57
        Multiprocessing 58
        Intel Microprocessors 59
        Memory 60
    Disk Storage 61
        Diskettes 62
        Fixed Disks 63
        CD-ROM Drives 63
PC Software 64
    Types of Software—A Model 64
        Application Programs 64
        Operating Systems 66
        BIOS 66
    Operating Systems 68
        The Disk Operating System (DOS) 69
        Advanced Operating Systems 70

Chapter 3:
IBM RS/6000   84

A Glance Backwards 84
Meet the RS/6000 Family 87

RS/6000 Models 89
    Micro Channel Systems 92
    PCI/ISA Systems 96
    POWERparallel SP 99
RS/6000 Hardware Architecture 102
    The Main Processor 103
    Main Memory 109
    Memory Management 111
    Symmetric Multiprocessing 114
RS/6000 Software 116
    Types Of Software—A Conceptual Model 116
        Application Programs 116
        Operating Systems 118
        Device Drivers 119
    RS/6000 Software Compatibility—Why It Is Important 120
    AIX for the RS/6000 121
        AIX Overview 122

Chapter 4:
IBM AS/400 Computers   126

A Glance Backwards 126
What Makes Up an AS/400 Computer System? 130
Meet the AS/400 Family 131
Inside AS/400 Systems 133
    Hardware Architecture Overview 133
        The Move from CISC to RISC 137
        Auxiliary Storage 138
        Storage Management 140
        Opticonnect/400 Systems 143
AS/400 Software 145
    Types of Software-A Model 145
        Application Programs 146
        Operating Systems 147
        SLIC Instructions 148
    AS/400 Operating Systems 149
        SSP 149
        OS/400 150

Chapter 5:
IBM S/390 Computers   153

A Glance Backwards 153
What Makes Up a S/390 Computer System? 160
Meet the Family 163
Inside S/390 165
    Storage Hierarchy—Making Data Available 166
        Processor Storage 166
        External Storage 168
    Parallel Sysplex 172
S/390 Software 172
    Types of Software—A Model 173
        Application Programs 174
        Operating System 175
        LIC 177
    Operating Systems 178
        OS/390 178
        VM 179
        VSE 181

Chapter 6:
Computer Networks   186

The Need to Communicate—An Introduction 186
IBM'S Overall Networking Blueprint 187
    Applications Layer 187
    Application Support Layer 188
    Transport Network Layer: SNA-TCP/IP-MPTN 189
    Subnetworking Layer 190
Local Area Networks 190
Wide Area Networks 191
What Is Client/Server Computing? 191
    What Makes Up a Client/Server Computing System? 192
    Common Approaches to Client/Server Computing 194
        Sharing Resources in Workgroups:
            The Resource Sharing Model 194
        Automating Process Flows:
            The Process-Driven Model 196

    Giving Applications Face Lifts:
        The Front-End Model 198
    Pointing and Clicking Over the Network:
        The Remote Presentation Model 200
    Dividing and Conquering:
        The Distributed Logic Model 205
    Keeping Replicas of Data Close at Hand:
        The Data Staging Model 205
Architectures for Client/Server Applications 206
    Two-Tiered Client/Server Applications 207
    Three-Tiered Client/Server Applications 208

Introduction

> *The bravest are surely those who have the clearest vision of what lies before them, glory and danger alike, and yet notwithstanding, go out and meet it.*
> —Pericles (c. 495–529 B.C.),
> Athenian Statesman

Technology can be daunting. Its fast pace of change can leave even technology experts in a daze. However, change means new opportunity. Since luck occurs when preparation meets opportunity, those who diligently prepare themselves are likely to find good fortune in the world of technology. This book is your first step in learning about the technology and products of a long standing industry leader—IBM. Best of luck.

What This Book Is

This book provides an overview of IBM's most popular technologies and products. It provides a basic foundation of knowledge about IBM's companywide network computing strategy, the four core IBM computer families, and computer networking. It is written using easy-to-understand language and all technical terms are defined as they are introduced.

The book includes a collection of excerpts taken from five books published by Maximum Press:

Exploring IBM's Bold Internet Strategy, Hoskins & Lupiano (IBM order number S246-0163)

Exploring IBM Client/Server Computing, Bolthouse (IBM order number S246-0098)

Exploring IBM Personal Computers, Hoskins & Wilson (IBM order number G325-0400)

Exploring IBM RS/6000 Computers, Hoskins & Davies (IBM order number GA23-2674)

Exploring IBM AS/400 Computers, Hoskins & Dimmick (IBM order number GA21-9990)

Exploring IBM's New Age Mainframes, Young (IBM order number G326-3006)

Consult these separate books for more detailed information on the topics they cover.

What This Book Is Not

This book is not a comprehensive IBM product catalog or technology encyclopedia. In the fast-moving computer world, any such book would be obsolete before it could be printed. Instead, this book presents basics about network computing, IBM's four main computer families, and networking. The companion web site for this book provides you with a way to quickly get the most current product information. Finally, this book does not expect you to be an engineer. Business people are typically short on time and patience as far as technical matters are concerned. Although some technical discussions are necessary, we have tried to keep these as simple and concise as possible while still conveying necessary and useful information.

How to Use This Book

Chapter 1 introduces IBM's network computing strategy. This companywide thrust is designed to make all of IBM's products able to share information and resources with any other via standards-based networks like the Internet and intranets.

Chapter 2 surveys IBM's diverse personal computer offerings. It explores the various brands of personal computer hardware as well as the all-important software including OS/2, Windows 95, Windows NT, application programs, etc.

Chapter 3 guides you through the RS/6000 world. This UNIX-based computer family can be used as a multiuser computer or a high-performance workstation.

Chapter 4 explores IBM's AS/400 computer family. The AS/400 is IBM's popular mid-range computer family that evolved from the IBM System/3X computer family.

Chapter 5 covers IBM's S/390 family. These are the largest computer systems offered by IBM and are used in the most demanding of environments.

Chapter 6 shows how IBM's various computer families can be networked with other computers for the purpose of sharing information, programs, and peripheral equipment. The most popular communications environments are explored.

To help you better understand the topics covered in this book, key terms and phrases are defined and **highlighted**.

Your "Members Only" Web Site

The world of IBM technology and products changes every day. That's why there is a companion web site associated with this book. On this site you will find news, expanded information on the topics covered in the book, and other resources of interest.

However, you have to be a member of the "IBM Insiders Club" to gain access to this site. When you purchased this book, you automatically became a member (in fact, that's the only way to join). So you now have full privileges of the IBM Insiders Club.

To get into the "Members Only" section of the companion web site, go to the Maximum Press web site located at *http://www.maxpress.com* and follow the links to the "IBM Technology Insiders Club" area. When you try to enter, you will be asked for a user ID and password. Type in the following:

For User ID enter: *ibmtech*
For Password enter: *bicycle*

You will then be granted full access to the "Members Only" area. Visit the site often and enjoy the updates and resources with our complements—and thanks again for buying the book. We ask that you not share the "user ID" and "password" for this site with anyone else.

1
Network Computing Basics

The Internet's rise in popularity has provided businesses of all types with a whole new world of network computing to pioneer. IBM, which finds itself beautifully positioned in the age of the Internet, is pulling out all the stops to help businesses tame this new frontier. This chapter starts with a quick review of Internet basics and then describes IBM's companywide vision and strategy for turning the Internet into a far-reaching business tool.

What Is the Internet?

The Internet is a public network of computers that spans the globe. What makes the Internet different from other private communications networks commonly used by businesses and other institutions is that anyone who wants to can get on the Internet. Individuals usually get on the Internet by subscribing to a service offered by an **Internet Service Provider** (ISP). These are companies that have a computer with a high-speed connection (over leased telephone lines) to the Internet and allow their subscribers' computers to communicate on the Internet computer system (Figure 1.1). Businesses and institutions

2 EXPLORING IBM TECHNOLOGY AND PRODUCTS

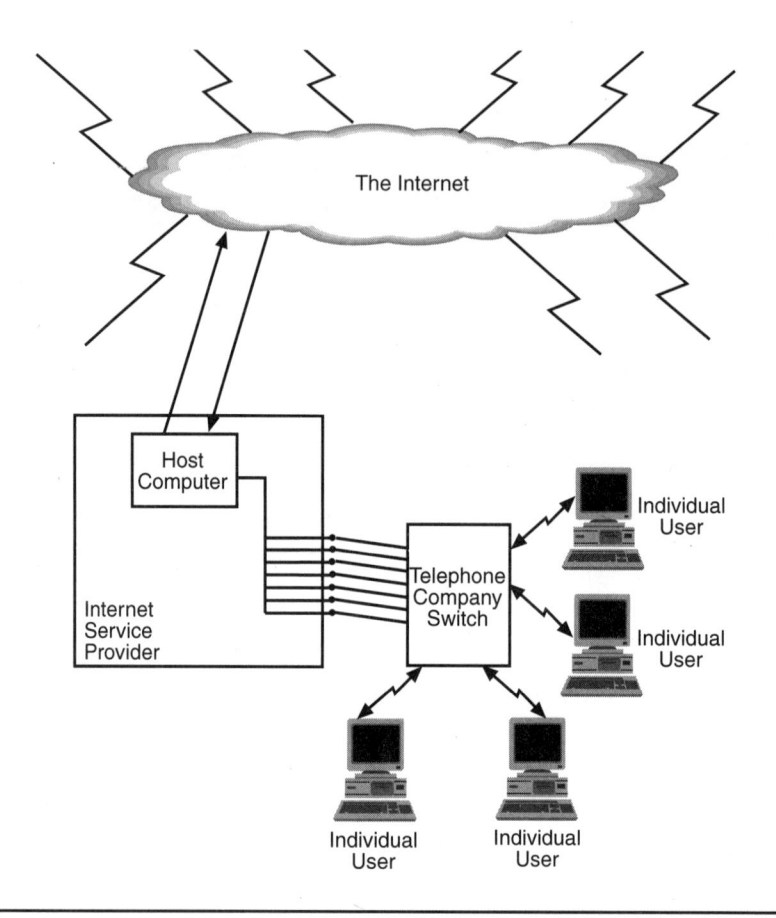

Figure 1.1. Individual Internet users typically access the Internet by dialing into the host computer owned by an Internet Service Provider. The users dial in over standard phone lines and share a high-speed connection between the host computer and the Internet.

often get on the Internet through their own high-speed connection to the Internet which is shared by multiple users within the organization (Figure 1.2).

Where Did the Internet Come From?

The great grandfather of the Internet was a network called **ARPANET** developed by the U. S. Department of Defense in 1969 to promote

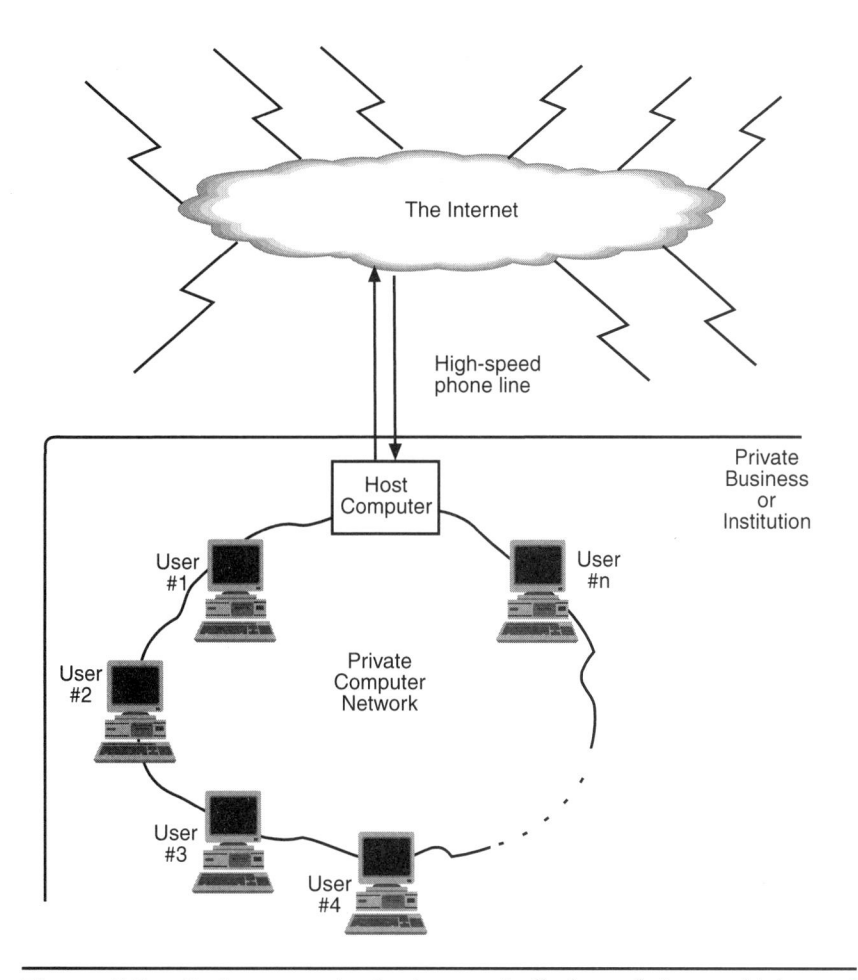

Figure 1.2. Businesses or institutions typically have their own high-speed connection to the Internet, which is shared by multiple users within the organization.

networking research (see the time line in Figure 1.3). Over the years, innovative individuals and government organizations like the National Science Foundation developed and adopted technologies and standards that allowed for the interconnection of all networks that adhered to the standards. The standard communications protocol (i.e., electronic language) used on the Internet since its adoption in 1982 is known as **TCP/IP** (Transmission Control Protocol/Internet Protocol).

4 EXPLORING IBM TECHNOLOGY AND PRODUCTS

1996 — U.S. Internet traffic now carried by commercial Internet service providers.

1995 — Number of Internet hosts reaches 12.8 million.
President Clinton announces "Next Generation Internet" initiative.

1994 — White House goes on-line with "Welcome to the White House."

1993 — President Clinton and Vice President Gore get e-mail addresses.
Mosaic, graphical "Web Browser" released by the NSF-funded National Center for Supercomputing Applications.
World Wide Web traffic explodes.

1991 — NSF lifts restrictions on commercial use of the Internet.
High Performance Computing Act is signed into law.
World Wide Web software released by CERN, the European Laboratory for Particle Physics.

1989 — Number of Internet hosts breaks 100,000.

1986 — NSFNET and 5 NSF-funded supercomputer centers created. NSFNET backbone is 56 kilobits/second.

1984 — Number of hosts (computers) connected to the Internet breaks 1,000.

1982 — Defense Department established TCP/IP (Transmission Control Protocol/Internet Protocol) as standard.

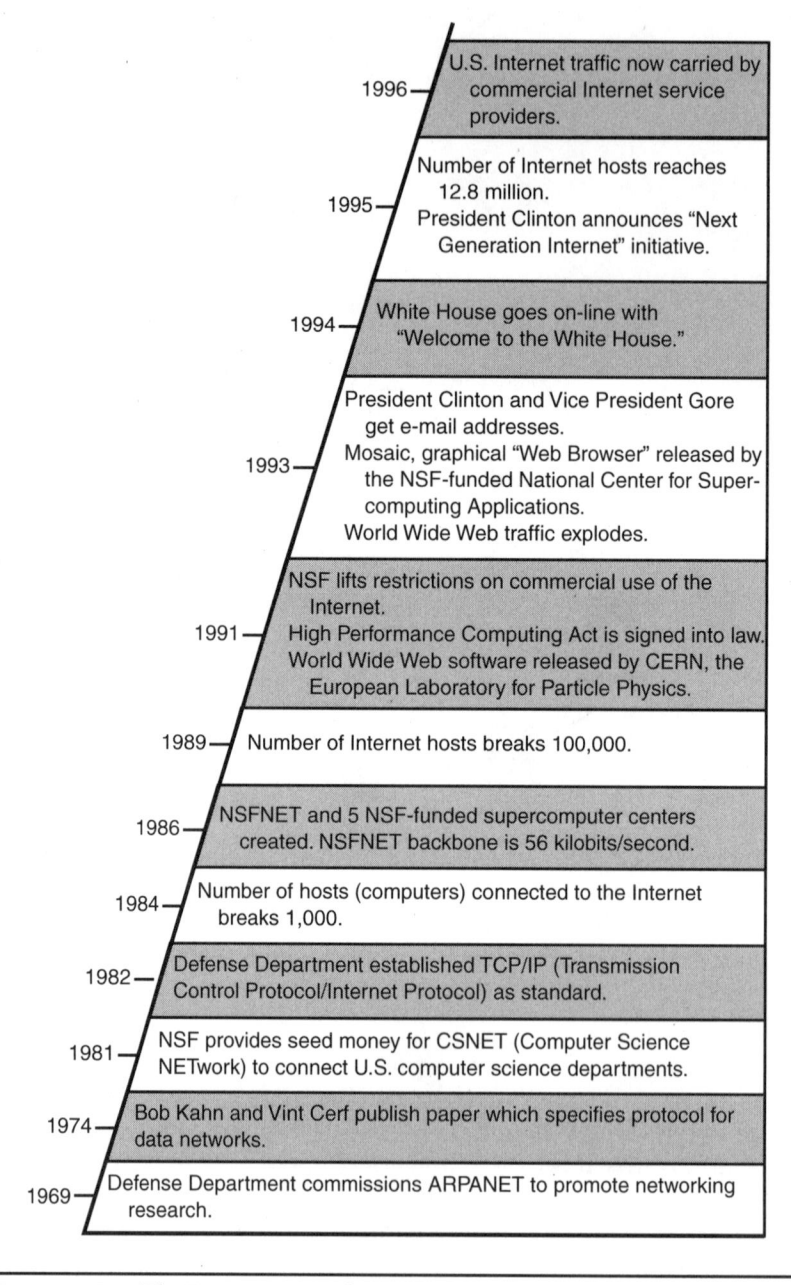

1981 — NSF provides seed money for CSNET (Computer Science NETwork) to connect U.S. computer science departments.

1974 — Bob Kahn and Vint Cerf publish paper which specifies protocol for data networks.

1969 — Defense Department commissions ARPANET to promote networking research.

Figure 1.3. The Internet started as a government project and is now emerging as a whole new business frontier.

By using this common language throughout the Internet, any computer on the Internet can communicate with any other computer on the Internet—that's the beauty of standardization. Other Internet software (running on all participating computers and using TCP/IP communications) implements the functions available on the Internet such as e-mail, World Wide Web browsing, sending information from one computer to another, chat sessions, and so on.

It's About Content

So, now that we have an Internet, what good is it? Well, it's only as good as the information it delivers. The Internet is like the plumbing going to everyone's house today. No one cares about the pipes themselves, it's the clear, pure, life-giving water the pipes bring that is important. Similarly, it is the text, sound, illustrations, images, and video (collectively called the **content**) the Internet brings to your home, school, and business that makes the Internet important—or not. Just as a dirty water system renders your home's plumbing worthless, poor-quality content would make the Internet nothing more than a collection of useless wires. So, if "content is king," where will it come from? Fortunately, the economic and social power represented by the Internet has attracted the best minds in the world, who are already delivering impressive content.

What sets the Internet apart from other important content delivery infrastructures (e.g., television, radio, and print media) is that the Internet is a two-way communications channel. This allows users to actively make choices that direct the flow of the content to suit their specific needs. It also allows users to communicate with the content provider and with other users—something the traditional media can't offer. This interactive capability allows users to execute transactions (e.g., buying and selling things or making reservations) and share content with others, providing a new way for people to work and play together in cyberspace.

What About Online Services?

Where do online service companies such as America Online, CompuServe, and Prodigy fit into the Internet picture? To answer this question, you must first realize that these online service companies were started before the Internet was popular with the general public. They offered their users access to a large body of well-organized information, all stored on their private computer systems. However, as the Internet gained popularity, much of the same information available from these online services (and more) started becoming available on the Internet. At the same time, people wanted to exchange e-mail messages with others who were on the Internet but not necessarily subscribers to a particular online service. This dynamic caused online service companies to offer their users e-mail exchange with Internet users, access the Internet's graphically oriented World Wide Web, and reduce their usage fees.

Another problem faced by the online services is a lack of speed. Since online services were not originally designed to provide their users with access to the Internet, the response time experienced by their users (the time from when you click your mouse to when you see the results on your screen) is typically longer, making for a more sluggish experience as compared to more direct connections to the Internet offered by ISPs. It's a tough time to be an online service company. To survive, they must find a way to offer things users want but can't get on the Internet—a challenge that seems to get harder every day. Time will tell if the online service companies can effectively adapt to the new world of the Internet.

What Are People Doing Right Now?

There is a flurry of business activity on the Internet going on right now. Here are just a few examples to get you thinking.

- *Mediconsult.com* is a virtual medical clinic on the Internet that offers peer-reviewed medical information on more than 50 chronic medical conditions and has logged more than 180,000 patient "visits" a month. It now is expanding beyond consulting and beginning to sell a line of hard-to-find medical products over the Internet.

- The American Schools Directory is developing Web sites for all K–12 schools in America. Currently 106,000 participating sites provide information about schools for educators, students, parents, and local communities.

- Lehigh Valley Safety Shoe Company (a 20-person company) is now doing all of its sales and distribution and wholesale business over the Web.

- Japan Airlines in Tokyo now allows its customers to make reservations over the Internet.

- The National Hockey League has a Web site that offers comprehensive news and information about the teams and games. You can buy team-related products from the NHL's online store.

- Electric Power Research Institute (EPRI) is a not-for-profit research organization that acts as a research clearinghouse for more than 700 utility companies. It now has a Web site at which members share text, charts, and graphics, making the exchange of ideas more efficient and interactive.

- The State Bar of California now has a Web site over which its members can access 15 years' worth of accumulated data from existing databases. The State Bar now posts bar exam results 48 hours earlier, provides consumer information for finding a lawyer, and invites public comment on pending state legislation.

- Charles Schwab, a leading discount brokerage company, is launching the e.Schwab stock market trading Web site which lets customers access their accounts and place trades from anywhere, 24 hours a day, over the Internet. Schwab did as much business through its Web site in the first year as it did in 13 years with its desktop software offering.

- Chrysler has built the Supply Partner Information Network (SPIN), a way for Chrysler to communicate over its corporate intranet with some 20,000 suppliers it relies upon. SPIN also provides a way for suppliers to submit cost-saving ideas, which already have realized $1 billion in cost savings.

- Borders, the multi-billion-dollar retail book/music store chain, is putting its entire book and music catalog on the Internet and allowing customers to shop and place orders from home. Borders also is providing access to its Web site through computers set up in all of its big stores so that if you can't find what you're looking for on the shelves, you can search for it online and then place your order.

- L.L. Bean, for example, has gone online live with electronic commerce at its Web site. Traffic on the site almost immediately exceeded expectations. During the first holiday shopping season, sales at L.L. Bean's Web site were twice what had been forecast.

- Auto-by-Tel uses the Web to take consumer order descriptions and match them with inventories of more than 1,500 car dealers who subscribe to the service. (They run at a rate of more than 40,000 requests per month, with more than $2 billion in sales generated this way.)

- In Japan, a project called VCALS (Vehicle Computer Assisted Logistic System) is building an electronic commerce environment that will include paperless design processes in a virtual enterprise environment and an electronics parts ordering and digital service manual covering the entire Japanese automotive industry between manufacturers and repair shops.

- In Europe, 30 European automotive and aerospace companies have embarked on a project called AIT (Advanced Information Technology) that intends to make the manufacturing segment more competitive. The initial focus is to define a common infrastructure to support interoperability between user environments.

- In Italy, Ente Lirico Arena di Verona (Verona Opera), which currently sells more than 500,000 tickets a year to opera fans, is creating a Web site that will let visitors browse information, check performance availability (in real time), make reservations, and pay for tickets with secure credit card transactions.

It is not difficult to imagine how these efforts (and a thousand others like them) will make our lives easier in the future as they permeate education, medicine, manufacturing, entertainment, travel, and so on. Over time, the use of Internet technology (and its derivatives) will enable businesses to become more and more competitive through quickly formed online partnerships with those inside or outside the company who can bring value to company projects. The ability to interact, using the Internet standards being established today, will undoubtedly permeate almost every aspect of our lives and businesses.

Through Internet technology, the cost of doing business will decline, much the same way costs declined with the proliferation of the telephone and all its adjunct services. The phone brought people together instantly: They no longer had to spend time composing and editing letters, then waiting during the time it took the letter to arrive at the addressee. As the phone became more and more fruitful, the cost of doing business decreased. Decisions were reached more quickly. The enormous costs associated with travel diminished as more and more people conducted business on the phone. Business people began to teleconference, further reducing travel costs and time. Customers no longer had to physically walk into a store to make purchases, these could be done on the phone. Today, customers don't have to "walk into" paper catalogs; they can shop at L.L. Bean on the Internet 24 hours a day, regardless of the weather.

During this transition from "no phones" to "all phones," business executives became more and more aware of the phone's potential just as they were totally aware of other basic business tools, such as the importance of location and advertising in order to reach customers. Any chief executive who, during this transition to an all-telephone world, was not aware of the emergence, the importance, and the impact of the telephone faced the prospect of not only falling behind the competition, but failing miserably. Similarly today, any chief executive officer who is not aware of the Internet's potential will inevitably be overrun by the giant wave of the technological progress and advantages inherent in the Internet. As we mentioned, seldom now does one see an ad on television or print without an Internet address. The phrases "e-mail" and "www dot com" are now an integral part of the world's lexicon, along with expressions like phone mail and fax.

Clearly, mainstream business is headed for the Internet while it is implementing internal company networks based on Internet technology, called **intranets**. A recent research report by Daniel Rimer of Hambrecht and Quist shows that 85 percent of the Fortune 200 companies now have an intranet strategy. That number is not apt to decline; quite the contrary. Ignoring the Internet phenomenon today is tantamount to saying that "The airplane will never fly," "Space travel is impossible," "Elvis Presley will last about a month," or "Close the patent office...everything's been invented."

IBM's Network Computing Vision

In a speech on September 9, 1996, IBM's Chairman and CEO, Louis V. Gerstner Jr., summed up IBM's vision of the Internet's potential. He said, "The rise of the Internet is connecting people with people, and people with content, in ways that weren't possible just a few years ago. But sheer connectivity, as important as it is, is not, and never has been, the holy grail. The payoff is what people and institutions do with this extraordinary capability—which literally has the power to change the way we work, and the way we live."

What IBM and the industry see is not only a business opportunity, but a sea change in the way businesses and people live today and tomorrow. For all its glamour, glitz, and hype, the Internet has the potential, the momentum, to make all our lives better.

To be able to capitalize on such potential is indeed a huge undertaking that requires vision, enormous effort, and the talent necessary to thrive in the frontier that is today's Internet. Think of it as electronic covered wagons riding toward new horizons. IBM refers to its broad Internet/intranet initiatives as **network computing**.

Why Does IBM Like the Internet So Much?

IBM views the Internet and its sibling intranets as opportunities for unprecedented growth, not only for businesses around the globe, but for the IBM corporation as well. Both the Internet and intranets are a means for users, large and small, to accomplish some basic business goals: disseminating information, cutting costs, and getting to market faster and more efficiently. At the same time the Internet is a device for accomplishing other things, too: forging tighter relationships with consumers, gaining an advantage over the competition, mobilizing global work forces, integrating supply chains, and reinventing the very souls of companies. Essentially, IBM perceives the Internet as a rare chance to help users harness today's newest technologies and achieve surprising goals.

Common sense says users want to do ordinary things over the Internet: check on their bank accounts from home, find the cheapest airline fare without leaving their office or den, get training from a far-flung campus without walking into a classroom, put in their two cents' worth about local politics—even though it's well past closing time at City Hall.

People will also want to perform complex tasks: conduct complex business transactions with business partners around the globe. Stamp out bureaucracy and get teams to work together better and faster. Improve efficiency by cutting out waste.

Another reason IBM is interested in the Internet is because of results of its own research. In August 1996, IBM conducted 36 one-on-one interviews with CEOs, division managers, vice presidents of marketing, sales, customer service, and so on. Simultaneously, IBM conducted focus groups with Fortune 1000 business executives, including many non-**IT** (**Informative Technology**) executives.

The findings confirmed that the most important business issues relate to growth, revenue, competition, and productivity. The research also indicated that the Internet is seen as a potentially powerful business tool that can and should be used to help with the issues of growth, revenue, competition, and productivity—a notion expressed even by those with limited Internet experience. Further, the studies found that security concerns are perceived as the final obstacle to Internet commerce: If a user buys something online, the transaction should be secure. If you want to send a private message to someone over the Net, it should remain private. If you want to see your checking account balance, only you should be able to. Systems should be secure, bulletproof, and reliable.

None of these challenges are new to IBM. As mentioned, IBM designed special hardware and software, and also provided operations and engineering support for the National Science Foundation

Network (NSFNet), which became the principle backbone network for the Internet. The people from IBM who were involved with this are now in the IBM Network Services unit.

In September 1996 IBM conducted additional research in the form of 250 market interviews of users and prospective users from all over the world. The interviewees consisted of enterprise, large, medium, and small companies (weighted toward large companies), cross-industry (banking, entertainment, government, health care, insurance, manufacturing, publishing, retail, communications, transportation, travel), **MIS (Management Information System)** senior management and functional heads (marketing, human resources, and operations). This list was supplemented by IBM partners and Lotus Premium Partners, market analysts, the Aberdeen Group, IDS, the Gartner Group, the Meta Group, Dataquest, and EDVenture Holdings.

Virtually all respondents envision developing Internet-based business processes that will improve the way their businesses are run, at a minimum risk to existing systems and data.

According to IDS, early adopter companies are currently deploying these Internet-based solutions, and the next wave of users is preparing to deploy in the next 12 months.

Currently, the Internet and the technology it's based on is the driving force behind the most sweeping change in computing history. The push is to move to content (information that includes text, numbers, graphics, images, sound, and video) and programs (used to manipulate content) from a user's personal computer (a **client**) and onto larger computers (**servers**) that can be accessed over the Internet. Why? Because there are costs to be saved, productivity to be enhanced, and new markets to enter and expand.

There are as many applications of the Internet and its technology as there are businesses. Let's look at some of the cost savings that can be realized:

In the past years, personal computers (PCs) have grown more powerful and more complex. This complexity is why studies have estimated that well over half of the cost of using a PC in your business is due to the time spent managing the PC—installing, upgrading, troubleshooting, helping users, and so on.

The cost of managing a large pool of high-powered PCs can be reduced by storing more, but not all, of the content and programs users need on a server shared by all the users. This centralized content and software can then be secured, diagnosed, repaired, updated, and otherwise managed once (on the server), rather than many times (once for each client).

The Internet's World Wide Web function is built around this centralized approach. The user needs only one program (a **Web browser**) to access any of the content offered on the World Wide Web. In fact, any type of computer—an IBM PC, Apple Macintosh, UNIX workstation, network computer, etc.—equipped with a Web browser program can access any of the content—and even run programs (written in languages like **Java**) offered on the World Wide Web. Since the same functions are available no matter what type of computer system or operating system you are using, the Internet represents a real threat to the dominance of Microsoft Windows and Intel microprocessors.

Until standards were imposed by the widespread adoption of the Internet, programmers and the business that paid them were in a never-ending struggle to make one type of computer system on one type of network that could share information with another type of computer on yet another type of network. Today the Internet has a set of rules, and since everyone uses the same set of protocols, content is viewable by all.

So, there are many benefits to standardizing and centralizing content as well as some of the programs. To centralize content, you must have a large-scale, powerful, secure, and reliable computer system (and the services to back them up) to act as servers (the points of centralization), and the tools to manage the sophisticated networks through which users access content.

Why is this important to IBM? As a long-time leader in the large computer arena, IBM is well positioned to help businesses implement their plans for leveraging the Internet to improve business results—a fact IBM is keenly aware of. As a result, every major segment of IBM is aggressively aligning its strategies, products, services and development priorities with the company's new Internet strategy, which IBM calls **e-business**. IBM's professional services organization—the fastest growing part of IBM—is better equipped than ever to provide the expertise and personnel to help design, implement, and manage these large-scale computing solutions.

In fact, IBM's Global Services unit is the world's largest consultancy, with more than 116,000 professionals in 160 countries, and since approximately 70 percent of the world's data resides on IBM computer systems, who is in a better position than IBM to help users enable their business information and processes for the Internet world?

While IBM is often a fairly strong competitor in the low-end commodity world—PCs, terminals, printers, etc.—IBM is at its best when there are large-scale problems to be solved, like designing powerful server hardware or secure and reliable software, managing large networks, and handling a large volume of transactions. These are the reasons why IBM loves the current trend toward centralization being driven by the Internet and intranets.

The market opportunity for products and services that enable people to use the Internet and intranets was about $200 billion in 1996, and expected to more than double by the year 2000. Sixty-five percent of this growth is expected to be in the area of services and solutions. Creating a leadership position in the development of Internet-based computing solutions is a top priority with IBM CEO Lou Gerstner. As a result, on December 1, 1995, IBM created the Internet Division, headed by Dr. Irving Wladawsky-Berger. The organization is responsible for defining and implementing all of IBM's software-based Internet and network computing initiatives. The division works across all of IBM's individual units to guide the development of IBM's e-business offerings. IBM's Internet Division is also responsible for branding, product integration, and marketing.

Another major move that bolstered IBM's ability to go after the opportunities presented by the rise of the Internet was the purchase of Lotus Development Corporation in July 1995. The unique combination of Lotus' end-user software expertise and IBM's scalable enterprise systems experience would enable them to quickly address brand, product, and technology-integration issues, thus leveraging the strengths of both companies and giving IBM a significant lead in the **groupware** world. With the advent of Domino, Lotus brings the substantial capabilities of Notes to the World Wide Web and further strengthens IBM's Internet hand. The strategy seems to be working because sales of Lotus Notes/Domino are way up. In fact, recent research conducted by International Data Corporation (IDC) showed that IBM/Lotus gained more new e-mail users during 1996 (8.4 million or 27 percent of all new users) than any other e-mail software vendor. More on Notes and Domino later.

Lastly, IBM is recruiting an army of smaller companies with its Internet Specialty Program through which qualified consulting and software development firms can get certified in commerce, security, intranet applications, and other topics. This strategy will help IBM quickly extend and deploy e-business applications.

Where Do Intranets Fit In?

Businesses are establishing **intranets** (private computer networks that use Internet standards and software but are electronically insulated from the Internet) at a phenomenal rate, which indicates a burgeoning opportunity. There are 23 million workers using corporate intranets worldwide. By the year 2000, there will be 180 million.

According to Forrester Research, 16 percent of the Fortune 1000 companies have intranets and another 50 percent are either in the consideration or planning stage. As companies build intranets for improving internal communications, streamlining processes such as purchasing and simplifying transaction processing, they are finding multiple sources of business value. They are reducing communication costs, increasing productivity and sales, and significantly improving the quality of work.

Today, businesses are only scratching the surface of a wellspring of possibilities. Intranets allow companies to reengineer processes as well as expand their business because of improved communications and greater productivity. Knight Ridder SourceOne, for example, quickly delivers documents—some rare and obscure—from internal digital and hard copy libraries from prestigious affiliated institutions around the world. Leveraging Intranet technology, Knight-Ridder SourceOne yielded impressive gains in efficiency and customer satisfaction. Further, companies such as Mason and Hanger, an engineering contracting company, are prototyping intranets for decision support systems. These are just two examples of the many intranet projects underway at businesses and institutions around the globe.

Many businesses which already have intranets up and running are quickly finding a need to securely provide outside trading partners with access to their intranet via the Internet. Intranets that allow select groups access over the Internet are called **extranets**. Businesses seem to be evolving intranets into extranets quickly.

Companies may be tempted to jump on the intranet bandwagon using the fastest means possible. This tactic may meet some basic requirements, but it often does not take into account future network growth, the advantages gained by leveraging existing data, nor how to add new intranet-enhancing products as they become available. These considerations demand that intranets be flexible, open, and integrated, and any time a company makes information accessible to a wide group of people or extends an intranet to suppliers or vendors, it must establish appropriate security mechanisms, ranging from **firewalls** (used to electronically isolate a company's intranet from the Internet) which control access to **encryption** (digitally encoding information to prevent unauthorized viewing). So how is IBM positioned to go after this intranet opportunity? Again—very well.

IBM has been managing and connecting enterprise computing environments for more than two decades. Many of IBM's loyal customers worldwide now want to reap the rewards that intranet technology can bring. IBM will start by helping these long-standing customers implement intranets and then use these successes to go after new customers.

IBM has the experience along with the depth and breadth of skills to help companies get intranets up and running quickly. IBM is focusing on creating new and tangible value for businesses on the Internet using a security-rich, integrated approach. IBM is leveraging their line of security products and technologies to help users build intranets that will safely handle mission-critical data and tasks. IBM's time-tested security products and technologies, combined with brand-new offerings from both IBM and its wholly owned subsidiary Lotus, will allow IBM to effectively compete in everything from the smallest departmental intranet to complex intranets connecting worldwide enterprises.

IBM research indicates that one of every three companies is pursing a strategy of *revolutionary,* as opposed to *evolutionary,* change. The business environment has become so competitive and customer expectations so high that it's a rare company that excels by doing business as usual. The competitive nature of business has led today's users to expect the highest quality at the lowest cost with impeccable service. Traditionally, most companies emphasized only one of three areas: quality, cost, service. To thrive today, it's imperative that they be strong in all three.

An IBM study of hundreds of senior functional and information technology executives found when companies don't take advantage of breakthrough advances, they limit their ability to keep pace with their competitors who do leverage technology. This yields a business cultural imperative: "change or die." Subjects of the study indicated that to get the most out of the change, it needs to be fast—at least as fast as competitors—and much deeper than cosmetic adjustments.

IBM understands the nature of this transformation not only as a supplier to businesses around the globe, but also through its own experience in the marketplace and its internal alterations in recent years.

Recently, the Internet and intranets have served as the impetus for positive change and new value. They have laid the groundwork for a surge of business transformations transcending industry, geography, or size.

Companies are fundamentally interested in intranets for enabling, enhancing, and extending effective communications with and among organizational communities of interest. There can be mutual benefits derived from intranetworking between synergistic businesses. Intranets also have allowed companies to enter new areas in their industry and expand elements within their businesses. Internet technology employed in intranets can be the base that a business uses to reinvent its entire operation.

This volatile but fertile business environment is the backdrop for IBM's e-business strategy. Every IBM offering in this arena is designed to optimize, expand, or transform new channels of business value. This translates into businesses successfully reengineering, broadening their scope, adding new areas of competence, and enhancing the way people communicate with one another.

Now, let's take a look at the specific direction IBM is taking in addressing opportunities offered by the impending mass migration to the Internet and intranets.

IBM's E-Business Strategy

Figure 1.4 depicts the three central themes that form the basis for IBM's new companywide e-business strategy: Commerce, Intranet/Extranet, and Content Management. This particular grouping of Internet application areas is the result of extensive IBM research into the way businesses use and will use the Internet and intranets. As depicted in the figure, there are sections of each ring that overlap with the other two rings. This illustrates the commonality across all three elements of IBM's strategy. There are also areas that are unique

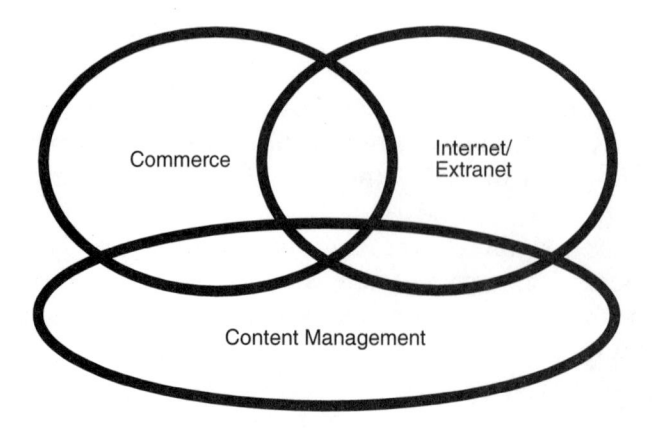

Figure 1.4. IBM's Internet strategy consists of three key areas: Commerce, intranet/extranet, and content management.

to each ring, representing the unique challenges presented by each application grouping. Simply put, IBM's e-business strategy is designed to create new value for businesses through the Internet and Internet technology.

IBM priorities are not focused on being the "commodity" side of the Internet world—Web browser software, client hardware/software, building simple Web sites, etc. Though IBM does offer products for the commodity side of the Internet, IBM's e-business strategy is more focused on *environments* that can benefit from the vast experience and expertise IBM can bring to solve end-to-end business problems with a combination of hardware, software, and services. Even if a project starts small, it must be designed to accommodate rapid—sometimes extremely rapid—growth. This is a key element of IBM's e-business approach.

While hobbyists, and now businesses, are already using the Internet for basic communications—e-mail and simple Web browsing, for example—IBM views transacting business on the Internet as a whole new world that is only now beginning to develop. IBM's approach is to *leverage* the Internet to help businesses decrease their time to market, open new markets, attract and retain customers, connect with partners and suppliers, and abolish barriers between teams.

If you are attracted to the glamour associated with a "cool" Internet startup company offering a revolutionary new technology, you will have trouble finding that image within IBM. What you will find is an extremely deep company with a proven track record of solving business problems in the real world. This heritage is clearly present in IBM's e-business strategy. It's important to keep in mind that IBM is not only focused on developing its own technology products (though it has an enviable R&D organization and budget). What is even more important to IBM is implementing technology (some developed by IBM and some not) as part of comprehensive business solutions. This requires the integration of new hardware and software technology with the existing infrastructure in such ways that create new business value. Now let's take a closer look at each ring in IBM's e-business strategy.

Internet Commerce

To IBM, Internet **commerce** means marketing, selling, and servicing customers over the Internet. That is, it involves all the interactions in support of a transaction between a company and its customer. It's one thing to simply put electronic brochures on the Internet for all to view. This is what most Web sites do today. But it's another thing entirely to transact business or "exchange value" through your Web site. To allow buyers and sellers to consummate sales completely online brings up issues of security, identification, electronic money, fraud, and more. But electronic commerce promises to be well worth the trouble. Experts predict that within five years Internet-based electronic commerce will reach $30 billion in the United States alone. By the year 2000, revenue from electronic payments is predicted to account for two-thirds of all non-cash transactions in the United States.

IBM's Internet commerce strategy is not narrowly focused on doing transactions or exchanging payment over the Internet. Rather, IBM seeks to differentiate itself from other vendors by focusing on the complete range of interactions between a business in customers, not just the sales transactions itself. IBM's Internet commerce strategy is to enhance all aspects of the customer relationship through the application Internet technology. That is why IBM has defined Internet commerce quite broadly and then divided it into three closely linked areas (Figure 1.5):

- Marketing
- Sales
- Customer Services

Marketing

The marketing segment of Internet commerce includes such things as brand management, corporate image, channel strategy, segmentation, customer profiling, market research, demand generation, campaign planning, managing responses, electronic catalogs, information requests, market intelligence gathering, and so on. In marketing products or services the Internet engages the user's interest with mass-market intelligence. Users proactively seek out Web sites from

- Advertising/Promotion
- Direct Marketing
- Public Relations
- Market Research
- Customer Relationship Building

Marketing

Customer Services

Sales

- Order Tracking
- Technical Support
- Warranty Support
- Complaints Mgmt.

- Lead Management
- Orders Gathering/Entry
- Payment Transactions
- Digital Product Delivery

Figure 1.5. IBM's definition of online commerce includes marketing, sales, and customer services.

anywhere in the world 24 hours a day, 365 days a year, and they never have to worry about the weather, parking, or store hours. The Web sites they settle on can hold the users' attention by providing an intimate one-on-one interaction tailored to each user's individual interests and needs. Thus, the Internet can play an important role in creating initial relationships with users at a very early stage that, ultimately, can develop into a long-term connection that might otherwise never develop. Based on a business relationship with a history, companies can provide tailored messages to their customers—quick, cost-effective ways to convey a variety of information, compared to direct mail or telemarketing efforts. Further, companies can track visits and interaction with their Web sites. This capability can present valuable, focused information for further marketing efforts, thus opening up commerce beyond traditional structured means.

Sales

The sales segment of Internet commerce is where the actual business transactions take place. This segment is where money is exchanged over the Internet and goods are shipped (or in some cases actually can be delivered over the Internet). Sales also includes managing leads, running promotions, submitting proposals, handling negotiations, selecting product configurations, managing standard and special pricing, order processing, billing, credit management, payment processing, and so on. During the sales transaction, you also must have a way to ensure that the entity you are dealing with is actually who it says it is (i.e., you must have **authentification**) and a means of consummating the transaction such that the parties involved can not later deny that a valid transaction took place (i.e., **nonrepudiation**).

With real Internet commerce, all of this and more is handled completely over the Internet in a secure and reliable way. Through Internet commerce, sales efforts reach a global 24-hour-a-day, self-selecting audience. Companies can offer prospects quick, easy access to up-to-the-minute information; in turn, that information can be updated instantly. Also, an effective Internet sales environment can enhance a user's trust while directly involving that user in the purchase process.

Customer Services

Another important part of IBM's Internet commerce strategy is on the customer service side. The idea is to enable customers to help themselves to the information they need before and after a sale, yet provide a smooth transition to human support when necessary. Such online customer service can reduce the cost of such things as technical support, a "help desk," complaint handling, cross-selling, loyalty programs, delivery tracking, warranty management, customer correspondence, delivery of electronic products, and more.

The intent is to build customer loyalty, brand value, and repeat sales while reducing costs. Viewing the openness, interactivity, and easy access to information, customers see the entire Internet process as an enhancement to their overall satisfaction. Done correctly, online customer service can improve customer satisfaction and loyalty while reducing costs by offering users the chance to help themselves through real-time access to databases, documentation libraries, and help information. Self-help customer service offerings can also free up customer support personnel to do more productive things such as look for new sales opportunities, deal with special circumstances, or provide more personalized service.

IBM's broad definition of Internet commerce as marketing, sales, and customer service reflects IBM's plans to differentiate its Internet commerce offerings from those of other companies. IBM will offer comprehensive solutions based on industrywide open standards that cover this broad Internet commerce definition. Rather than going head to head with the competition on individual pieces to the Internet commerce puzzle, IBM will bring a broad range of integrated products in concert with services that offer end-to-end Internet commerce solutions covering the whole of IBM's broad definition. These offerings will also include services that give users the option of outsourcing their Internet commerce infrastructure to IBM when that makes sense.

Overall, the IBM strategy is to offer an Internet commerce infrastructure that enhances the entire online customer relationship. Such a comprehensive approach will be difficult for companies without the diverse product lines, expertise, and services infrastructure of IBM to offer. This strategy is how IBM is differentiating itself from other Internet commerce vendors.

Net.Commerce

Net.Commerce is a key product in IBM's electronic product portfolios. It is a prepackaged set of software components that work together to provide an infrastructure for creating and managing retail stores on the Internet. It allows users to create customized **virtual storefronts** to display product lines, initiate immediate purchases, accept payment information through secure credit card transactions, and perform accounting and tax handling functions. It enables the construction of an environment in which the online shopper is led through the decision-making process with feature information and product comparisons. The shopper then selects items from a graphical and interactive product catalog and makes payment through secure payment technology that monitors the purchasing process, and ensures confidentiality, integrity, and authentication. Security is implemented using the **Secure Socket Layer** (**SSL**) standard or the Secure Electronic Transaction (SET) standard. Security in payment will be achieved using Net.Commerce Payment. There are Net.Commerce versions for various operating systems. Check this book's companion web site (described on page xiv) for more information on Net.Commerce and other key IBM products in the electronic commerce arena.

Net.Commerce is designed for use by mail-order catalogs and retailers, telecommunications service providers, and new Web-based businesses. Among the first users of Net.Commerce were the Atlanta Committee for the Olympic Games (which sold over 100,000 tickets worth over $5 million) and L.L. Bean (selling its well-known lines of outdoor equipment and apparel).

Intranets and Extranets

Whether we are talking about a two-person startup company or a 200,000-employee multinational conglomerate, good communications are vital to the efficiency and therefore the competitiveness of a business. That's why businesses have long been overrun with telephones, fax machines, memos, filing cabinets, and Post-Its. Business computers, which started out to be large accounting systems, evolved into small personal productivity tools and became important communications devices for the employees of a business (e.g., e-mail over a local area network). As the computer's role as a communications tool grew, a classic headache for users became that one group's internal e-mail system generally would not let them exchange electronic messages with the users of another.

That was then and this is now—the age of the Internet. The rise in popularity of the Internet established clear and nonproprietary standards (i.e., **open standards**) and caused the various developers of e-mail systems to make the changes necessary so that their users could exchange e-mail with other users over the Internet. Suddenly, everyone could exchange e-mail over the Internet with everyone else, the long-standing but hitherto unattainable goal of many information systems departments.

Once Internet standards were widely adopted, businesses began to tie their own private and disparate networks together, adhering to these same Internet standards—and intranets were born. The adoption of Internet standards for electronic communications over the Internet and intranets marked the beginning of the move from relatively limited electronic communications to widespread deployment of intranets and extranets, which offer virtually limitless sharing of information over the Internet and intranets to facilitate business activities. The need to work together with individuals, groups, and other businesses has often provided a clear need to carefully and methodically offer Internet access to selected intranet resources—and the extranet was born.

With intranets and extranets, users can exchange e-mail, efficiently publish information via Web sites and electronic distribution, hold interactive electronic discussions across time and space, and create electronic workflow models that implement and streamline business processes.

Intranet/extranet environments enable teams with members located around the world to quickly form and maintain effective and well-documented communications without regard to geographical distances, time zone differences, or computer system incompatibilities. The result is increased speed—in the development of a new product line, in the creation and execution of a new marketing program, in the processing of expense reports, or in the dissemination of important company information.

Before intranets, employees working on a specific project or activity had no option but to create and use systems of paper documents. If team members were not colocated in the same office building, they had to either wait for the mail or work with faxed documents—neither of which lent themselves to modification, version tracking, interactive development, distribution to multiple team members, gathering input from multiple people, and so on. Each person who received a document made edits/comments, which would then be passed along either to the originator or someone else in the development or approval chain—with each step adding delays and changes unknown to those earlier in the chain. With intranets and extranets, such things as e-mail, online discussion groups, online publishing, and electronic workflow systems provide users with much faster, more expeditious tools for allowing teams (colocated or geographically disbursed) to work together, share information, and remain up to the minute.

Leading companies throughout the world are implementing intranets that address a wide range of objectives: improving and reducing the costs of doing internal business, providing the new information technology systems infrastructure for global reengineering projects, and creating competitive marketing advantages with new customer acquisitions and customer service approaches and systems. In general, companies are finding that intranets can provide solutions to their challenges.

Years ago, such companies might not have sought outside solutions to internal problems and had found a lack of tools to facilitate the efficient communication between employees as well as customers—a laborious, time-consuming, costly process—but, with the Internet and intranets standards and the wide range of software tools available today, working together over time and distance is now more feasible.

Most companies today are in the "Business Foundation Phase" of Web site development (see "Vassos' 17 Stages" later in this chapter). That is, they've launched a Web site and are using that site to broadcast and publish information. They are ready to evolve to the next phase (Business Extension Phase), which provides more tools for working together over time and distance—Web-based interactive communications and discussion databases, which shape the foundation for the development of further, more sophisticated, integrated applications.

When the business is ready to enter the third phase (Business Transformation), workflow and process management applications, such as human resources, sales force automation, customer service and support, customer relationship management, product development and logistics processes are added. You should bear in mind that later-stage decisions you will make will be influenced by technology and infrastructure decisions that are made earlier. It pays to look well down the road early in the project.

IBM has divided its intranet/extranet strategy into three areas or application groupings, each more sophisticated than the previous (Figure 1.6). We will take a closer look at each of these application groupings:

1. Message and Information Sharing

2. Authoring and Publishing

3. Collaboration

Message and Information Sharing

Electronic mail (e-mail) is the simplest intranet application and is typically the starting point for intranet initiatives. E-mail allows us-

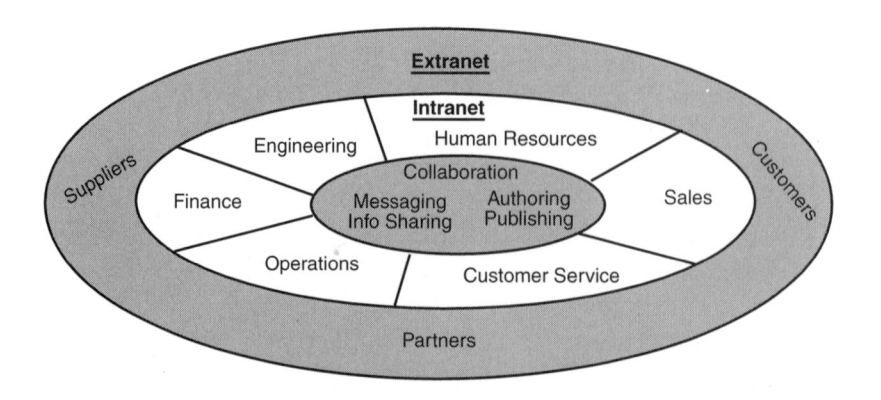

Figure 1.6. IBM's intranet/extranet application grouping.

ers to send messages through computer networks to one another across the hall or around the globe in seconds. Until the rise in popularity of the Internet, incompatibility between the plethora of e-mail systems in use caused users difficulty when trying to exchange e-mail messages with users on different systems (e.g., nonemployees such as customers, consultants, or vendors). Many companies are addressing this problem by migrating to Internet technology and standards on internal networks (i.e., building intranets). By attaching a business's intranet to the Internet (typically through a security connection called a **firewall**), the users can freely exchange e-mail with anyone on the Internet (a fast growing population, especially among businesses). This universal e-mail initiative, although easy to visualize, is often difficult or expensive to achieve due to past investments in proprietary e-mail systems. This is why IBM and Lotus have developed products and services to help users integrate disparate e-mail systems or aid in the migration to Internet-based e-mail systems.

Traditional e-mail messages consist of only textual information. However, today's e-mail messages can also contain graphics, sound, animation, and video. E-mail is also used to share information by exchanging computer files, which can contain most anything that can be encoded (photographs, sound recordings, spread sheets, long documents, computer programs, etc.)

Authoring and Publishing

The next group of intranet/extranet applications goes beyond the simple exchange of messages and computer files to enable **joint authoring** of documents and **electronic publishing.** Joint authoring means that many people can work together in creating a single document. This is accomplished through the use of a shared document database (e.g., Lotus Notes/Domino) in which each individual author can post work for other authors to see with a full audit trail and version control. This **shared document database** can also take the form of a **discussion database** (not unlike the forums of online services and the newsgroups of the Internet). A discussion database can be used by team members to post questions to the other team members, report status, the others, document the project as it evolves, report a problem, etc. All postings to the discussion database are immediately available for all authorized users to see. This type of free-form communication allows geographically dispersed individuals to quickly form teams and efficiently work together on almost any type of project. Management (or any authorized individual) can monitor the progress, see what problems arise and how they are handled, provide the answer to a team member's questions, and so on—all from anywhere in the world.

Web sites and related technologies offer another way to communicate—electronic publishing. When applied within a company, electronic publishing allows businesses to save money by distributing information to employees without the need for paper, printing, and postage. Further, information can be quickly changed without causing the scrap associated with printed documents. Electronic publishing techniques can also be used to distribute information outside the company to customers, vendors, members, investors, and so forth (e.g., corporate Web sites on the Internet).

Traditional Web sites use a **pull method** to distribute information. This means the employees must actively visit the company Web site to get the latest information (not unlike a company bulletin board over the water cooler). There is also a **push model** for electronic publishing, which can be used to distribute news (similar to a company memo or newsletter stuffed into an employee's mailbox). Later, in the case studies given in the chapter, we will see examples of both electronic publishing approaches.

Collaboration

The most advanced application of intranet/extranet technology is collaboration or the invention/reinvention of core business processes (e.g., purchasing, expense reporting, asset tracking, regulatory and environmental compliance, customer service, product development, logistics, etc.). Almost any existing business process can be implemented and streamlined through this aggressive use of intranet/extranet technology. Collaboration also offers a chance to invent whole new categories of business processes to add value to the business. While this level of sophistication promises to be the most valuable to business, it is also the most complex and difficult to achieve.

Online collaboration tools can be applied to almost any business function, including human resources, sales, customer service, operations, finance, engineering, and so on. For example, collaboration tools can be very useful to a human resources department in managing the recruitment of new employees and in meeting the needs of current employees through a "self-service" option. In the area of sales force automation, intranets can be used to provide a highly mobile sales force with the most current product information, configuration tools, promotions, order processing capability, and so forth—all while on the road. Lotus Notes/Domino are examples of two key IBM products in the intranet/extranet environment.

Introducing Lotus Notes/Domino

Groupware is one of the hottest buzzwords in the intranet/extranet jargon today. The objective of groupware is to improve the sharing of information among members of a group or team. **Lotus Notes/Domino** is the leading groupware product available today and is central to IBM's intranet/extranet strategy. To see Notes in action, consider a simple example in which a team of writers wants to work together to create a group of articles to be published in a newsletter. In our example, a Notes database is used to hold the articles as they are created. Each writer can add his or her own article and create comments about the articles of others. These comments are stored in the database associated with the article, and, again, all writers can "share" the comments. By adding an approval form (used by the authors and editors to approve an article), which also resides in the Notes database, everyone can be made aware of the progress of any article in the newsletter. This is an example of the way people can work together with the help of groupware.

Notes can also be used to support **workflow.** Workflow is generally described as a business process where a sequence of activities by a team results in a useful work. To extend our newsletter example, consider the value of creating an approval process in which the final version of each article is automatically routed (via e-mail) to the lead editor and then to the publisher for approval before publication. Further, if the newsletter is published on an Internet Web site, the newsletter can be automatically published upon final approval of all articles by the publisher.

Documents in a Notes database can contain **rich text.** Rich text describes a document that can contain text, graphics, scanned images, audio, and full-motion video data. Sometimes such documents are called **compound documents.** This feature alone can improve the communication quality of shared information.

Notes incorporates a shared, distributed, document database which resides on a server, an easy-to-use graphical user interface, a built-in e-mail function, and built-in security to allow access control for critical information. A notable feature, called **rapid application development,** means that users can create custom application programs to run on top of Notes, enabling Notes to work the way a business wants it to. Spectacular benefits can be achieved if business processes are reengineered and groupware applications are developed to support them. In effect, the groupware application is the embodiment of the process. In this way organizations can gain a competitive advantage with improved coordination of effort between members of local or widely dispersed teams. This, in turn, improves their responsiveness to the marketplace. Visit this book's companion web site (described on page xiv) for the latest information on Notes/Domino and other key IBM intranet/extranet offerings.

Content Management

For our purposes, the term **content** refers to the text, relational data, graphics, animation, sound, video, Java applets, and so forth that are offered to a community of users. **Content management** then refers to the creation, maintenance, distribution, and protection of this content. IBM's content management offerings form the foundation upon which Internet commerce and intranet/extranet applications are built (Figure 1.7). However, the lines of distinction between content, intranet/extranet, and commerce are often blurry with many areas of overlap.

When you mention content, people's first thoughts are typically of the content specially designed for delivery over the Internet such as HTML pages, graphics files, and compressed sound recordings. Of course these things are important content which needs management. However, don't forget that much (if not most) of the content businesses today want to offer their customers, employees, business partners, and vendors is critical business information that already exists within company computers but is only accessible by an isolated group (e.g., a location or department). Presenting this existing and vital information to a broader audience over the Internet/intranet holds great

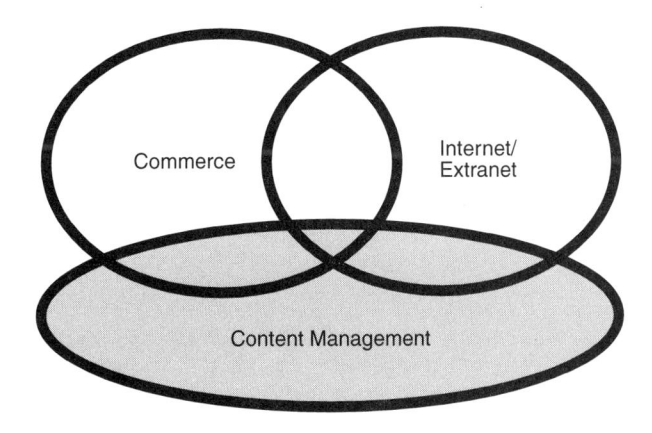

Figure 1.7. Content management disciplines and tools provide the infrastructure for Internet commerce and online collaboration.

value to businesses, perhaps more real value than the glitzy graphics and sound effects specially created for online consumption.

By some estimates, about 70 percent of the mission-critical business information in the world is currently stored in IBM computer systems. This, again, gives IBM a competitive advantage as businesses search for ways to **leverage** their existing investments in information systems by delivering this existing content to the relatively new online community. It's understandable, then, that IBM is focused on helping users enable the vast information stores in their current business systems for viewing over the Internet/intranets. IBM's strategy also includes tools and infrastructure that let a business uncover patterns, predict trends, and address their customers' needs in new ways. The goal is to allow a business to extract new value from existing information, which ultimately leads to a business advantage.

IBM's content management strategy has three segments (Figure 1.8), which we will examine more closely here:

1. Legacy System Enablement

2. Business Extension

3. Business Process Transformation

Business Extension
- Internal Publishing
- External Publishing
- Two-way Communication

Business Process Transformation
- New Business Models
- Re-inventing Business Processes

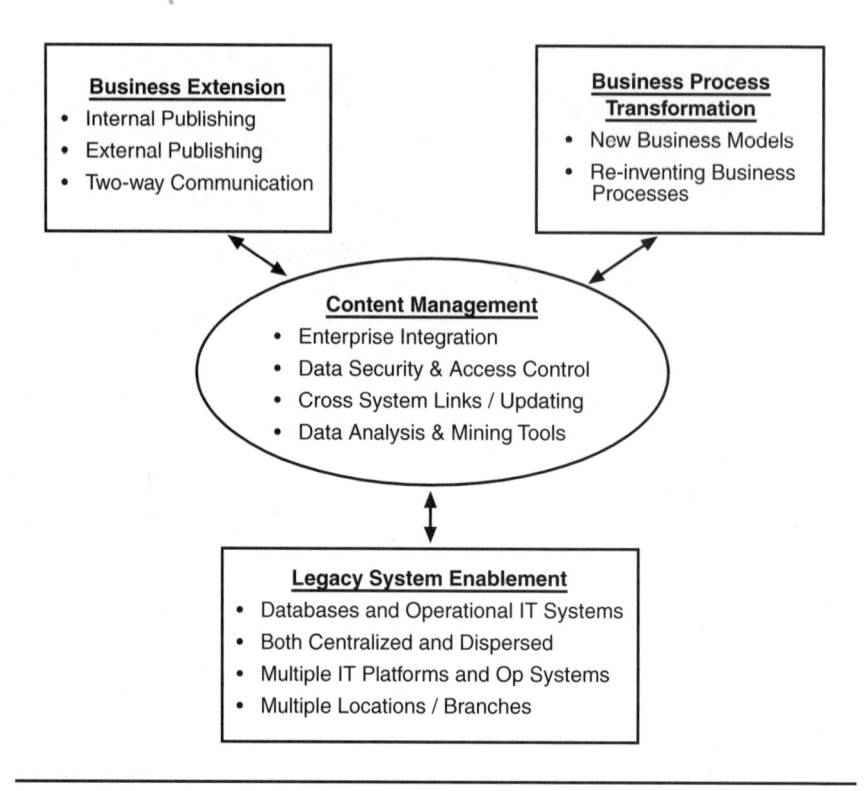

Content Management
- Enterprise Integration
- Data Security & Access Control
- Cross System Links / Updating
- Data Analysis & Mining Tools

Legacy System Enablement
- Databases and Operational IT Systems
- Both Centralized and Dispersed
- Multiple IT Platforms and Op Systems
- Multiple Locations / Branches

Figure 1.8. Content management can be broken down into three application groupings.

Legacy System Enablement

As mentioned earlier, about 70 percent of today's business information is stored in IBM computer systems. The vast majority of this information (and the software tools originally used to manage it) was never intended for distribution over the Internet. Herein lies an enormous opportunity to leverage existing information technology investments. Through Internet-based standards and technologies, businesses have an opportunity to bring existing information stored in long-used systems (called **legacy systems**) to a much broader audience. Today's Internet-enabled content management tools allow a business to link the new world of the Internet with its universal access and consistent user interface (e.g., the Web browser) to the world of inconsistent and specialized internal systems, and that's where the information is.

In combination, the two worlds hold more promise than either one by itself. Legacy System Enablement is about freeing existing information for distribution to more people, either within a company via an intranet or both inside and outside via an extranet.

Business Extension

Since the world is "tuning in to the Internet," business has a new vehicle to reach customers, vendors, and business partners. IBM sees this outreach opportunity as a way for businesses to extend their reach to a new community, the online community. You can think of this segment as an open invitation by businesses for their customers to visit them, learn about them, and interact with them over the Internet. While the Business Extension opportunity benefits from the broader distribution of legacy data (just discussed), it goes beyond that by enabling a business to build new ways to actively interact with its customers, vendors, and business partners.

Business Process Transformation

The two previous segments of content management have dealt with increasing the availability of legacy information and endeavoring to increase a company's interactions with its customers in evolutionary ways. In this Business Process Transformation, the approach is more revolutionary in that it refers to the opportunities to completely reinvent core business processes. By exploiting new content management offerings built on Internet technology, a business can reduce costs in some cases and increase sales in others. For example, a business might completely redesign paper-intensive processes through the use of electronic workflow tools over an intranet to improve cycle time, increase productivity, and decrease physical storage requirements.

Alternately, a business might simultaneously reduce expenses and reach a whole new market by opening an electronic storefront built on content management tools. When you think of the Business Process Transformation segment, think of completely rebuilding a business process on top of the most current content management tools available. One of the important products in IBM's content management line is DB2 Universal Database.

IBM's Database 2 (DB2) has long been a popular family of database management software for use in decision support and transaction processing applications. **DB2 Universal Database** is a new version of DB2 which fits nicely into the Network Computing Framework since it has been enabled for access directly using Internet standard protocols, that is, it has been **Web-enabled.** DB2 Universal Database is capable of storing traditional text and numerical data as well as multimedia content such as graphics, scanned images, sound, and video. This capability allows users to store all forms of information in a structured way which can then be queried and used to populate a Web page on the fly. Visit this book's companion Web site (described on page xiv) for the latest information on DB2 Universal Server and IBM's other content management offerings.

Vassos' 17 Stages

To get a feeling for what it takes to execute an Internet presence capable of doing e-business, consider the work of Tom Vassos of IBM Canada. In his book *Strategic Internet Marketing,* Vassos describes 17 stages (within three phases) that a business Web site typically evolves through (Figure 1.9):

Business Foundation Phase

1. Launch: planning your strategy

2. Repository: publishing your content

3. Link: connecting to other Web sites

4. Cool: using advanced Internet technologies

Business Extension Phase

5. Interactive: interacting with your stakeholders

6. Database: extending the reach of your corporate databases

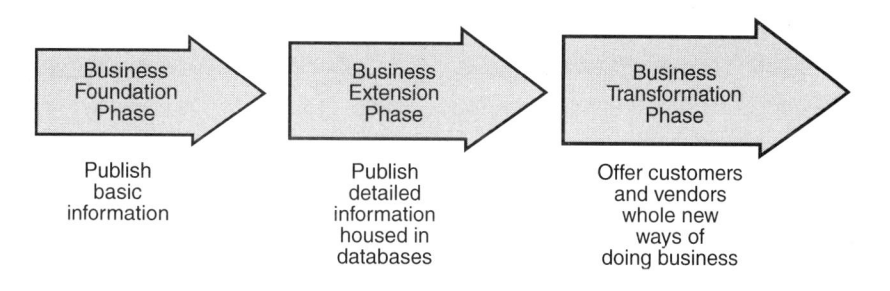

```
Business              Business              Business
Foundation    >       Extension     >       Transformation
Phase                 Phase                 Phase

Publish               Publish               Offer customers
basic                 detailed              and vendors
information           information           whole new
                      housed in             ways of
                      databases             doing business
```

Figure 1.9. Business Web sites typically evolve through three phases, each more valuable to the business than the last.

7. Advanced repository: using advanced content update strategies

8. Advanced interactive: using instant and automated interactive strategies

Business Transformation Phase

9. Mass customization: creating customized content for individual visitors

10. Outbound: reaching out to stakeholders rather than waiting for them to come to you

11. Integration: integrating with content of services from other Web pages

12. Commerce: conducting commercial transactions

13. Personality: giving your Web site character

14. Application: extending the reach of your corporate applications

15. Global: meeting the needs of the global community

16. Strategic alliance: aligning with corporate partners

17. Closed loop: monitoring results and evolving your strategies

Most companies today are in the first phase: Business Foundation (stages 1 through 4). They have a Web site with a primary function to publish information about their company, products, and services. Many businesses have moved on to the second phase: Business Extension. Here a business has learned to make available detailed information typically contained in internal databases. Its Web site becomes more useful to and interactive with the business customers and vendors.

The third phase of Internet presence—Business Transformation—has only been reached by a relatively small number of early adopter companies. The Web sites of these companies have transformed the way they do business with their customers. They have leveraged the Internet to offer their customers and vendors whole new ways of transacting business with them, including end-to-end online transactions.

By considering these steps in the evolution of business Web sites, you can begin to see that the most useful Web sites are those in the latter phases. IBM's focus is on moving companies into the extension and transformation phases —which provides a greater return on investment and more overall business value.

The Foundation Supporting IBM's E-Business Strategy

We have seen how IBM is defining today's users needs through the three application groupings: commerce, intranet/extranet, content management. Now let's take a quick look at some underlying infrastructure components upon which IBM will deliver its Internet/intranet offerings.

- Network Computing Framework

- Java, the Key to Independence

- IBM Server Families

- The IBM Global Network

- Security

Network Computing Framework

In April of 1997, IBM announced its **Network Computing Framework** (Figure 1.10). This framework is a software roadmap for those who will be developing Internet or intranet-based application programs (i.e., independent software developers, IBM business partners, IBM customers, etc.). It is an architecture based on industry standards that provides a foundation upon which software developers can efficiently develop e-business applications that link people, information, and business processes to a Web site.

The heart of the framework is the five servers that link information (Web pages and legacy business data) to the Internet and intranets:

- Lotus Go Webserver

- Lotus Domino Mail

- Lotus Domino

- IBM DB2 Universal Database

- IBM Transaction Series

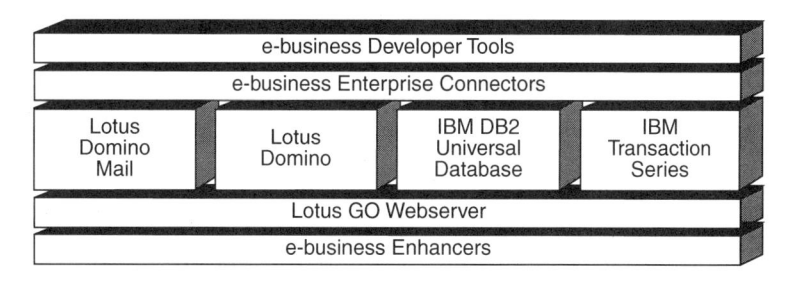

Figure 1.10. IBM's Network Computing Framework.

Below the servers are the e-business Enhancers. These are products that improve the security, scalability, interoperability, and ease of administration of the Web such as the Network Dispatcher (which balances Web site traffic among a group of servers), IBM Firewall (a security layer between an intranet and the Internet), and systems management products for IBM's Tivoli Systems subsidiary.

The e-business Enterprise Connector layer of the framework is for software that provides linkage between existing application programs and the rest of the framework infrastructure. Examples of products in this layer include Net.Data, Domino.Connect, and the IBM CICS Gateway for Java.

Finally, the e-business Developer Tools layer includes a set of visual programming tools for creating Internet and intranet-enabled application programs.

IBM has defined six key concepts that went into the development of the Network Computing Framework:

1. **Servers.** At the heart of IBM's framework are a set of integrated IBM and Lotus Internet/intranet software servers. These servers can be accessed using standard Internet protocols as well as a component interface based on JavaBeans.

2. **Clients.** Clients are used by people to interact with servers and can be anything from a single-purpose application that supports standard browsing protocols (HTTP) and Java applets up to a full-service client which supports additional standard protocols (IIOP, LDAP, IMAP, POP, NNTP, and so forth) and offers offline access to key information and applications. The model leverages the power of the server to provide functionality on client devices—thin clients, fat clients, and everything in between. That functionality is achieved by a set of components that are delivered to the client just in time and on demand, based on the task at hand. By having the server bear a larger part of the workload, the Network Computing Framework enables companies and end users to take advantage of more cost-effective client-side devices, thereby reducing overall technology costs.

3. **Java.** The Network Computing Framework leverages Java as its unifying programming model (i.e., all development efforts

take advantage of Java's "write-once, deploy-everywhere" approach). The JavaBean component standard is used to create client-side applets, server-side applications (called **servlets**), and components to access enterprise services. The Network Computing Framework provides a new set of Java-based tools designed to improve programmer productivity and enable the reuse of virtually all code in future development efforts.

4. **Standard linking.** All components in the model can be linked via open Internet standards such as HTTP and **Internet InterORB Protocol** (IIOP), ensuring that all components in the framework work in harmony to deliver functionality to the user. This enables companies to distribute services over the network, deploying them on whatever platform—client-side or server-side—that makes the most sense. Furthermore, these standards enable the NCF to be an open model that can interact with the Object Request Brokers (ORBs) from HP, Sun, and others.

5. **Groupware.** More and more, companies want to augment the human-centered processes in their companies by adding Internet or intranet functions. The Network Computing Framework employs a set of **groupware** functions—mail, discussions, chat capabilities, group scheduling, contact management, customer service, and others—to enable this trend.

6. **Connectors.** Today companies also want to tie their Internet and intranet facilities to existing enterprise systems and services. The Network Computing Framework provides a set of JavaBean components that access network connectors to enable development teams to leverage enterprise systems, such as CICS, Encina, and DB2.

Java, the Key to Independence

Java technology is a central part of IBM's overall e-business strategy because it gives users more flexibility, offers economies to software developers, and tends to loosen the iron grip of proprietary operating systems (such as Microsoft Windows) and computer system implementations (Intel microprocessors) in favor of open industry standards. Java promises to let any computer exchange information with any other computer, a long sought-after goal in business computing. Let's take a closer look at Java to see how it is accomplishing this feat.

Java technology was announced by Sun Microsystems in 1995 and is now strongly supported by additional companies including IBM, Netscape, and Novell. Java technology consists of two basic elements: the Java programming language used by a programmer to write programs for users, and the Java-enabled browser software that runs Java programs on the user's computer (i.e., the Java Virtual Machine).

There are many programming languages available today, but what sets Java (a derivative of the C++ language) apart from the others is that a program written in Java can be run on any type of computer system. With traditional programming languages, the programmer writes a program which is then **compiled** (translated) into digital codes that can be executed only by a particular computer—the one targeted by the particular compiler used. With Java, the programmer writes the program in much the same way, but it is then translated into Java **byte codes,** which can be executed on any type of computer running a Java-enabled browser program. It is this Java-enabled browser program on the user's computer that does the final translation from Java byte codes to the digital codes that are actually executed on the particular computer in use. This is how any Java program can run on any type of computer system—because the Java-enabled browser on each user's computer system does the final step in the translation.

You will recall that **browser programs** (most of which are now Java-enabled) are needed to access the Internet's, or an intranet's, Web sites. A programmer can write a Java application and put it up on a Web site. Anyone using a Java-enabled browser (running on any type of computer) who visits that Web site can automatically download and run that Java application program by clicking on a hypertext link. This gets us close to software nirvana—where the programmer writes an application program (in Java) one time and distributes it over the Internet, where it can be downloaded (with virtually no distribution costs) and run on any type of computer system (one version for all). Since the Java language was designed for delivery over networks, the resulting programs are compact, for quick downloads to the user's computer.

For users, Java promises pay as you go simplicity with no upgrade headaches to manage. Users may even choose to purchase a low-cost and simplified computer called a network computer, which is only capable of running Java applications resident on a Web server (either on the Internet or an intranet).

IBM is betting heavily on Java technology. In December 1995, IBM announced its licensing of Java technology. IBM then formed the Center for Java Technology in Hursley, England, to deploy Java technology throughout the IBM product line, including key operating systems (e.g., AIX, OS/2, OS/390, and OS/400), databases (e.g., DB2), groupware (e.g., Lotus Notes), transaction systems (e.g., CICS), and development tools (e.g., VisualAge).

IBM has also licensed some related technologies from Sun including JavaOS and HotJava. JavaOS is a compact operating system that can be used in things like cell phones and network computers (simplified low-cost computers that get their programming from an intranet or the Internet). HotJava provides building blocks that can be used to more quickly develop network-based application programs. Thanks to open standards, the HotJava building blocks of one company can work with those of any other. IBM created the first Java Validation Centers, where Java program developers can test their programs on Java systems from companies like Sun, HP, IBM, and others at no charge. If you still want more Java—Sun, IBM, Lotus, and others are working on, yes!, Java Beans—a specification that allows Java application programs to interoperate over networks. IBM is betting heavily on Java.

Server Hardware

It's the job of the server to offer resources (e.g., Web content, disk space, transaction processing, access to other networks, etc.) to clients (e.g., an individual using a PC to access resources available on the network). While the terms "server" and "client" are applicable to any type of computer network, for our purposes we will concentrate on the Internet/intranet environment.

IBM has four primary families of computer systems appropriate for use as Internet or Intranet servers. The chapters that follow will explore each of these computer families more closely:

1. The Personal Computer Server Family (PC Servers)

2. RS/6000 Servers (RS/6000)

3. Application Server/400 Advanced Servers (AS/400)

4. System/390 Servers (S/390)

IBM Global Network

The IBM Global Network is IBM's private worldwide network, which provides communications products and services (including Internet access) to its users. Its focus is to help businesses integrate the Internet into its overall business strategy. The IBM Global Network is one of the largest data networks and Internet service providers, supported by some 5,000 networking specialists serving 28,000 users in 850 cities and some 100 countries around the world. Users can subscribe to the services and applications of their choice and access those applications from virtually any location, through land lines or wireless connections. The user's connection to the IBM Global Network can extend a private network to the Internet without jeopardizing security.

The IBM Global Network plays an important role in IBM's overall e-business strategy. It allows users to outsource much of their Internet and intranet-related infrastructure if they so choose. In later chapters, we will explore some specific services relevant to IBM's e-business strategy. For now, just think of the IBM Global Network as more "plumbing" IBM is leveraging to implement online commerce, intranet/extranet, and content management.

Security

Few Internet subjects are more important than security. To make commerce and intranets pervasive and successful, users must be certain that, unequivocally, transactions and communications can be conducted securely. One of the major cornerstones of transacting business on the Internet is the notion that one's business can be truly private and restricted to specific eyes, very much like the mail we send and receive or the phone conversations we have. As a result, security on the Internet is a major consideration for today's businesses, regardless of their size or scope.

The subject of security involves more than a safe connection to worldwide networks. Surveys have indicated that most businesses incur losses that could be prevented because computer viruses infect their business systems, or that individuals have inappropriate access to sensitive information. Such losses have cost businesses millions of dollars in lost revenue and productivity. Essentially, business cannot be effectively conducted on the Internet without security.

Here again, IBM's heritage gives it advantages in the all-important area of Internet/intranet security. IBM practically invented security in the computer world many years ago. For years, the company has controlled access to the first mainframes, and today it continues to build its experience in securing information across distributed networks around the globe. Thus, in the arena of security, the company has a reputation for innovation and leadership. It has skilled security consultants, technology that has been awarded numerous patents, experience in security services, and the tools necessary for conducting business.

In December 1996 at Internet World in New York City, IBM introduced a broad security framework for conducting business online—called **SecureWay**. This framework makes it possible for diverse security offerings to work together allowing businesses to mix and match security products. SecureWay provides the easy adoption of new and existing technologies; at the same time, it doesn't disturb existing cryptographic and other security functions and operations. It does this by effectively isolating an application from the unique properties of a specific recovery implementation.

A Story of Three Businesses

So far, we have covered many pieces of the e-business puzzle. To help you see how all these pieces can come together to solve problems and create new business opportunities, let's look over the shoulder of three hypothetical companies—small, medium, and large—as they investigate and implement Internet technology. By doing so, you will likely get some ideas on how Internet technology might be used in your environment.

Small Business—Ned Connolly's Auto Parts

Ned Connolly's Auto Parts is a small distributor of high-performance automobile engine parts for American cars. For the past eight years, Connolly's has been comfortably profitable and growing steadily under Ned Connolly's leadership. Connolly's started by selling a basic line of high-performance auto parts through direct mail in Phoenix, Arizona. Now, they offer an expanded line of parts through direct mail and advertising in regional newspapers and magazines. Over the years, Connolly's has earned a reputation for low prices and speedy delivery. Their customers include the major auto parts chain stores and many independents. They have 10 employees who work from a large warehouse. Connolly's currently uses a few personal computers for basic accounting and mailing list management.

Like any good businessman, Ned is always looking for ways to reach new markets. Ned's daughter introduced him to the Internet one weekend, and Ned began to think of ways to use this new technology in his business. He has been looking for a way to sell his parts to more people throughout the United States and Canada. In fact, he also would like to start selling his line to European and Japanese dealers who need American auto parts—a strong and fast-growing market. Ned began to think that the Internet might help him reach these new markets, but he was not knowledgeable about computer technology (or particularly interested in it).

Ned decided to contact a computer consultant in his area who was recommended by a friend. The consultant came in and spent some time learning about the way Connolly's Auto Parts currently does business and their plans for the future. After careful consideration, the consultant recommended that Connolly's Auto Parts put their parts catalog on the Internet and then launch a marketing campaign to inform new customers about their current strengths (low prices and fast delivery) along with secure and convenient online shopping. After reviewing several alternatives, Ned selected the **Domino.Merchant** product as the foundation for his new Web site.

Ned retained the consultant to customize the ready-made Domino.Merchant templates to meet the needs of Connolly's new online storefront and create an online version of their catalog.

After the site was up and functioning, Ned hired an Internet publicist to announce and promote his new online store. The first thing the publicist did was to get Connolly's Online listed in the many online **directories** and **search engines** (e.g., Yahoo!, Lycos, Excite, etc.). Once this was done, the online publicist began posting information about the new store in the automotive-oriented areas of the Internet and online services (i.e., news groups, mailing lists, forums, Web site, etc.). The online publicist also negotiated links to Connolly's online store from heavily traveled Web sites that cater to auto enthusiasts.

As online visitors (from all over the world) began to arrive at Connolly's Online, they were greeted by grand opening specials featuring prices and terms sure to keep buyers coming back. Ned and his staff can easily manage the online store (change prices, add products, etc.) from a personal computer at their convenience. Ned selected the Domino.Merchant product because it was easy, it was low cost, it could be operated at low risk, and he didn't need to invest in and learn to manage a complex computer system.

Medium Business—Blue Sky Musical Instruments

Blue Sky is a medium-sized manufacturer of high-quality musical instruments sold throughout the world. The Business employs 270 people and has shown consistent growth during its 12-year history. When Blue Sky was a smaller company with only one location, internal communication between employees and from management to employees had been done through traditional means including phone calls, face-to-face meetings, and a company newsletter. However, now that Blue Sky has grown considerably and spread out into three different locations, internal communications have become more complicated, and sometimes problematic. So Bill Thompson, Blue Sky's president, commissioned a task force to investigate the internal communications situation and make recommendations. After conducting extensive employee interviews, the task force found that company news and word of personnel policy changes were often slow to circulate among employees. This lack of communication sometimes caused personnel problems and generally eroded morale.

The task force also found that teams consisting of engineers, programmers, and quality personnel, which had been assembled to develop a new line of electronic keyboards, were frustrated. It seems that the team members, often selected from more than one company site due to their unique skills, had difficulty coordinating their activities. Telephone tag, time zone differences, frequent trips between company sites, and mail problems all resulted in delays in their development schedules.

The conclusion of the task force was that Blue Sky had grown to a point where their existing internal communications methods no longer met the needs of the business. The recommendation was to implement an intranet, which could be used as a whole new internal communications infrastructure. The Domino server was recommended for the intranet Web site because of its broadcast and collaboration capabilities. **Domino.Broadcast** along with the new intranet Web site would allow Blue Sky to communicate instantly detailed information about company happenings or policy changes directly to employees. The development team members would use the discussion database, e-mail, and shared document capabilities of Domino to work together online and reduce frustrating delays.

With the approval and active support of president Bill Thompson, a team was assembled and the intranet project was carefully planned and implemented with the help of an authorized Lotus business partner firm. While the implementation ran into several hitches along the way, the final result helped improve communications in the ways anticipated. There were also some unanticipated benefits that resulted from this intranet project. For example, a college co-op employee used Domino's workflow functions to implement an electronic expense-report routing system that streamlined the processing of employee travel-expense reports.

Now that personnel from various functions within Blue Sky better understand what the intranet can do, new ideas for improvement are surfacing regularly. Blue Sky now wonders how they ever did without their company intranet.

Large Business—Stonefield Audio/Video

Stonefield, a large audio/video direct-marketing company, sells a complete line of audio and video equipment including automobile stereos, speakers for cars and homes, television sets, VCRs, telephones, and answering machines. It also sells a full selection of music CDs including pop, classical, jazz, and rock categories. Stonefield's strategy is to sell at less-than-retail prices, purchase in large volumes to reduce inventory costs, and keep overhead and marketing expenses relatively low. Its primary marketing tools are its direct-mail catalog and its in-bound telemarketing organization. It has a liberal return policy and a reputation for providing quality service through its courteous phone reps. It has been in business for nearly 20 years and has recently begun to enjoy a worldwide reputation. Because of thousands of in-stock items which are warehoused and a continual stream of phone calls, Stonefield uses a large S/390 mainframe computer system. It provides its telemarketing staff complete information on its customers, product line, special promotions, and inventory status using the DB2 relational database.

Stonefield has the products that appeal to hundreds of thousands of customers throughout the world. It has been eyeing the Internet as a way to reach new global markets and reduce the cost of reaching existing markets. After mining demographics in the Stonefield's DB2 database, management concluded that the average customer age, yearly income, and so on match the average Internet user. This is a fact that Stonefield wants to exploit. To test the Internet commerce waters, Stonefield decided to start by setting up a new Web site, called Hot Pop, and test-market its line of pop music CDs. This first step out onto the Internet will give Stonefield invaluable experience and lead the way for Stonefield to sell its entire product line over the Internet.

Since Stonefield currently has a large investment in S/390 hardware and DB2 software, IBM's **Net.Commerce** product is a natural choice as the foundation for the Hot Pop Web site. Net.Commerce, if you recall from our earlier discussion, is a set of integrated software products that will allow Stonefield to set up its own "retail store" on the Internet. This product includes accounting, tax handling, and an intuitive user interface. With this product, Stonefield will be able to create a "virtual storefront" to display its line of music CDs. Net.Commerce is also a good choice for Stonefield because it will allow the Hot Pop Web site to link directly to the company's existing DB2 product and customer databases. That is, Net.Commerce will allow Hot Pop visitors to see dynamically generated Web pages that pull directly from the DB2 product database. These visitors will be able to select items from a graphically rich, interactive product catalogue, make sure the desired CDs are in stock (by directly querying the DB2 inventory information), and then securely purchase the desired music CDs online using their credit card.

The secure payment technology **Net.Commerce Payment** will be used to monitor the entire purchasing process, ensuring confidentiality, integrity, and authentication. In the long term, Stonefield expects to realize increased sales and a reduction in normal business operating costs such as staffing, printing, processing, and mailing expenses normally associated with print catalogs.

Stonefield also wants to experiment with another Internet commerce model. The company wants to see if it can sell and deliver music directly over the Internet. While it would be nice to be able to deliver the entire contents of a music CD over the Internet, the limited speed of most Internet connections today makes that impractical. However, a single song off of the CD is of manageable size and can be downloaded in just a few minutes.

Stonefield started by contacting a major record label and negotiating the permissions and royalty arrangements that will be in force during the test-marketing phase. Then 10 popular songs from leading pop artists were selected and stored (in digital form) in files on Stonefield's Web site. A visitor can now visit the Web site and purchase one of these singles for $2 during the test marketing phase. When purchased, the file containing the song is automatically **encrypted** (using IBM's Cryptolope Databolt) and **downloaded** to the visitor's computer over the Internet, right then and there. Once the file is received, the customer can decrypt the song and play it over and over again on any multimedia computer system. Stonefield knows that the Internet market for downloading these files is likely to be small for now but expects that it can increase the sales of music CDs through the publicity and traffic it can generate since it is a leading-edge Web site doing something new. The company also will gain valuable experience and competitive advantage as it monitors the growth of an emerging online delivery market.

2

IBM Personal Computers

This chapter looks at the very popular IBM personal computer line. This broad family ranges from desktop models for the home to high-performance servers. We will start with the groundbreaking history of this family and then take a look at today's IBM PC hardware and software.

A Glance Backwards

IBM entered the small computer business on August 12, 1981, when an informal leg of IBM (called an Independent Business Unit) in Boca Raton, Florida, announced the **IBM Personal Computer (IBM PC)**. The IBM PC was an experiment conducted by 12 developers under the leadership of Philip (Don) Estridge. The small computer system was designed in 12 months from "off-the-shelf" components. Designed primarily for small to medium-size businesses, the IBM PC had an 8088 microprocessor, 16K of standard memory, 160K diskette drives, a text-only monochrome display, and a cassette port. How undemanding we were back in 1981!

Today, just a few short years later, a Personal Computer with such characteristics could hardly satisfy a preschooler playing video games, let alone any serious business needs. However, at that time it fit the needs of the users. Not even the 12 developers imagined that the seed they planted with the IBM PC would grow to become a cornerstone in businesses of all types.

As time went on, IBM developed a family of Personal Computers, and the Independent Business Unit became a full division, the Entry Systems Division (ESD). IBM published all of the PC's technical information, inviting third-party manufacturers to develop and market their own hardware and software for the PC—which they did. This practice of publishing technical details about a product is known as adopting an **open architecture policy.** As more and more third-party hardware and software became available for the PC family of computers, their popularity grew, prompting even more third-party development activity. This self-fueling cycle was beneficial to IBM, third-party developers, and the end users. The success of the open architecture policy has prompted IBM to continue publishing technical details about all subsequent Personal Computer systems.

The Personal Computer family included a wide range of products in terms of both function and price. Let's quickly look at the two core PC family members: the **Personal Computer XT**, shown in Figure 2.1, and the **Personal Computer AT**, shown in Figure 2.2.

The Personal Computer XT was based on the 8088 microprocessor used in the original PC. It was the first PC family member to support a fixed disk. The Personal Computer AT introduced the 80286 microprocessor to the PC family. It offered enhancements in the areas of performance, disk storage, and memory size.

Many of the other PC family members, such as the IBM 3270 PC, the IBM PC/370, and the IBM Portable PC, were developed directly from these core PC family members. All of these PC family members retained a high degree of software compatibility with preceding products.

Then, on April 2, 1987, IBM announced a new generation of personal computers called Personal System/2 computers. The first four models of the IBM Personal System/2 (PS/2) family (Models 30, 50, 60, and 80) were announced on that day. Over the next few years, the PS/2 family grew to include many different models and configurations. The current PS/2 family is part of IBM's enhanced desktop line and employs the best of IBM's technology and design. It is in-

IBM Personal Computers **51**

Figure 2.1. IBM Personal Computer XT.

Figure 2.2. IBM Personal Computer AT.

tended for use by small, medium, and larger business. Not long after the PS/2 announcement, the Personal System/1 (PS/1) family of computers was introduced and targeted at individuals and small business users, being sold primarily through retail outlets.

Then, in September, 1992, IBM turned its Entry Systems Division into the IBM PC Company. This reorganization was designed to give the Personal Computer part of IBM more autonomy and flexibility. On the heels of this reorganization (October, 1992) came the introduction of the ValuePoint and ThinkPad families of Personal Computers. The ValuePoint family—also intended for small, medium, and large business users—has been IBM's low-cost, industry-standard line of Personal Computer. The ThinkPad family consists of battery-powered notebook and subnotebook computers for those needing to compute outside the office.

By far the most sweeping change in the use of PCs in the last few years has been the rapid movement to get connected to the public network of networks called the Internet (and private networks based on the same technology called intranets). Whether we connect from home by modem or through a **LAN (Local Area Network)** at our business, the Internet is truly changing the way we communicate, share information, and do business. So important is the Internet, President Bill Clinton has set forth the goal for all schools in the U. S. to be connected by the year 2000. This book will introduce you to IBM's PC solutions for the Internet, from connecting to the **Web (World Wide Web, or WWW)** at home to building an Internet PC Server for your business. As a result, the IBM PC Server systems began to take on a unique functional and brand identity as well.

Meet the Family

What started out to be a small-scale experiment back in 1981, the IBM Personal Computer, has now grown into several complete families of Personal Computers. The families (also called **brands**) that make up IBM's Personal Computer line are the **IBM Aptiva** family, the **IBM Personal Computer (PC)** family, **IBM Personal Computer (PC) Server** family, and the **IBM ThinkPad** family. Though not a formal member of the IBM PC family, the **IBM IntelliStation** family is a close cousin. The IntelliStation represents IBM's high-end PC Workstations that run technical applications under a Microsoft/Intel platform. Each family is designed to suit the needs and buying habits of specific user communities (with some overlap between the families).

The Aptiva family is designed for use by individuals, in very small businesses and at home. It currently consists of two series of different models, all with standard multimedia capabilities. Figure 2.3 shows a member of the Aptiva S family. The focus is on low cost, convenience, and ease of use. Unlike most of IBM's other PC families, Aptiva computers are offered only through general retailers rather than computer dealers or IBM marketing representatives. Since Aptivas are primarily for the individual and home market, they are not intended (or supported) for use in complex local area networks. PC families designed for use in networks undergo additional and extensive testing in various network environments, which adds costs consumers do not require. However, Aptivas do come with fax/modems and com-

Figure 2.3. A member of IBM's Aptiva S Series.

munications software that allow for everything from Internet access to telephone answering machine functions. The new Aptivas, based on Intel's Pentium and Pentium MMX microprocessors, come with the Windows 95 operating system and several basic application programs preinstalled.

IBM has consolidated its line of commercial desktop systems under the IBM Personal Computer (PC) brand. The IBM PC brand is also known under the umbrella name of **Client Systems,** denoting systems that can attach to a server over a network. This also means that the systems are network certified and supported in a network environment. IBM's commercial systems also provide many features that help businesses manage and protect their PC assets. The newer models in this family are identified by the IBM PC name and a product number such as PC 300GL and PC 365. The IBM Personal Computer family (Figure 2.4) covers a wide range of performance, features, and functions. There are IBM PC models based on the full range of Pentium microprocessors and incorporating both **ISA (Industry Standard Architecture)** and **PCI (Peripheral Component Interconnect)** expansion buses.

IBM has also consolidated its line of server systems under the IBM Personal Computer (PC) Server brand. The newer models in this family are identified by the IBM PC Server name and a product number such as PC Server 325 or PC Server 704. The new line of IBM PC Servers (Figure 2.5) covers a wide range of performance, features, and functions. There are IBM PC Server models based on a broad range of microprocessors extending from a single 100 MHz Pentium

Figure 2.4. IBM PC family.

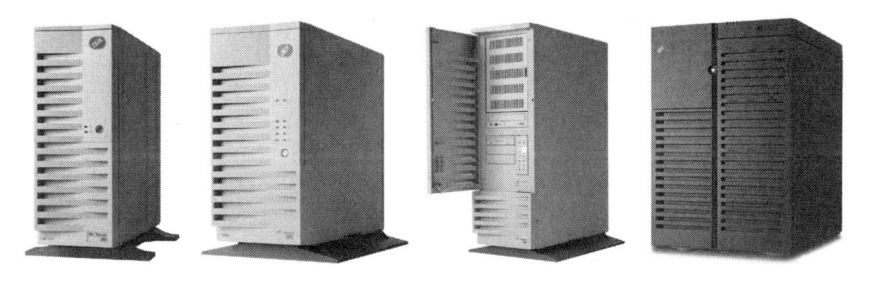

Figure 2.5. IBM PC Server family.

processor to systems with as many as four **Symmetric MultiProcessing (SMP)** 200 MHz Pentium Pro processors sharing the same PC Server. Industry Standard Architecture (ISA), Enhanced Industry Standard Architecture (EISA), Peripheral Component Interconnect (PCI), and Micro Channel Architecture products are offered in the IBM PC Server family. All of IBM's PC Servers come with an array of software including Lotus Notes Server software, TME 10 Netfinity, and Server Guide.

The IBM ThinkPad family (Figure 2.6) of computers is designed to be used both in and out of the office environment. Their key features are small size, light weight, and battery power. All ThinkPad computers have built-in color displays. Some models are capable of recognizing your handwriting; others are capable of recording and playing back speech and music. The power and flexibility of these systems combined with the available optional features allows a single system to satisfy all computing needs of a traveling professional.

Finally, the IBM IntelliStation family of computers is intended for the business professional who requires very high-end workstation performance to run graphically and compute intense 32-bit applications such as Computer Aided Design (CAD) and statistical modeling. The IntelliStation bridges the gap between the traditional UNIX/RISC workstation and the PC by using high-end Intel-based processors running Microsoft's Windows NT.

Before leaving this overview section, we should mention IBM's new Network Station, which is meant to replace **Non-Programmable Terminals (NPTs)** that connect to servers and mainframes. The IBM Network Station with its PowerPC Microprocessor is marketed

56 EXPLORING IBM TECHNOLOGY AND PRODUCTS

Figure 2.6. IBM ThinkPad family.

through the IBM PC Company dealer channel. It provides users with a lower-cost access to the network than traditional PCs, but with many popular PC features such as SVGA graphics and mouse support that are lacking in a Non-Programmable Terminal.

Also worth mentioning is IBM's Industrial Computer line, which is intended for nonoffice environments. These PC compatible systems are designed and packaged so that they can withstand harsher environments (e.g., higher temperatures, particulates, power surges, shock, vibration, and longer power-on hours) than mainstream personal computers.

So much for an overview of IBM's Personal Computer families. Now let's go back and take a closer look at each family. Since the PC world is a fast changing one, be sure and check this book's companion Web site (see page xiv for the address) frequently for news, updates, and expanded information.

Hardware Architecture

There are many elements that together provide the functions and performance of a computer. The remainder of this chapter provides a closer look at the following elements of IBM's Personal Computers:

- Microprocessors
- Memory
- Disk storage

Microprocessors and Memory

Although there are many electronic circuits in Personal Computers, two key elements contribute the most to the system's capabilities and performance. These are the **microprocessor** and the **RAM (Random Access Memory)**, called simply the **memory**. The microprocessor and memory, along with other circuits, reside on a circuit board called the **system board** in most Personal Computers. In some, however, such as the PC Server 720 and 704, this circuitry is packaged on a **processor card** installed in a special slot on the system board.

Microprocessor Basics

The microprocessor is typically the most important item in a computer system because it executes the instructions that make up a computer program, acts as the control center for information flow inside the computer, and performs calculations on the data. It is a single computer chip containing many thousands or even millions of microscopic circuits that work together to execute computer programs. The microprocessor does the data manipulation or "thinking" necessary to perform tasks for the user.

The microprocessor is the central processing unit (CPU) of the computer. It is the place where most of the control and computing functions occur. All operating system and application program instructions are executed here. Most information passes through it, whether that information is a keyboard stroke, data from a disk, or information from a communication network.

The processor needs data and instructions for each processing operation that it performs. Data and instructions are loaded from memory into data-storage locations, known as **registers**, in the processor. Registers are also used to store the data that results from each processing operation until the data is transferred to memory. The microprocessor is packaged as an integrated circuit that contains one or more **Arithmetic Logic Units** (ALUs or execution units), a floating-point unit, an on-board cache, registers for holding instructions, data, and control circuitry. This circuitry is used to perform the binary mathematics electrically inside the microprocessor.

A fundamental characteristic of all microprocessors is the rate at which they perform operations. This characteristic is called the clock rate and is measured in millions of cycles per second or **megahertz (MHz)**. The maximum clock rate of a microprocessor is determined by how fast the internal logic of the chip can be switched. As silicon fabrication processes are improved, the integrated devices on the chip become smaller and can be switched faster. Thus, the clock speed can be increased.

Multiprocessing

The speed of the microprocessor has a significant effect on the performance of the computer. The internal structure or architecture of the microprocessor also determines the inherent capabilities of the Personal Computer in which it is used. Another way to increase the performance of the computer is through the use of multiple processors in a system. This is called **multiprocessing**. The two main types of multiprocessing are asymmetric and symmetric. In **asymmetric** (or loosely coupled) processing, the CPUs are dedicated to specific tasks, so a CPU can be idle if a specific task is not needed. Asymmetric processing is no longer commonly used in the PC environment. In **symmetric** (tightly coupled) processing, each CPU is available for any process task. An **SMP (Symmetric MultiProcessing)** system enhances performance by allowing the computer's whole workload to be distributed among all the CPUs. Additional CPUs act like all the others in processing tasks or threads of execution.

As there is overhead in managing additional processors, the system performance gain will be less than 100 percent for each processor. The **performance gain** is dependent on the operating system and type of application used. An operating system must support SMP. Applications also need to be designed for SMP (i.e., multithreaded) to realize the full potential of SMP.

IBM's new PC Servers and IntelliStation PCs have support for SMP. For example, the PC Server 320 supports dual Pentium processors and the PC Server 720 supports as many as six processors.

Intel Microprocessors

Since the beginning of the PC, IBM has continued to make computers based on Intel's line of CISC microprocessors. Figure 2.7 shows a history of the generations of Intel's processors. Although IBM manufactured some number of their own 386- and 486-compatible processors, the majority of IBM's PC models have used Intel processors.

Introduction Year	Internal Processor	Clock	Bus Width	Number of Transistors	Addressable Memory
1971	4004	108KHz	4 bits	2,300	640 bytes
1972	8008	108KHz	8 bits	3,500	16K
1974	8080	2 MHz	8 bits	6,000	64K
1978	8086	5 MHz	16 bits	29,000	1 MB
1979	8088	5 MHz	16 bits	29,000	1 MB
1982	80286	8 MHz	16 bits	134,000	16 MB
1985	80386 DX	16 MHz	32 bits	275,000	4 GB
1989	80486 DX	25 MHz	32 bits	1,200,000	4 GB
1993	Pentium	60 MHz	32 bits	3.2 million	4 GB
1995	Pentium Pro	150 MHZ	64 bits	5.5 million	4 GB
1997	Pentium MMX	166 MHZ	32 bits	4.5 million	4 GB
1997	Pentium II	233 MHZ	64 bits	7.5 million	64 GB

Figure 2.7. History of major Intel processor introductions used in computers. (Not all variations are listed.)

IBM PCs have evolved from Intel's 8088, 8086, 286, 386, and 486 to today's Pentium and Pentium II microprocessor architectures.

Memory

The memory is also a very important part of a computer. **Memory** is the set of electronic chips that provide a "workspace" for the microprocessor. The memory holds the information being used by the microprocessor. This memory, as mentioned before, is called RAM (Random Access Memory) because it can store and retrieve any piece of information independent of the sequential order in which it was originally stored. The smallest piece of information that can be stored in memory is called a **bit**. These bits are grouped into **bytes** (8 bits), **words** (16 bits), and **double words** (32 bits) to form the computer's representation of numbers, letters of the alphabet, and instructions in a program.

The amount of memory in IBM Personal Computers ranges from 8 MB (IBM ThinkPad Model 365) to 2 GB (PC Server 704). As memory increases, so do the chances of having a **memory failure**, which can cause the computer system to deliver erroneous information or abruptly halt the system altogether. To combat this problem, the IBM Personal Computers that can be configured with the largest memories, including the IBM PC Server systems, employ schemes to detect and correct memory defects, thus protecting the integrity of the information stored in the computer system's main memory. These schemes, called **error checking and correcting (ECC)**, can detect both single- and double-bit errors and correct single-bit errors.

At this point it is prudent to mention three other types of memory in Personal Computers: **read only memory (ROM)**, **flash erasable programmable read only memory (EPROM)**, and **complementary metal oxide semiconductor (CMOS) memory**. Each Personal Computer contains some amount of ROM, which permanently stores some special housekeeping programs used to manage the internal operation of the computer. The memory is called ROM because information it contains cannot be altered or written to—it can only be read. The information stored in ROM is preserved even when the computer is turned off. In many of the newer Personal Computers, flash

EPROM is used to store the same housekeeping programs that were traditionally stored in standard ROM. As the name implies, the flash EPROM is a read-only memory that can be erased and reprogrammed using a special technique. Like standard ROM memory, the information is preserved even when the computer is turned off. However, since the flash EPROM can be altered, the information can be loaded into the EPROM from a diskette, using the utility software that comes with the system. This provides an easy way to correct possible errors once you have already purchased the system or to add enhanced function to upgrade performance or function.

CMOS memory gets its name from the transistor technology used to build the memory. The information in CMOS memory, unlike the information in ROM, can be altered at any time. The low power consumption inherent in CMOS technology allows the internal battery to preserve the information stored in CMOS memory even when the computer is turned off. The CMOS memory is used to store system configuration and diagnostic information. The CMOS memory chip also has circuitry that automatically keeps track of the current time of day and date. This time and date information is available for use by an application program and is used by operating systems to track when disk files were created, when files were last modified, and so on.

Disk Storage

Disk storage, commonly used in Personal Computers, provides a relatively inexpensive way to store computer data and programs. The information stored on disk can be easily modified or kept unchanged over long periods of time as an archive. The information remains intact whether the computer is turned on or off. Thus, disk storage is said to be **nonvolatile**. All Personal Computers (except for medialess workstations) utilize two types of disk storage: **diskettes** and **fixed disks**.

It is also worth mentioning here that optical disk storage (discussed in Chapter 4) is growing in importance as multimedia applications become more prevalent. For now, let's look at the diskette and fixed disk storage commonly used with Personal Computers.

Diskettes

Diskettes are portable magnetic storage media that can be used to record and later retrieve computer information via a **diskette drive**. All IBM Personal Computers use 3.5-inch diskettes as opposed to the 5.25-inch diskettes used by earlier Personal Computers. These diskette types are compared in Figure 2.8. The outer case of the 5.25-inch diskettes is flexible and doesn't completely cover the sensitive magnetic material actually containing the information. The 3.5-inch diskette has a rigid outer case that completely encloses the magnetic material. A sliding metal cover, which protects the magnetic material, is retracted only while the diskette is inside the diskette drive. For these reasons, the 3.5-inch diskettes are less susceptible to damage that may result during normal handling. Further, the 3.5-inch diskettes are small enough to fit conveniently into a shirt pocket or purse. The write protect switch (not visible) in the lower-left corner on the back of the diskette allows you to prevent the accidental overwriting of information. When the switch is positioned so that the square hole in the lower-left corner is open, the diskette is write protected. When the switch is blocking the square hole, information can

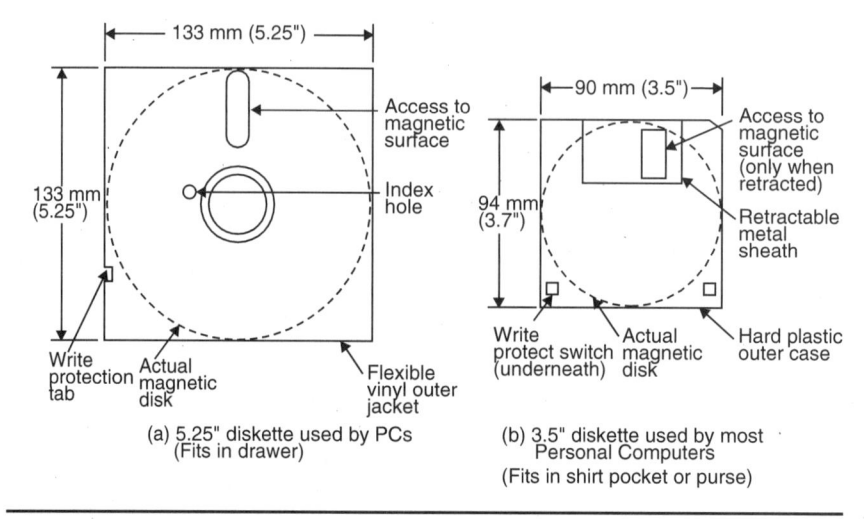

Figure 2.8. The 5.25-inch and 3.25-inch diskette.

be written to the diskette. Some diskettes, such as the Reference Diskette, will not have this switch and are therefore permanently write protected. One of the primary functions of the diskette is to provide portable disk storage, allowing for the transfer of programs and data between computers.

Fixed Disks

Another kind of disk storage used with IBM Personal Computers is called a **fixed disk** (or simply a **disk**). Fixed disks are high-capacity magnetic storage devices commonly used in most Personal Computers as well as in the largest computer systems. They consist of a drive mechanism with permanently installed metallic disks coated with a magnetic material. An **activity light** is usually provided and is illuminated when a fixed disk is being accessed. The circuitry that controls these fixed disks is packaged with the fixed disk drive itself (called an integrated **controller**), on the system board, or on a separate feature card.

CD-ROM Drives

CD-ROM drives use the same technique to store information as audio compact disks. Rather than using magnetics, CD-ROM systems use optical techniques to achieve their much higher density. A single disk used in CD-ROM drives can hold about 600 MB of information. That's enough storage to hold over 300,000 sheets of computer output, or a stack over 90 feet high. CD-ROM drives are **read only**. That is, Personal Computer users can view the information but they can't change it. The information is prerecorded on the disk using specialized equipment and then distributed to Personal Computer users for their use. The primary use of CD-ROM storage is to distribute large amounts of information in a convenient package. Potential uses for CD-ROM include distribution of program libraries, financial reports, operations manuals, phone directories, or any large (and relatively stable) database.

The extremely high storage capacity of CD-ROMs can be attributed to the technique used to store the information. When the

CD-ROM is first recorded, a laser beam is used to burn tiny patterns on the reflective surface of an optical disk according to industry standards. Later, by bouncing the low-power laser beam in the CD-ROM drive off the optical disk's surface, a series of mirrors and sensors can read back the information burned into the disk. Although this optical technology lends itself quite well to the information distribution applications mentioned earlier, their limited speed (as compared to fixed disks) and inability to record information preclude using CD-ROM disks as normal fixed disk storage. Two CD-ROM drives that can be used with IBM Personal Computers are the IDE CD-ROM Drive and the Enhanced SCSI CD-ROM Drive.

PC Software

The term "software" is analogous to the term "publication." Newspapers are a category of publication. Annual reports, novels, and *Who's Who* directories are some other categories of publications. These different categories fill very different needs. The same situation exists with software. The different categories of software are diverse in function and purpose. Here we will explain how the various unique and highly specialized programs interact, through descending levels, to communicate with the hardware in your CPU.

Types of Software—A Model

The basic categories of real software used with all Personal Computers to perform useful work can be understood through the simple software model shown in Figure 2.9. There are three basic categories or software layers commonly used with Personal Computers: the **application program** layer, the **operating system** layer, and the **Basic Input/Output System (BIOS)** layer. Although each software layer performs a completely different job, all three work closely together to perform useful work for the user. Some special-purpose programs don't fit neatly into any of the three categories, but the majority of the software commonly used to perform business tasks does. Software programs for the various IBM families will be further discussed in later chapters.

```
                User's view of Personal Computer

                  ↓    ↓    ↓    ↓

              ┌─────────────────────┐
              │  Application Program│      Memory
              │ ┌───────────────────┤
              │ │ Operating System  │
              │ │ ─ ─ ─ ─ ─ ─ ─ ─ ─ ┤ ─ ─ ─ ─ ─
              │ └──┬────────────────┤
              │    │   BIOS         │
              │    │                │      System
              │    Hardware         │      Board
              └─────────────────────┘
```

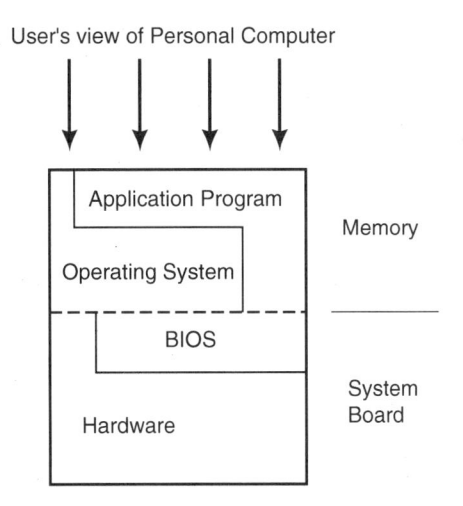

Figure 2.9. Conceptual software model of the basic software structure of Personal Computers. The three layers of the software model work together to perform useful work for the user.

Application Programs

The top software layer in the software model is the application program layer, highlighted in Figure 2.10. The programs in this layer apply Personal Computers to specific tasks such as word processing and communications. Thus, they are called application programs. They actually perform the task the user purchased the computer for, while the other two layers play important support roles.

The "User's View" arrows in Figure 2.10 indicate that the user usually interacts with the application program layer and less frequently interacts with the operating system. By working closely with the other software layers, the application program processes the various keystrokes made by the user and responds by displaying information on the computer's display or some other output device.

As we see later in the chapter, newer Personal Computers can execute most of the programs written for the original IBM PC. This allows Personal Computer users to capitalize on the thousands of application programs originally developed for IBM PCs and compatibles. Common functions that application programs perform in

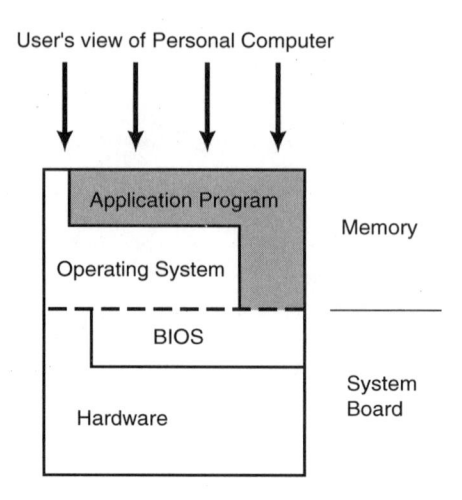

Figure 2.10. The application program software layer, highlighted in the software model above, defines the particular task the computer is performing for the user.

the business environment are accounting, financial modeling, word processing, database management, communications, and computer graphics. There is an application program that can help the user with just about anything he or she wishes to do. Look around—it may be hard to find, but it probably exists.

Operating Systems

The next layer in our software model, called the **operating system,** is highlighted in Figure 2.11. The operating system must manage the hardware resources of the computer system and perform tasks under the control of application programs and keyboard/mouse/touch-screen input from the user. The application program can rely on the operating system to perform many of the detailed housekeeping tasks associated with the internal workings of the computer. Thus, the operating system is said to provide the environment in which application programs execute. Operating systems also accept input directly from the user to perform such tasks as formatting diskettes and clearing the screen.

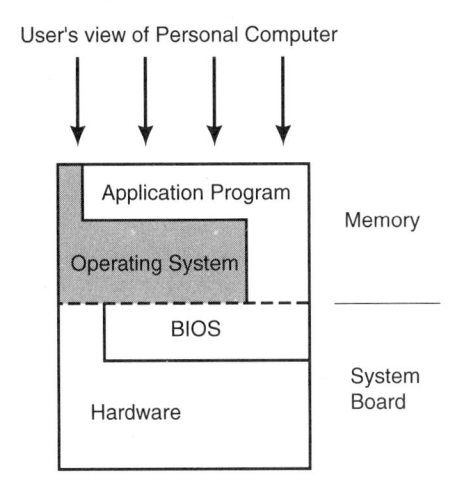

Figure 2.11. The operating system software layer, highlighted in the software model above, provides the environment in which the application program(s) run.

BIOS

The third and final layer of software in our software model is called the Basic Input/Output System (BIOS) layer, highlighted in Figure 2.12. BIOS is a set of specialized programs that, unlike application programs or operating systems, are used only by other programs. BIOS never interacts directly with the user and exists only to help application programs and operating systems perform tasks. In fact, the user never even knows it's there. BIOS assists the operating system and application programs in performing tasks directly involving details of the computer hardware. BIOS also shields a computer program from the hardware specifics of computers, allowing these specifics to evolve as new computers are designed without causing software compatibility problems.

Unlike operating systems or application programs that must be loaded into memory from disk, BIOS is permanently stored in the read only memory (ROM) chips within the Personal Computer along with the POST program. Many of the newer Personal Computer models store a large portion of the BIOS in flash memory, which can

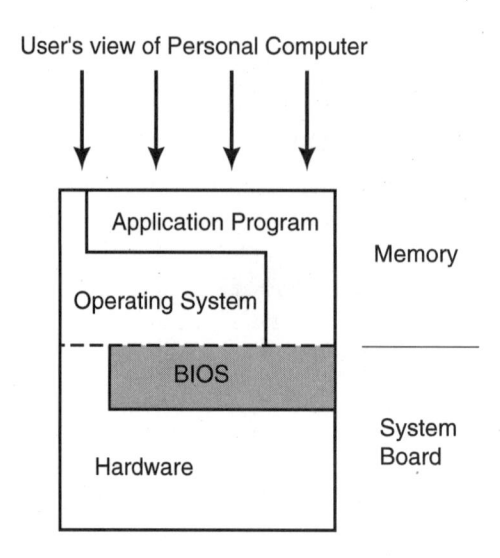

Figure 2.12. The BIOS software layer, highlighted in the software model above, directly controls the hardware elements of Personal Computers and shields application programs and operating systems from the hardware details.

be easily updated using special information provided on the reference diskette.

Most Personal Computers have both a **compatibility BIOS** and an **advanced BIOS**. The compatibility BIOS is provided to preserve software compatibility with PCs. This same type of BIOS was supplied with all earlier PC computers. The advanced BIOS is a completely independent set of programs, also stored in the Personal Computer's ROM (or flash memory). Advanced BIOS provides a more advanced set of programming tools used by operating system programmers and provides specific support for the multi-application environment.

Operating Systems

Few topics in the personal computer area create more confusion and apprehension than the operating system. Never before has the user had more operating system alternatives. This section will help remove some of the mystery associated with operating systems used on IBM Personal Computers. It is designed to familiarize you with operating system topics, such as multi-application and extended memory, and how these concepts apply to the business environment. It also discusses specific operating system products for IBM Personal Computers.

The Disk Operating System (DOS)

The PC Disk Operating System, commonly called DOS, was the operating system originally offered for the IBM Personal Computer. It was primarily designed to provide a single-application, single-user environment—though today's extensions to DOS (such as Windows, covered later in the chapter) can make it a multi-application environment.

Since its introduction in 1981, DOS has become widely accepted. As PCs evolved, DOS was revised to support the enhancements in the computer hardware. Although each new version of DOS provided additional functions, compatibility with earlier application programs was maintained. Each version of DOS was numbered to distinguish the different levels. The original DOS was called DOS 1.0. The most recent version of DOS as of this writing is DOS 7.0, which is currently the entry-level operating system for IBM Personal Computers.

DOS provides an IBM PC-compatible, single-application environment. It consists of a set of programs designed to perform many diverse hardware housekeeping tasks under the control of either the user or an application program. As the name DOS implies, many of these housekeeping tasks deal with the fixed disks in personal computers. Other tasks performed by DOS include starting application programs, setting the computer's date and time, sending information to a printer, and managing files.

DOS operates personal computers primarily in **Real mode.** In this mode, the microprocessor appears to have the same basic architectural structure as that of the 8088 microprocessor used in the original IBM PC. The architectural similarities afforded by Real mode allow current IBM Personal Computers to execute software written for the original IBM PC.

Advanced Operating Systems

The full capabilities of IBM Personal Computers are not unleashed unless the operating system fully exploits the advanced features offered by the advanced microprocessors (386 and above). The **Protected mode** of the advanced microprocessors provides an effective and fully architected path to overcoming the 640 KB memory limitation of the original PC design.

In addition, there are other advantages offered by advanced operating systems. For example, the **Virtual 8086 mode** of the 386/486 family of microprocessors allows Personal Computers to behave as if there were several independent computers cooperating to perform work for one user.

There are several different operating system environments that more fully exploit the advanced capabilities of the microprocessors used in IBM Personal Computers. Now let's take a closer look at the advanced operating system alternatives.

DOS Extended with Windows

The Windows program, developed by Microsoft Corp., can be used to extend the basic DOS functions in the area of multi-application and maximum memory size. Windows version 3.0 introduced some major enhancements to the Windows product. The 3.1 version of Windows includes additional enhancements in the areas of performance, file management, font capability, reliability, and network integration.

Because Windows is built on the DOS base, you cannot run OS/2 application programs under Windows. For DOS or Windows application programs, Windows helps overcome the **640 KB memory limit** of the original IBM PC, which is still with us in today's DOS environment for the sake of compatibility. It is important to somehow overcome this 640 KB limit, because as you begin to load multiple application programs into memory, you quickly run out of space in the 640 KB area. Depending on the mode in which you operate Windows, the 640 KB limitation is overcome in different ways (more on that shortly).

In the area of multi-application, Windows allows the user to start up and run more than one application program at a time (i.e., multi-application support). To manage these applications, Windows subdivides the display screen into multiple rectangular areas called **windows**. Each application program then resides in its own window to facilitate quick and convenient switching from one application to another (i.e., program switching). A mouse is used to interact with Windows for things like selecting which window is the active window, starting programs, resizing windows, moving windows around on the screen, and so on. Small images called **icons** are drawn on the display to indicate that application programs are loaded but not currently shown in a window. This type of user interface based on icons, windows, and so on, is called a **Graphical User Interface (GUI)**. Some application programs can remain active (in the background) while you are interacting with another (in the foreground). However, because Windows works in conjunction with DOS (a non-multi-application operating system), there are limitations to the multi-application environment provided by the DOS/Windows environment. These limitations depend on the Windows mode being used.

With Windows, there are three different modes of operation: **Real mode, Standard mode,** and **Enhanced mode.** (*Note:* Version 3.1 dropped Real mode.) Chances are, you would run Windows in Real mode only if you had to. You would have to if you use Windows in a computer based on the 8088 or 8086 microprocessors (e.g., a very old system by today's standards). In Real mode, Windows gets around the 640 KB memory limit through the **Expanded Memory Specification (EMS)** for applications written for Windows (Windows applications) and for regular DOS applications (non-Windows applications) if the application program supports this standard. EMS (originally developed by Lotus, Intel, and Microsoft) is a bank-switching technique that tricks the application program into thinking there is more memory than 640 KB. Like PC DOS 7.0, Windows in Real mode can use another trick to make the memory seem larger than 640 KB for non-Windows applications that do not support EMS—namely, swapping DOS applications to the fixed disk and recalling them when needed. The application program(s) need not be specially written to support this swapping. However, the extra work of swapping from memory to fixed disk and back to memory can make the computer system respond sluggishly.

If you have a more current Personal Computer based on one of the more advanced microprocessors (286 or greater), you can use Windows in its Standard mode. In Standard mode, Windows gets around the 640 KB memory limitation by exploiting the Protected mode functions designed into these more advanced microprocessors. A special part of Windows called a **DOS extender** switches back and forth between the microprocessor's Real mode (where the 640 KB limit is in force) and Protected mode (where the limit is 16 MB). This allows multiple Windows application programs to reside in a memory space larger than 640 KB and facilitates program switching. However, all non-Windows application programs must still coexist within the 640 KB limit, along with DOS and a portion of the Windows program. For this reason, Standard mode users of non-Windows applications will often find that the system reverts back to disk swapping (discussed earlier). Further, non-Windows application programs will usually not remain active when in the background.

For Personal Computers based on the 386 SX microprocessor or higher, the full power of Windows Enhanced mode is available. In Enhanced mode, Windows utilizes the Virtual 8086 mode of these more advanced microprocessors to overcome the 640 KB limit and provide for program switching and multitasking of non-Windows application programs. The Virtual 8086 mode of these more advanced microprocessors allows a Personal Computer to behave as if it had multiple 8086 microprocessors, with one 8086 dedicated to each non-Windows application program. The performance of 486 and Pentium microprocessors also makes for a more productive computing environment than that provided by older 8088, 8086, or 286 computer systems.

Windows 95

Windows 95 is the most current version of Microsoft's Windows. Windows 95 is a 32-bit operating system that can also run 16-bit Windows 3.1 programs. The graphical user interface has a different look and feel from Windows 3.1. Navigating the system is now easier with this new interface. First, Windows 95 features a new "Start" button and taskbar at the bottom of the screen as shown in Figure 2.13. The "Start" button is located at the far left with a Windows logo as part of the button. You can click your mouse on the "Start" button to open programs, find documents, and use system tools. Another way to open the Start menu is by using a Windows 95 key-

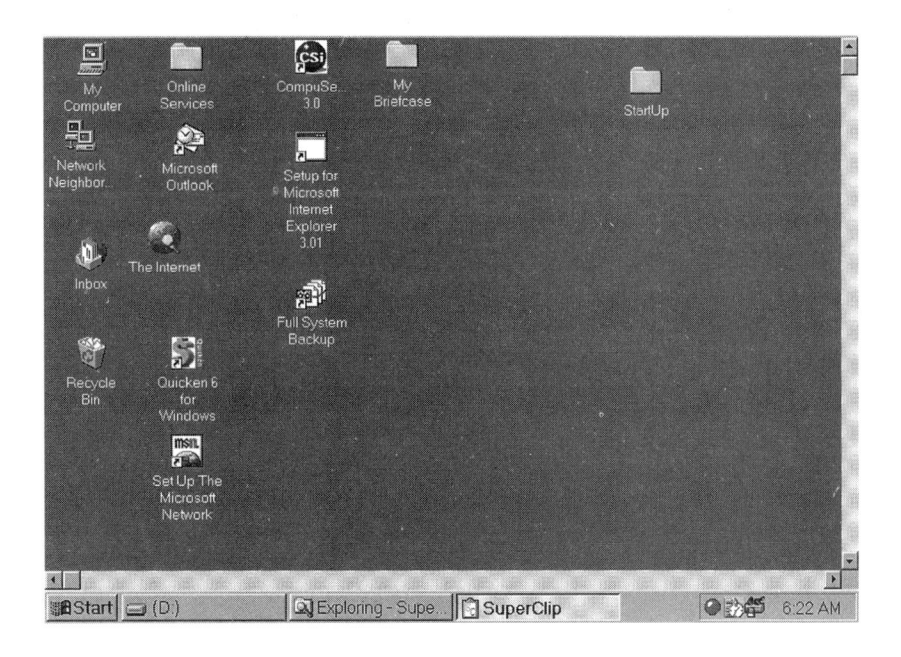

Figure 2.13. Windowing environment presented by Windows 95.

board. A Windows 95 keyboard has an additional Windows 95 key that you can press to open the Start menu without using a mouse.

The Windows 95 taskbar, at the bottom of the screen, makes it easy to switch between programs. Every time you start a program or open a window, a button appears in this area representing that window. To switch between windows, all you need to do is click the button for the window you want. To the right side of the taskbar is a "Notification Area" that can be used by programs as an indicator of program activity such as printing. The system clock is displayed on far right side of the taskbar. To change the clock settings all you need to do is double-click your mouse on the clock.

Second, Windows 95 now supports longer filenames (up to 250 characters). The use of longer filenames can make it easier to organize and locate programs and documents on your computer. For example, you can now have a spreadsheet file called "*Bobjohnsons_1997income_tax*" rather than "*BJOHN97*" Files are stored in **folders** in Windows 95. A folder is like a directory in Windows 3.1 and may also contain other folders. Windows 95 uses a folder icon to represent directories.

Another significant advancement is with DOS compatibility. Windows 95 does not require DOS to run, but includes an MS-DOS kernel for compatibility as part of the Windows 95 operating system. MS-DOS can be started from the Applications menu in Windows 95.

Windows 95 lets you use many programs at once through 32-bit preemptive multitasking. However, multitasking and performance improvements require applications to be written for 32-bit operations. (This means you will need to update your applications to a 32-bit Windows 95 version to get the most improvement.)

Windows 95 has a large number of accessories including a built-in Internet browser, system backup, hard disk scanning, and data compression. Windows 95 also includes an icon for signup and access to the Microsoft Network. The **Microsoft Network** is an on-line service that allows you gain access to the Internet. The Microsoft Network is a growing Internet service provider and provides its own set of information, news groups, bulletin boards, electronic mail, and download software.

Also, there are interactive on-line help guides called **Wizards** that walk you through many of the tasks in Windows 95. One last key feature, called **Plug and Play**, makes installing new hardware options easier by automatically detecting the new option. You should be aware that new hardware options must be Plug and Play compatible to take advantage of this feature.

Operating System/2 Warp

Operating System/2 Warp, Version 4 is the latest version of IBM's OS/2 operating system. It is designed to concurrently run three types of application programs effectively: DOS application programs, Windows application programs, and OS/2 application programs. The standard version of OS/2 Warp is designed to be installed with Windows 3.1 in order to support Windows applications. The enhanced capabilities of OS/2 Warp are built around the Virtual 8086 mode provided in the 386 SX and higher microprocessors (but not provided in the 286). This prevents OS/2 Warp from running on older 286-based computer systems. Before we look at OS/2 Warp's compatibility with

DOS, Windows, and OS/2 native application programs, let's look at some things about OS/2 Warp that apply across the board.

The first thing you will notice about OS/2 Warp is the **OS/2 Workplace Shell** (Figure 2.14). The Workplace Shell is the graphical user interface for OS/2. It combines the functions of a desktop manager, print manager, and file manager, which Windows 3.1 has as separate interfaces. This provides a more consistent, usable, and powerful interface than the standard Windows 3.1 program manager. In OS/2 Warp, the Workplace Shell has been enhanced even further with the addition of new three-dimensional and animated icons. An animated icon is one that changes its appearance to indicate the status of a function, such as a folder being opened or closed. This greatly improves usability because the status of the workplace can be deter-

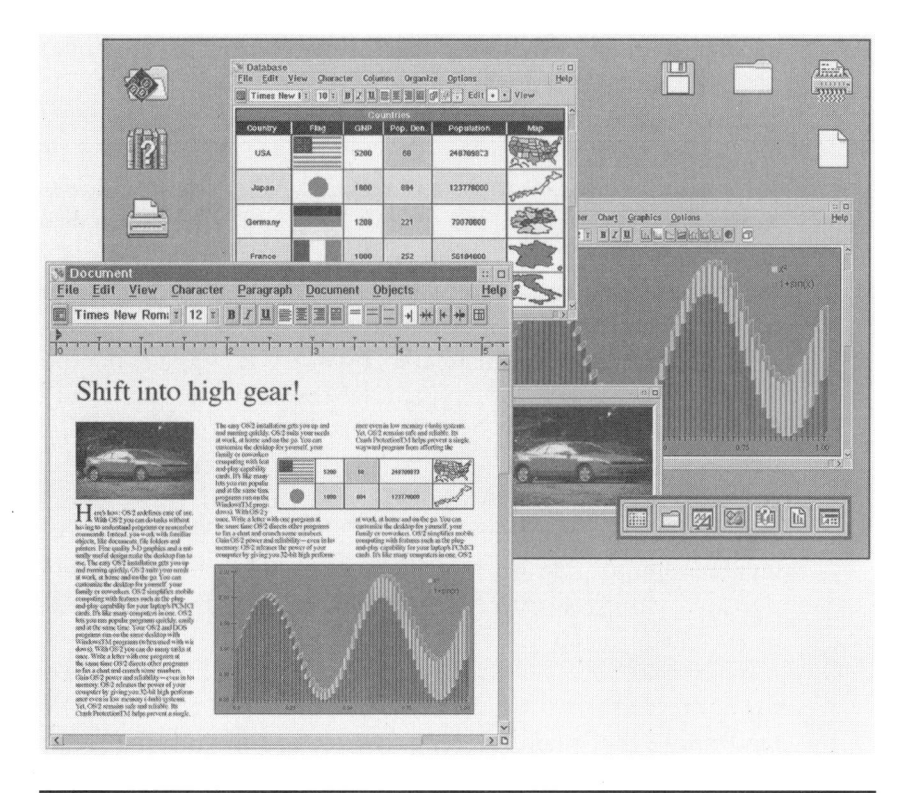

Figure 2.14. Screen presented by the OS/2 Warp, Version 3 Workplace Shell.

mined at a glance. Tutorials and numerous help functions are available to help new (or forgetful) users through any problems they may encounter. The OS/2 Workplace Shell allows different operating system elements or "objects" (programs, data files, printers, etc.) to be manipulated in a consistent fashion.

Since OS/2 Warp fully exploits the 32-bit architecture offered in the 486 and Pentium family of microprocessors, OS/2 Warp is called a **32-bit operating system.** Since OS/2 Warp is a 32-bit operating system, it (and any 32-bit OS/2 application program) exploits the 32-bit registers in the 486 and Pentium microprocessors to more efficiently address memory, thus providing better system performance. Other performance improvements have been made in OS/2 Warp in the areas of file drivers, the OS/2 Workplace Shell, and memory management. Some performance benefits are enjoyed whether running DOS, Windows, or 16-bit OS/2 native application programs originally written for earlier versions of OS/2. Additional performance improvements are enjoyed when running 32-bit application programs specially designed to take full advantage of OS/2 Warp. An on-line tutorial and games are provided to help new users learn how to interact with OS/2 Warp. Further, the on-line contextual help and on-line documentation are easier to access in OS/2 Warp than in previous versions. This helps reduce the need to go to reference manuals when the user needs more information. Also provided with OS/2 Warp are a set of robust personal productivity applications including word processing, spreadsheet, graphics, database, and fax programs.

In addition to sophisticated memory management and performance features, OS/2 Warp includes several other powerful features. OS/2 Warp includes multimedia presentation functions. These functions add digital audio, Musical Instrument Digital Interface (MIDI), Compact Disk-Digital Audio (CD-DA), digital video, and software motion video capabilities to OS/2 Warp. Like DOS 7.0, OS/2 Warp includes support for portable computers by including PCMCIA support, Pen support, and Advanced Power Management (APM) support. OS/2 Warp is now available on CD-ROM to make the installation process even easier. Product documentation and technical library information can also be purchased on CD-ROM with a read utility that makes it very easy to find the information that you need.

OS/2 Warp, Version 4.0 became available in 1996, offering several enhancements. Included with OS/2 Warp, Version 4.0 are enhancements to OS/2 Warp's Internet capabilities. Java for OS/2 provides native Java support in OS/2 Warp on the desktop. Version 4.0 also added support for Netscape Navigator with a voice-navigable interface to the Internet. The speech navigation and dictation function included with Version 4.0 adds a new way to interface with your computer. Speech navigation is currently supported in six national language versions. Other new features include enhancements to device driver support, Plug and Play for ISA, and systems management functions.

OS/2 LAN Server

The OS/2 LAN Server extensions (Advanced and Entry versions) to OS/2 allow a Personal Computer to offer its resources (fixed disk storage, printers, etc.) to other Personal Computers in the LAN. When a Personal Computer offers resources to others in a network, that Personal Computer is called a **server**. The computer system accessing those resources is called a **requester** or a **client**. The server would have OS/2 and the OS/2 LAN Server extension installed. The client can have DOS, DOS extended with Windows, or OS/2 LAN Client installed.

Windows NT Workstation

Windows NT (NT stands for "New Technology") is Microsoft's flagship operating system for high-end Personal Computers and high-performance workstations. With the introduction of operating systems like Windows NT (and OS/2), performance and capabilities that a few years ago were only available on much larger, more expensive workstation and mainframe computers are now available on relatively inexpensive personal computers. These operating systems are designed to provide the robust software platform required to exploit the price and performance advantages of personal computing and apply them to enterprise-wide mission-critical applications.

Windows NT 3.5 offers a user interface that is nearly identical to that of Windows 3.1, and the Windows NT 4.0 user interface is like Windows 95. Due to the widespread use of Windows and the comprehensive availability of personal productivity applications for the

Windows environment, Windows users should be able to easily upgrade to Windows NT with a minimum of training. Although the OS/2 Warp Workplace Shell is more object-oriented and has several additional advanced features, it may take more time and effort for a Windows user to adapt to the OS/2 environment and take advantage of its functions. Even though the user interface of NT looks like Windows 3.1, it is much more like OS/2 from an internal design standpoint and in terms of the functions that it offers. Early in the development of Windows NT, while Microsoft and IBM were jointly developing earlier versions of OS/2, Windows NT was named OS/2 3.0. Although starting from the same base, Microsoft's and IBM's operating system strategies have diverged considerably. The result is two very powerful 32-bit, multitasking operating system alternatives focused on solving the same fundamental problems and limitations of DOS, but executed and optimized in slightly different ways.

Windows NT overcomes the limits of DOS by implementing huge memory addressing for each application. It has an architectural limit of 4 GB of memory addressability, like OS/2. NT reserves 2 GB for its own use and allows up to 2 GB for applications. In practice, however, the amount of memory that NT can actually supply to applications is typically limited by the sum of the amount of physical memory and the amount of free fixed disk space. As with OS/2, the use of fixed disk space as virtual memory can make each application believe it has more memory than it really does. This can be a problem if you are running applications that need a great deal of memory. Do not underestimate the performance improvements possible by installing only a couple of extra megabytes of memory if you find that the operating system is extensively swapping data and programs to and from the fixed disk.

Like OS/2, Windows NT is capable of running applications developed for several other operating environments. An NT system can simultaneously run most DOS and Windows 3.1 applications, as well as many character-based (nongraphical) OS/2- and POSIX-compliant applications. NT is not compatible with every application, and its performance may suffer in comparison to computers running only DOS-based Windows, OS/2, or UNIX. Windows NT, however, offers a good blend of compatibility and performance for multiple-operating-system networks and applications.

Windows NT runs DOS programs within a **virtual DOS machine (VDM)**. One VDM process is created for each DOS program running under NT. The VDM supports well-behaved DOS applications—that is, DOS applications that use system calls for all I/O. Applications that attempt to bypass DOS to directly access fixed disks or other mass storage devices typically do not run. Standard DOS I/O requests are intercepted by the VDM and executed by either the Windows API or the NT executive. Therefore, DOS I/O does not violate NT's system integrity features, and multiple DOS processes can share devices.

You can run 16-bit Windows applications under Windows NT. Launching the first 16-bit Windows program starts a new VDM. The VDM, in turn, loads an environment called **Windows on Win32 (WOW)**. The WOW VDM is based on the DOS VDM. It includes a "simulated" version of Windows 3.1, with multitasking removed, in addition to the 16-bit Windows application and DOS. The result is that some existing 16-bit Windows programs that bypass the API and go directly into the Windows window manager for better graphics display performance will not run under WOW.

Windows NT offers compatibility with some OS/2 applications. Since OS/2 applications are designed to run in a multitasking, 32-bit environment, there is no need to have a virtual machine environment to safeguard Windows NT's system integrity. Instead, OS/2 applications are clients to the OS/2 API-protected environment. This API supports only character-mode applications, so Presentation Manager-based OS/2 applications are not compatible with NT.

Windows NT also offers limited compatibility with POSIX-compliant applications. **POSIX** is a standardized UNIX variant designed to ensure software source code portability and facilitate program maintenance. Instead of having a unique program for every UNIX variant, only one version of the program's source code is required for any POSIX system. Like the OS/2 API, the POSIX API in Windows NT supports only character-mode applications.

OS/2 Warp either incorporates or adds to Windows 3.1 code to provide application compatibility. In many cases, even somewhat ill-behaved applications will run in the OS/2 Warp environment, offering even more complete DOS application compatibility than Windows NT. OS/2 Warp obviously provides increased compatibility for OS/2 applications, both character based and Presentation Manager based. OS/2 does not currently offer any support for POSIX-compliant applications.

Like OS/2, Windows NT implements a Protected mode environment for all running applications. If one DOS application does something it should not, Windows NT detects the error and prevents the fault from causing any side effects on the operating system or with any other application that may be executing at the same time. On Intel processors, Windows NT uses the hardware protection features built into the processors to provide this function. On non-Intel processors, these features are provided by software emulation via the **virtual DOS machine (VDM)**.

Because Windows NT offers many of the same features as OS/2 Warp, either operating system is able to form the software base of a robust client/server environment. OS/2 offers the advantages of the object-oriented Workplace Shell, slightly better connectivity support, and the reliability inherent in being at a its fifth major release level. What advantages does Windows NT have in its current release that differentiate it from OS/2 Warp? A few important areas in which NT currently differs from OS/2 are portability, extensibility, and the NT file system. IBM has already announced plans to add most of these features to OS/2 or to its future line of operating system products called Workplace OS.

Being able to move an operating system from one style of computer to another is a feature called **portability**. For an operating system to be moved, this feature must be built in. Portability for operating systems is of great interest to system software developers because it enables them to move their products at a reasonable cost into multiple marketplaces on multiple hardware platforms. Windows NT has a **Hardware Abstraction Layer (HAL)** that isolates function calls to hardware. To port Windows NT to other systems, all that is needed is a new HAL for that computer. Microsoft has already committed to support Windows NT on both the DEC Alpha and Silicon Graphics MIPS processors. The advantage that portability offers to users is the ability to select from a broader base of hardware while maintaining a common software base. Also, the wider base of available hardware encourages increased software development for the Windows NT platform, providing more options for the user and access to applications that might not be available otherwise.

Extensibility, like portability, is a way for end users and application developers to protect their current investments in software. The architecture of Windows NT allows new subsystems to be added to NT to support other types of applications, such as OS/2 Presentation Manager applications. With an extensible operating system such as Windows NT, end users will have the opportunity to adopt popular applications from a variety of current and future operating systems without abandoning NT as a whole.

Both Windows NT and OS/2 support **File Allocation Table (FAT)** and **High Performance File System (HPFS)** file systems. The FAT file system was originally introduced with DOS and is required to maintain compatibility with DOS filenames and DOS applications. The HPFS file system offers higher performance when accessing data on very large fixed disks as well as adding other features such as support for long filenames and extended attributes. In addition to these file systems, Windows NT offers a third option called the **NT File System (NTFS)**. The NT File System includes all of the features of the HPFS and adds greater security, greater data reliability and recoverability, and support for fault-tolerant features. It also supports larger file volumes and even longer filenames.

Windows NT Server

While Windows NT Workstation incorporates peer-to-peer networking as an integral part of the operating system, Windows NT Server, a separate product, offers significantly enhanced functions to implement advanced domain-administered networks. The capabilities of NT Server can be grouped into four basic categories: network management and administration, security and log-on control, reliability, and client support. NT Server adds the concept of domains to the Windows environment. A **domain** is essentially a group of servers that can be managed as a group from a single system. This **centralization** allows user profiles and information to be stored in a single location, simplifying the management of large networks.

The Windows NT Server 4.0 is the latest version of NT Server and includes SMP support for multiprocessing and expanded Internet, intranet, and communications services. NT Server also incorporates support for **RAID (Redundant Array of Inexpensive Disks)**, which increases performance and reliability by spreading data across any array of disks and protects that data with a parity check. In addition, NT Server makes it easier to configure clients via directory replication. This feature lets a server automatically load files from a particular server directory into designated clients. Remote users are also supported through **Remote Access Services (RAS)**.

Advanced Interactive Executive

The IBM Advanced Interactive Executive (AIX) operating system provides an environment very different from that of DOS, DOS/Windows, or OS/2. AIX is a multiuser, multi-application operating system for Personal Computers. It requires a 386 SX microprocessor or higher. It is based on the **UNIX** operating system, first developed by Bell Labs in the late 1960s. Over the years, UNIX has been expanded and enhanced by Bell Labs as well as many other commercial and academic organizations. AIX, IBM's version of a UNIX-type operating system, borrows concepts from other implementations and adds some of its own, such as improved networking capabilities and a DOS affinity. The strengths of UNIX include its industry-standard-driven or **open systems** architecture, which gives users a lot of flexibility when deciding which brand of computer hardware and software to buy.

AIX was first introduced for the IBM RT/PC family of computers in 1986. IBM now has a complete line of AIX operating systems for computers ranging from Personal Computers to the company's largest ES/9000 mainframe computers. Since AIX exploits the advanced capabilities of the 386 SX microprocessors and higher, only systems using these microprocessor families can run AIX. AIX can be used in a single-user environment or a multiuser one with up to 16 users. It provides all of the basic hardware support necessary to make a complete system. Because UNIX has been around for so long, a large number of UNIX application programs are available.

The base AIX operating system provides a base to which these application programs (written for UNIX System V Release 2) can be easily migrated. DOS and OS/2 application programs, however, are not compatible with the base AIX offering. The user interfaces included with AIX (called the **user shell**) are known as the **Bourne Shell** and the **C Shell,** both of which are command-driven interfaces (as is that of DOS 6.3). Also provided with AIX is the OSF/Motif user interface. Motif provides a graphical user interface not unlike Windows 3.1 and the OS/2 Presentation Manager. Other extensions to AIX add database and communications capabilities to the base offering, resulting in built-in functions similar to (but not compatible with) CM/2 and DB2/2.

Many extensions to AIX are offered (e.g., AIXwindows Environment, AIX Usability Services, and the AIX Network File System) that allow users to tailor the system to meet their needs. This is indicative of the broad number of people and organizations who have improved UNIX—and thus AIX—over the years and exists because of UNIX's open architecture approach.

3

IBM RS/6000

This chapter first provides an overview of the RS/6000 family of computers, covering the highlights of these new systems. The latter part of the chapter then moves in for a closer look at the design features that make the RS/6000 family unique.

A Glance Backwards

To understand the full intent of the RS/6000 family and its AIX operating system, one must be familiar with some basic history. The AIX operating system is IBM's version of the **UNIX operating system**, which was originally developed by AT&T Bell Labs in 1969. The original UNIX was not intended to be a commercial product, but rather a tool for use by computer programmers internal to AT&T. In fact, at that time AT&T was not in the business of selling computers or operating systems. However, in 1975 AT&T began to license universities to use the UNIX operating system at no charge. This practice caused the UNIX operating system to become widely used in the academic community. Students quickly took advantage of the freedom in the academic world to make their own improvements to the UNIX operating system, often resulting in new commands that, although obvious to the creator, sometimes seemed cryptic to other users. For example, the BIFF command used to pick up electronic mail stored in the computer system was added to the UNIX operating system. Why BIFF? Because the student who made the enhancement owned a dog named Biff that was trained to go out and get the newspaper every morning. Although this freedom to make unstructured improvements to the UNIX operating system at will helped UNIX become more powerful, it also left holes in areas such as data security and reliability.

In 1981, the University of California at Berkeley offered its own version of the UNIX operating system with many enhancements of its own. Berkeley's version of the UNIX operating system, known as Berkeley Software Distribution 4 (BSD 4), became a very popular operating system in its own right—so much so that most of the enhancements contained in the Berkeley version were incorporated by AT&T's later versions of the UNIX operating system.

Meanwhile, IBM was busy working on the "801 project," which was started in 1975. Named after the building in which it was resident, the 801 project was an experiment to develop a minicomputer that bucked the existing trend toward complex computer programming instructions. Under the leadership of IBM scientist John Cocke, the 801 approach was to simplify the range of instructions used to perform tasks and optimize the computer to execute this limited range of instructions with extreme efficiency. Born of this approach is **RISC (Reduced Instruction Set Computer)**.

In January 1986, IBM announced the first product to utilize the RISC approach in the IBM RT PC (for RISC Technology Personal Computer) shown in Figure 3.1. At the same time, IBM introduced its own version of the UNIX operating system to run on the RT Personal Computer, called the **Advanced Interactive eXecutive (AIX)** operating system. Later, IBM released versions of the AIX operating system for the smaller IBM Personal System/2 computers and the larger S/370 mainframe computers.

In early 1986, IBM hardware and software engineers in Austin, Texas, took on the task of designing a new product family. It would represent IBM's second-generation RISC technology, combining the RISC philosophy with more traditional concepts, the goal of which was to achieved balanced performance. The result of that effort is the RS/6000 family of products and AIX Version 3—both introduced on February 15, 1990. Since that time, the RS/6000 family of hardware

86 EXPLORING IBM TECHNOLOGY AND PRODUCTS

Figure 3.1. IBM RT system. The System Unit can be seen beside the desk, and the associated display and keyboard are on the desktop.

and AIX have been enhanced through a continuous stream of product announcements. The remainder of this book will focus on the most current RS/6000 family and the latest version of the AIX operating system.

In general, the UNIX marketplace can be divided into two camps. First there is the "technical and scientific" community. These users are typically crunching numbers to do things like predict the weather or design the latest high-tech aircraft. The primary concerns of these users are floating-point performance and graphics features/performance. Typically they will be looking at the desktop, deskside, or parallel RS/6000's. According to IBM, these kinds of users and applications make up about 40 percent of the current RS/6000 users.

The other primary camp within the UNIX marketplace is typically termed "commercial." This camp is dealing with banking, manufacturing, and retail to name a few. Their primary concerns will be database performance, reliability, and communications with their older systems. Typically, commercial users look at the deskside, rack, and

Symmetric Multi-Processing (SMP) models of the RS/6000. This segment of the market is probably 60 percent of the RS/6000 install base.

These definitions of "technical" and "commercial" are certainly not exact. I'm sure lots of banks crunch lots of numbers. Similarly, our national labs have large databases of information. But this does give us an idea of the general distribution of RS/6000 users and can also give you and idea of where your application and requirements fit into this market.

Hundreds of thousands of RS/6000s are currently in use. This market is extremely competitive from a performance and price standpoint. If IBM announces a hot new machine, you can rest assured that other vendors will react by dropping their prices and/or six months later, announcing their new performance topping box. So, when you ask why IBM and the RS/6000, a number of different factors account for IBM's continued leadership in this market: worldwide service, technological research and innovation, and one-stop shopping.

Meet the RS/6000 Family

The IBM RS/6000 family is IBM's second generation of computers based on the **RISC** architecture (described above) developed by IBM in the late 1970s. With this concept, a very simple set of programming instructions is used to perform all work within the computer system. Because the instructions are very simple, they can be executed at very high speed, and they also lend themselves to a more efficient implementation of the program being executed. The RISC architecture was first introduced in the IBM RT Personal Computer, later renamed the IBM RT System. The RS/6000 family is based on a second-generation RISC architecture, called the **Performance Optimized With Enhanced RISC (POWER)** architecture, and its PowerPC and POWER2 derivatives. The POWER architecture combines the concepts of the original RISC architecture with a sprinkling of more traditional concepts to create a system with optimum overall system performance.

The RS/6000 family uses the AIX (Advanced Interactive eXecutive) operating system. The AIX operating system is IBM's version of the

UNIX operating system, originally developed by AT&T Bell Labs. As mentioned earlier, in the AIX operating system, IBM has combined the basic functions of the UNIX operating system with enhancements made by many other companies and academic institutions. IBM has added many enhancements to the AIX operating system and has adhered to the mainstream industry standards developed to make the systems from various vendors more compatible.

Because the AIX operating system conforms to many industry standards, the RS/6000 family is considered an **open system**. This term simply means that the AIX operating system conforms to standards (programming interfaces, communications protocols, and so on) defined by independent standards bodies rather than utilizing an IBM proprietary set of standards not generally adhered to by other computer manufacturers. The advantage of the open-system strategy comes when an independent software development company writes an application program conforming to these industry standards. Because many computer manufacturers offer open-system computers conforming to these industry standards, the software development company can offer its application program on many different brands of open-system computers. The advantages of open systems to computer users are that (1) after selecting the application program that best meets their needs, the users have more flexibility as to which brand of open-system computer system to buy; (2) after users have purchased an open-system computer, they can choose from the large body of open application programs to meet new needs as they emerge; and (3) users have the flexibility to purchase multiple open-system computers of different brands knowing that they will be able to interoperate over a communications network.

The open-system concept is not without its difficulties, however. First, there are multiple organizations simultaneously defining standards for the same open-system environment. This leads to conflicts and incompatibilities. Further, although open-system computer manufacturers conform to industry standards, they also offer proprietary extensions to help differentiate their open-system computers from those of others. The more a software development firm exploits these proprietary extensions, the more it diverges from the spirit of the open-system concept. Even with these difficulties, the open-system approach provides the most widely compatible environment today and shows great promise for the future.

RS/6000 Models

As of this writing, 16 models make up the RS/6000 family. For our purposes, we will divide them into three groups: (1) **Peripheral Component Interface (PCI)** and **Industry Standard Architecture (ISA)** based, (2) **Micro Channel**-based, and (3) **SP** systems. *Note:* IBM frequently introduces new RS/6000 models so visit this book's companion Web site (see page xiv for the address).

PCI/ISA based systems include:

- Desktop or Deskside Models: 43P-140, 43P-240

- Deskside-only Models: E30, F40, F50

- Rack Mounted: F3L, H10, H50, S70

Micro Channel based systems include:

- Desktop or Deskside Models: 39H and 397

- Deskside-only Models: C20, 595, J50

- Rack Models: R20, R50

SP systems include:

- Rack Mounted RS/6000 SP

Figure 3.2 shows the RS/6000 family at a glance. Let's pause here to take a quick look at IBM's **naming convention** on these systems. Notice that a four-digit heading precedes the system description (e.g. 7013 Systems). This numeric designation gives a general classification for the system like many other products that IBM sells. All systems in the same classification are very similar in design and often only differ in performance or capacity. For example, all 7013 Systems have eight Micro Channel slots and are similar in size. Three digits then indicate the actual system (e.g. *595*). The first of these is another general indicator of similarity with the last two being an

90 EXPLORING IBM TECHNOLOGY AND PRODUCTS

System	Processor(s)	SPEC int95	SPEC fp95	Rel. OLTP/ tpmC *	Key point of system
7006 Systems					
41W/41T	PowerPC 601 (80 MHz + 0 - .5 MB L2)				HighEnd Graphics
42W/42T	PowerPC 604 (120 MHz + 0 - .5 MB L2)	4.01	3.53	234.13*	Better Performance
7009 Systems					
C10	PowerPC 601 (80 MHz + 0-1 MB L2)			485.88*	Low Cost Server
C20	PowerPC 604 (120 MHz + 0-1 MB L2)			2.1	More Performance
7011 System					
250/25T	PowerPC 601 (80 MHz)	1.82	2.32	1.0	Server or Workstation
7012 Systems					
390/3BT	POWER2 (67 MHz + 0-1 MB L2)	3.21	7.52	3.0	Good DB Performance
39H/3CT	POWER2 (67 MHz + 0-2 MB L2)	3.31	9.35	3.3	Best FP Perf Desktop
G40	1,2,4 (PowerPC 604 112MHz + .5 MB L2)			8.8	Mini-Tower SMP System
7013 Systems					
590	POWER2 (66.5 MHz)	3.33	10.4	3.9	Entry Deskside
591	POWER2 (77 MHz)	3.84	12.4	4.5	More FP Performance
595	POWER2 (135 MHz)	5.90	17	5.8	Best FP Performance
J40	2,4,6,8 (PowerPC 604 112MHz + .5 MB L2)			5774.07*	Deskside SMP System
7015 Systems					
R20	POWER2 (66 MHz + 1 MB L2)	3.31	9.34	4.4	Entry Rack System
R24	POWER2 (71.5 MHz + 2 MB L2)	3.53	9.98	1470.06*	Better DB Performance

Figure 3.2. The IBM RS/6000 family at a glance. (Continued on next page)

IBM RS/6000

System	Processor(s)	int95	SPEC fp95	SPEC tpmC*	Rel. OLTP/ Key point of system
R40	2,4,6,8 (PowerPC 604 112MHz + .5 MB L2)			5774.07*	Rack SMP System
PCI/ISA Bus Systems					
7024 Systems					
E20	PowerPC 604 (100 MHz + .5 MB L2)	3.67	3.13	735.27*	Entry PCI-Based Server
E30	PowerPC 604 (133 MHz + .5 MB L2)	4.74	3.49	2.8	More Performance
	PowerPC 604e (166 MHz + .5 MB L2)	6.19	4.77	3.7	More Performance
7025 Systems					
F30	PowerPC 604 (133 MHz + .5 MB L2)	4.74	3.49	2.8	More Capacity than E30
	PowerPC 604e (166 MHz + .5 MB L2)	6.19	4.77	3.7	More Performance
F40	1,2 PowerPC 604e (166 MHz + .5 MB L2)			4.2	First PCI-based SMP
7043 Systems					
140	PowerPC 604e (166 MHz + .5 MB L2)	6.15	4.83	2.9	PCI-based Workstation
	PowerPC 604e (200 MHz + 1 MB L2)	7.22	5.23	3.6	More Performance
240	1,2 PowerPC 604e (166 MHz + .5 MB L2)			4.2	First Desktop SMP
7248 Systems					
43P	PowerPC 604 (120 MHz + .5 MB L2)	4.24	3.41	1.9	Low Cost Desktop
	PowerPC 604 (133 MHz + .5 MB L2)	4.72	3.76	2.1	Higher Performance
	PowerPC 604e (166 MHz + .5 MB L2)	6.19	5.01	2.6	Best Performance
Notebook Systems					
860	PowerPC 604ev (100MHz + .25 L2)	3.94	2.71		Portable Workstation

Figure 3.2. The IBM RS/6000 family at a glance. (Continued from previous page)

indication of the system's relative performance level. So now we can decipher that a 7013-591 (now withdrawn) is the same size as the 7013-595, but a bit slower and, by the way, a bit less expensive. The 7013-J50 is similar to other 7013s in size and slots, but the "J" indicates that something is different from the 5xx's. These rules-of-thumb still leave much to be desired in understanding the RS/6000 family.

With that, let's take a brief look at each of these systems. Because the first RS/6000 systems were based on the microchannel architecture, we'll start with them and work our way to the PCI/ISA systems which have become predominant. In general, the desktop systems provide from 2 GB to 18 GB of internal disk storage, up to 1 TB of external disk storage, from 64 MB to 1 GB of memory, and 4 or 5 expansion slots. This small number of slots might seem to be a limitation, but all of these systems will include Ethernet LAN and SCSI expansion capabilities on the planar or motherboard without requiring any slots. In addition, like many of today's personal computers, a business audio capability is included in some of IBM's desktop RS/6000s. Standard and maximum configurations will obviously vary from system to system, but this gives you a general idea. Desktop systems will also operate while on their sides, but the deskside-only systems are strictly floor-standing models. They typically provide more capacity both in internal bays and memory than the desktop systems. The rack systems provide the greatest capacities of memory, disk, slots, and easy expansion. Now let's take a look at the three basic groups of RS/6000 systems.

Micro Channel Systems

The Micro Channel-based RS/6000 systems consist of desktops, desksides, and racks. The 300 series systems (Figure 3.3) utilize a system frame that has been a mainstay of the RS/6000 family since its beginning in 1990 with the original Model 320. Today two systems are available in these frames. If you are looking for floating-point performance, the 300s are excellent price/performers.

The Model 39H uses a 67 MHz POWER2 processor with the L2 cache capability of 1 MB or 2 MB. This L2 cache offers a particular advantage for database applications. As a result, although the 39H is in the compact form of a desktop system, it is best suited as a technical or commercial server. Also, if you have applications that for some

Figure 3.3. An IBM RS/6000 300 series system in an office setting.

reason require version 3.2 of AIX, this is one machine that will still run this older version of operating system.

A much newer offering in the 300 series, introduced in October, 1997, is the model 397. This model contains the 160 MHz **Power2 Super Chip (P2SC)**. It is designed for floating-point performance and has a high-performance graphics card available for complex 3D graphics workloads. This model will most often be used as a single-user workstation.

Now to the deskside-only, Micro Channel machines. Depending upon the model, these systems provide from 16 MB to 4 GB of memory, from 2 to 60 GB of internal disk, over 3 **TB** (**terabytes**) of external disk storage, and 3 to 16 slots. They span nearly the full range of performance for the RS/6000 product line.

The first of the floor-standing systems is the Model C20 Compact Server (Figure 3.4). It uses a 120 MHz PowerPC 604 and sup-

Figure 3.4. RS/6000 Compact Server (C10, C20).

plies a generous offering of slots and internal bays. It provides an excellent compact solution for server and multiuser commercial environments that require Micro Channel adapters.

The very first RS/6000 deskside systems used the 500 mechanical enclosure. Today, this packaging, shown in Figure 3.5, is used in the Model 595. The System Unit is sitting on the floor beside the desk in the center of the photo, with the associated display on the desktop.

The Model 595 uses a 135 MHz POWER2 Super Chip and delivers very high performance on floating-point workloads. This system comes standard with 64 MB of memory and 2 GB of disk storage.

The RS/6000 Models R20 and R50 use a completely different approach to physical packaging. These System Units reside in larger, floor-standing racks as shown in Figure 3.6. In fact, the rack itself is offered as the Model R00 without a CPU. Other than the R00, these models offer performance comparable to that of the deskside series, but offer more expansion capability than any other members of the RS/6000 family. The rack systems have from 8 to 16 Micro Channel slots, 128 MB to 4 GB of memory and over 3.4 TB of external disk storage. These models are designed to be shared by multiple users— each provided with a low-cost terminal directly connected to the sys-

Figure 3.5. An IBM RS/6000 500 series system in an office setting. Notice that users are sharing the single System Unit seen beside the desk.

tem or an intelligent workstation (such as a PC or X-terminal) attached to the system via a LAN.

In October, 1994, IBM introduced its first Symmetric MultiProcessor (SMP) systems in the RS/6000 product line; the Models G30 minitower, J30 deskside, and R30 rack. All of these SMP systems used multiple PowerPC 601 processors running at 75 MHz. IBM has subsequently announced the 604 and then 604e upgrades to these machines. The G-series has been replaced by the newer, PCI-based F-series; the J and R series are still current. Today, IBM sells only the 604e version of these systems called the J50 and R50 (Figure 3.7). These two workhorses can support 2, 4, 6, or 8 processors. The earlier J30, J40, R30 and R40 can be upgraded to the J/R50 by changing the processor cards. This built-in upgrade path has allowed easy capacity upgrades as performance requirements have grown. Like the rack systems, users of database and transaction processing environ-

96 EXPLORING IBM TECHNOLOGY AND PRODUCTS

Figure 3.6. An IBM RS/6000 rack system in an office setting.

ments (commercial processing) will find these systems well suited for attaching large numbers of terminals or as servers in a LAN environment. These systems can be further upgraded to the brand new, higher performing S70 which is in the newer PCI family of products.

PCI/ISA Systems

At a technical level, one might say simply that the PCI/ISA-based RS/6000 systems support both the Industry Standard Architecture (ISA) and Peripheral Component Interconnect (PCI) bus structures.

J50

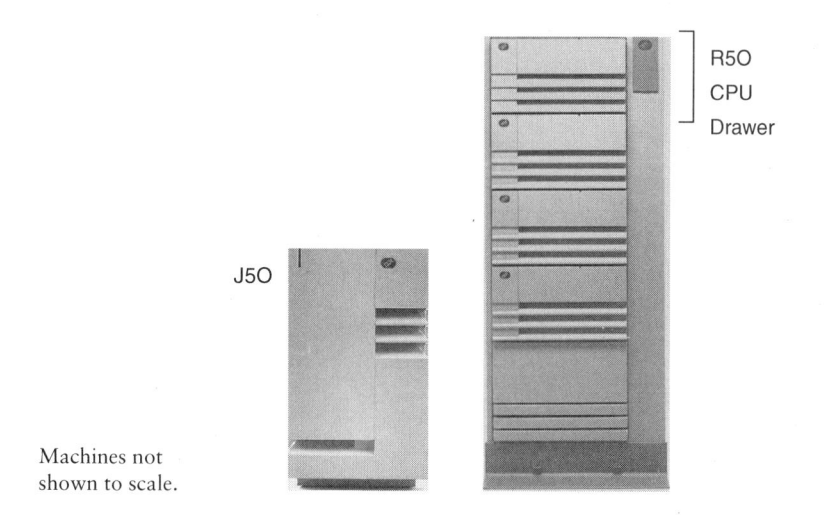

R50 CPU Drawer

Machines not shown to scale.

Figure 3.7. The RS/6000 MicroChannel SMP Servers.

This is 100 percent true, but there is more to the story. The PCI/ISA systems represent a major paradigm shift for the RS/6000 product line. This may be an overworked phrase in our industry, but it represents a different way of building systems for IBM's Austin-based division. In general, the RS/6000 Division is moving from a line of specialized machines with custom-built components in fairly low volumes, to a more generalized line of systems with common off-the-shelf components. There are advantages here for both the user and IBM. IBM can now design new systems faster and release them to the market faster than their competition. Plus, due to the use of fairly common, high-volume parts from the Personal Computer line (like power supplies, cables, disks, memory, etc.) prices to the user continue to drop.

The 43P model 140, like most of IBM's PCI based RS/6000s, provides a mixture of PCI and ISA slots. It comes with a choice of PowerPC 604e processors with speeds of 200, 233, 332 MHz. The 43P is an ideal entry system for applications such as retail, insurance, finance industry applications, and web serving. With the variety of graphics adapters available, the 140 is also an excellent choice for 2D and 3D graphics applications. The 140 can also act as a very cost-effective entry-level server.

The 43P model 240 represents IBM's first desktop system with more than one processor under the covers. The 240 supports one or two 604e processors running at 233 MHz.

The larger enclosures of the deskside-only models we will now talk about are designed to sit on the floor and allow these models to accommodate more main memory, more disk storage, and more I/O adapters. Do not discount these systems from your single-user graphics environment that is more typical for the 43P-140, and 240. Armed with a graphics adapter and monitor, the deskside systems below can make excellent workstations.

The Model E20, announced in October, 1995, was the first deskside system to use a mixture of PCI and ISA slots instead of the typical Micro Channel. IBM uses the phrase "8 by 8" to describe this and the E30 systems because they provide 8 slots and 8 internal bays. The E20 has been replaced by the E30 which sports a 233 MHz PowerPC 604e and 1 MB L2 cache. This system has similar low cost and small size as the C20, but with a PCI/ISA bus structure.

The model F40 expands upon the number of slots and bays in the E30 and goes a step further with the option of adding an additional processor. This makes the F40, along with the 43P-240, the first Symmetric MultiProcessors (SMP) that have a PCI bus.

RS/6000 model F50 is a powerful new deskside, PCI-based, SMP system which supports one to four 604e microprocessors at 166 MHz as well as 256 MB L2 cache for each processor. The F50 is the first PCI system capable of true enterprise workloads. Price performance as an **online transaction processing** (OLTP) system, a web server, and a Lotus Notes server is outstanding.

Two rack systems are based upon the previously mentioned F-series deskside systems. The model H10 is essentially a rack form factor for the model F40. Also, similar to the F50 in design, but now rack mounted and sporting a much faster 332 MHz PowerPC 604e, is the H50. IBM began a practice of offering this additional form factor for its PCI SMP systems a short time after they were introduced as deskside systems.

Finally, for the first time, a PCI system has taken over the leadership performance position in the RS/6000 line. The model S70 is a 12-way rack-based system which introduces the PowerPC RS64 microprocessor with 4 MB of L2 cache per processor. The S70 is a full 64-bit system and is supported by IBM-s 64-bit AIX Version 4.3. This system is designed to give superior performance in addition to price performance in commercial applications such as OLTP. As we will see in the detailed discussion of this model, it is a large system built with high-availability standard features as well as consideration for future growth.

The RS/6000 family of computers includes systems designed to meet the needs of either technical users (engineers, scientists, economists, and so on) or general-purpose commercial users (executives, accountants, clerks, secretaries, and so on). The various models offer many different levels of performance, capacity, and function.

POWERparallel SP

The IBM Scalable POWERparallel System 9076 SP1 was the first system to employ multiple RS/6000 main processors in a single system. The family of IBM's parallel processors continued to be enhanced with the SP2. Recently the numeric designator was dropped, they were moved into the mainline of the RS/6000 family, and the systems are now simply called RS/6000 SP (Figure 3.8).

Figure 3.8. The IBM Scalable POWERparallel SP system.

Systems that employ multiple main processors working in parallel can achieve extremely high levels of performance and are called highly parallel or massively parallel systems (depending on the number of main processors used in the system). A common industry term is **Massively Parallel Processing (MPP)**. This may sound very much like the SMP systems that we discussed earlier, but in fact, the SP is quite different. Since the processors within the SP do not share a single operating system, disk, memory, or adapters, the SP is called a **shared nothing environment.** It is this fact that allows hundreds of processors to be combined in an SP rather than only a few in the SMP. Later in this chapter we will discuss both the SMP and parallel processing environments in more detail.

From a hardware perspective, the SP consists of a frame, which then contains the various processing nodes. **Nodes** can be of various types: thin (having only 1 microprocessor and 4 slots), wide (having one processor and 7 slots), or the latest addition, high (an SMP with 14 slots). These nodes can also be of different processor speeds. See Figure 3.9 for a summary of the various nodes. The frame provides the interconnection between all of the nodes. This interconnection can be either just Ethernet LAN or an additional **SP Switch (SPS)**. The SP Switch provides a high-speed, low-latency, point-to-point connection for all nodes in the frame, making distributed applications more efficient. An SP system can have as few as 2 nodes or as many as 512 nodes contained in 1 to over 30 frames.

Frames come in two different sizes (see Figure 3.10), short (49 inches with four drawers) and tall (79 inches with eight drawers). A drawer contains the space and appropriate mounting hardware and connections for the various nodes. **Thin nodes**, as the name suggests, are small and take up only half of a drawer. However, thin nodes are typically purchased in pairs, thus consuming an entire drawer of space. **Wide nodes**, due to their additional slots and bays, take up a full drawer. IBM's newest type of node, first announced in July of 1996 is the high node. The **high node**, again as its name implies, takes up twice the space as wide nodes, thus consuming two drawers within an SP frame. Currently, IBM only supports up to 64 high nodes in a single SP system. Also, look for new nodes in the near future with multiple processors (SMPs) as well as the PCI bus in the thin and wide form.

An additional piece of hardware called the **Control Workstation (CWS)** is required to complete the SP. This is a stand-alone RS/6000

	Node Type	Thin	Wide	High
CPU	P2SC	160 MHz	135 MHz	—
	PowerPC 604e	—	—	2, 4, 6, or 8 at 200 MHz
Slots (Micro Channel)		4	7*	14*
Bays	Media	—	—	—
	Disk	2	4	4
Memory (MB)	Standard	64	64	256
	Maximum	1024	2048	4096
	Slots	4	8	4
	Level 2	—	—	2 (per CPU)
Disk (GB)	Internal Standard	4.5	4.5	4.5
	Maximum	18.2	36.4	18
	External Maximum	1.7 TB	3.4 TB	3.4 TB
Performance	SPECint95	7.6	6.17	"rate" 445
	SPECfp95	23	17.6	"rate" 320
	Relative OLTP	—	5.8	30.6
Additional Standard Features		Integrated SCSI-2 F/W Controller & Ethernet	SCSI-2 F/W Controller & Ethernet	—

* Dual Micro Channel busses

Figure 3.9. Comparison matrix for SP nodes.

(frequently a model 3xx or 5xx with graphics) that manages all the nodes within the SP. The CWS is the repository for the **Single System Image (SSI)**. The SSI gives a single interface to the users and systems administrators of the SP. This is typically the most daunting challenge to putting tens or hundreds of processors together on a single task; that is, making it look like just one system when, in actuality, it is hundreds of systems. The SSI provides a single copy of the AIX operating system which is then proliferated to each node.

The SP was originally very popular for large-scale numeric computing environments such as research centers and universities. This was an area typically dominated by supercomputers like Cray, Convex, or IBM mainframes. With the appearance of parallel databases

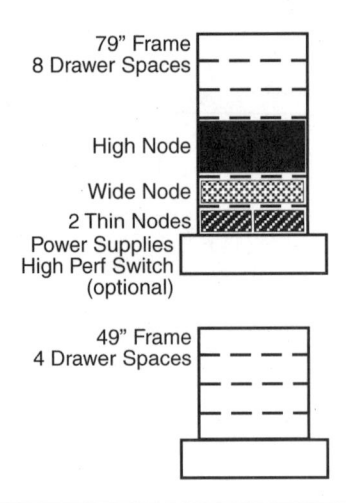

Figure 3.10. The POWERparallel SP frames are either 79" or 49" tall.

like Oracle Version 7 and 8 and IBM's DB/2 Parallel Edition, the SP has also been very popular in commercial database processing as well. A third application area has emerged for the SP called **LAN consolidation.** Instead of having RS/6000 servers geographically distributed throughout an enterprise where systems administrators might not be on-site, some users find that using the SP can be a very cost-effective alternative. By using a common pool of administrative personnel, backup devices, printers, and storage, the SP provides the benefits of high-performance RISC workstations with centralized, cost-effective systems administration. Today, use of the SP in the commercial market has outpaced that of the technical.

RS/6000 Hardware Architecture

The internal organization of the hardware elements comprising the RS/6000 system is known as its hardware architecture. The architecture of RS/6000 computers contributes a great deal to the performance offered by these systems. The RS/6000 architecture is an enhanced version of the earlier RISC architecture. As explained earlier, with RISC the instruction set or total number of programming instructions that can be executed within the computer is reduced compared with more traditional **CISC (Complex Instruction Set Computing)**. Because the instructions in RISC systems are very simple, they can be executed using high-speed computer hardware within the computer system in a very short period of time (for example, one clock cycle). Further, the simple instruction set of a RISC computer typically can be carefully employed to perform even complex functions in a more efficient manner.

This original RISC architecture was first used in the earlier IBM RT system, which had limited success. The RS/6000 family employs IBM's second-generation RISC architecture, called the POWER (Performance Optimized With Enhanced RISC) architecture. As previously discussed, this architecture utilizes a blend of the original RISC architecture and some traditional CISC concepts with an emphasis on doing multiple operations at the same time. The new PowerPC architecture, developed jointly by IBM, Apple, and Motorola, is a highly compatible derivative of the POWER architecture. Currently, the PowerPC architecture is implemented on most of the RS/6000 models. Other systems in the RS/6000 family are based on the POWER architecture and implemented either with the POWER2 multichip main processor design or the more powerful POWER2 single chip design, called the POWER2 Super Chip (P2SC).

To understand the POWER architecture, it is necessary to look at two key pieces of RS/6000 systems—the main processor and the main memory system. The main processor and the main memory system, along with other circuits, make up the **Central Processing Unit (CPU)** circuit board found inside the RS/6000 chassis.

The smallest piece of information the main processor and main memory can use is called a **bit**. These bits are grouped into **bytes** (8 bits), **half-words** (16 bits), and **words** (32 bits) to form the computer's representation of numbers, letters of the alphabet, instructions in a program, and so on. With this basic knowledge, let's take a closer look at the RS/6000 system's main processor and main memory.

The Main Processor

The main processor is the heart of a computer system because it is the control center for information flow inside the computer. It is the main processor that does the data manipulation or "thinking" necessary to perform tasks for the user. The speed of the circuits making up the main processor, along with the architecture of the main processor, determines the overall processing speeds achievable by the computer system.

Several different (though compatible) main processor designs have been used in the RS/6000 product line including:

1. The original implementation of the POWER architecture still used in some current RS/6000 models

2. A RISC Single Chip (RSC) implementation of the POWER architecture built within a single chip

3. PowerPC 601, 604, and 603 microprocessors that provide significant performance at low costs

4. A POWER2 implementation of the POWER architecture that provides high-speed performance for numeric- and graphics-intensive applications

We can get a feel for the strengths of the POWER architecture by taking a quick look at the original implementation.

There are five basic elements in the original RS/6000 main processor architecture, each made up of thousands of circuits packaged in several specially designed chips:

1. Instruction cache/branch processor

2. Fixed-point processor

3. Floating-point processor

4. Data cache

5. I/O unit

Figure 3.11 is a block diagram showing how these elements are organized to make up the RS/6000 hardware architecture. To see how this architecture can do multiple operations at the same time, let's quickly trace the flow of information through the system. It all starts when the user executes a command to start a program, which causes the instructions of that program to be retrieved from disk storage and loaded into main memory (shown at the bottom of the diagram).

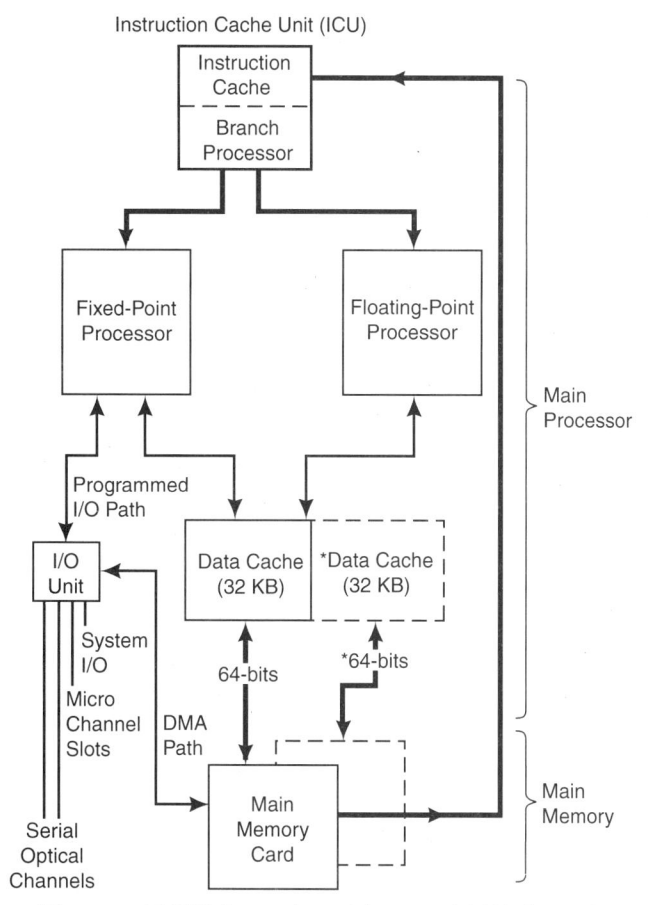

*The second 32 KB data cache and the second 64-bit data path are only provided on the larger RS/6000 Models.

Figure 3.11. RS/6000 POWER architecture original multichip implementation.

After the program is loaded into main memory, the RS/6000 main processor requests the very first instruction (4 bytes) in the program. In compliance with the request, the first instruction, along with the next several instructions (a total of 64 sequential bytes), is retrieved from the main memory and loaded into the **Instruction Cache Unit (ICU)**. The instruction cache is a group of very high-speed memory circuits contained in the ICU chip. It is used as a temporary holding area (8 KB in size) for programming instructions that are likely to be next in line to be executed.

When the main processor requests the next instruction, it will first look in the ICU. Most of the time, the next instruction needed will already have been loaded into the ICU, eliminating the delay associated with getting the instruction from slower main memory. This is called a **cache hit**. Because the instruction cache can respond much more quickly than the system's main memory, the system's performance is dramatically improved with every cache hit. If the needed instruction is not already loaded into the ICU (called a **cache miss**), another 64 bytes starting with the needed instruction are automatically loaded from the main memory into the ICU. In the case of a cache miss, loading the ICU takes longer than simply getting the needed instruction from main memory (that is, a cache miss results in a penalty to RS/6000 system performance), so it is a game of statistics. Because most computer programs will experience many more cache hits than misses during normal operation, the cache technique usually increases overall RS/6000 system performance significantly.

So far, then, we have gotten the first few programming instructions loaded into the 8 KB of instruction cache memory located in the ICU. Next, the branch processor component of the ICU examines each programming instruction in turn and independently executes any condition register or branch instructions. Condition register instructions manipulate the contents of working storage locations (a **condition register**) within the main processor that stores information about the results of calculations performed earlier in the program. **Branch instructions** are a commonly used type of programming instruction that directs the flow of the program, usually taking different paths depending on the contents of the condition register. Branch instructions that are executed completely within the ICU (while other operations are happening in the other processor elements) are said to occur in zero system clock cycles. These branches are therefore said to be zero cycle branches.

While the branch processor intercepts and executes branch and condition register instructions, the remaining instructions are simultaneously fed to and executed by the fixed-point processor and the floating-point processor. The **fixed-point processor** performs mathematical and logical operations with things that don't have decimal points, such as whole numbers (for example, the integers 1, 5, and 6) and numeric representations of text (such as ASCII codes). These fixed-point instructions are common in almost any computing environment. The **floating-point processor** performs mathematical and logical operations (IEEE 754-1985) with things that have a decimal point (that is, real numbers such as 53.254376, 4.6, and 3.1313). These floating-point instructions are common in engineering/scientific applications and others requiring sophisticated computer graphics.

For those who aren't counting, that makes four independent operations going on inside the RS/6000 at the same time:

1. A branch instruction

2. A condition register instruction

3. A fixed-point instruction

4. A floating-point instruction

In fact, if the floating-point instruction happens to be the multiply-add (A x B + C) or the multiply-subtract A x B - C) instruction, these can be counted as two floating-point operations, making a total of five operations being performed at once. This architecture is therefore said to be a **superscalar** implementation.

The instruction cache and processing units in the main processor allow an RS/6000 system to execute a great many programming instructions in a very small amount of time. However, it's not enough to make a main processor architecture that offers high performance. You must also be able to efficiently move the data on which the programming instructions are to operate between the RS/6000 main processor and main memory. This is where the **Data Cache Unit** comes in. The data cache unit operates much like the instruction cache unit, only the data cache unit provides a temporary holding area for data needed during program execution rather than programming instructions. When a program instruction requires data on which to operate, the data cache unit is first checked to see if the needed data has already been loaded. If the data cache unit contains the needed data (a cache hit), it can very quickly provide the needed information and dramatically boost RS/6000 system performance. If the data cache unit does not have the requested data, a cache miss occurs, which negatively impacts system performance. In the event of a cache miss, the needed data plus the next few words of data are automatically loaded from the slower main memory to the data cache unit.

In this way, the data cache unit continuously accumulates the data most likely to be needed during upcoming calculations, increasing the likelihood of cache hits. As with the ICU, the more cache hits, the better the system performance. Statistically speaking, the larger the data cache, the higher the percentage of cache hits, and thus the higher the overall system performance.

The base models of the RS/6000 family have a data cache 32 KB in size, whereas the larger models have a 64 KB data cache, accounting in part for their higher performance. Still other processors, such as the PowerPC 601, have a combined 32 KB data and instruction cache. Those models with the 64 KB data cache are also designed to move twice as much information between main memory and the data cache. That is, the models with the 64 KB data cache provide a more efficient path (for example, a 128-bit-wide data path vs. a 64-bit-wide data path on models with the 32 KB data cache) between main memory and the data cache, which also serves to boost system performance. All RS/6000 models use a scheme called **set associativity** to reduce the number of instruction and cache misses by allowing for more efficient sharing of the data cache among multiple programs running simultaneously.

Finally, the **Input/Output Unit (I/O Unit)** element of the RS/6000 main processor manages data transfers between all input/output devices and the rest of the RS/6000 system. These include things such as the disks, communications adapters installed in the Micro Channel slots, and any devices attached to Serial Optical Channels. Often, the information will flow directly between the I/O device and main memory. This is called **Direct Memory Access (DMA)**. Other times, the program may directly control the information between the main processor and the I/O device. This is called **programmed I/O**.

The activities of the five RS/6000 processor elements are coordinated by an electronic signal called the **system clock**. The system clock is the heartbeat of the computer system. It steps the main processor through each step in the execution of a program. It is the time reference of the main processor and sets the pace for all main processor activity. The speed at which the system clock runs is called the **system clock rate** and is measured in millions of clock steps per second, or **megahertz (MHz)**. For example, the RS/6000 Model 595 runs at 135 MHz and the Model E30 runs at 133 MHz. All other things being equal, the performance of the computer system is directionally proportional to the system clock rate. However, there are many other things inside a computer (such as main processor architecture/implementation, instruction sets, main memory system speeds, disk speeds, I/O bus speeds, and so on) that together define the overall performance of a computer system. Therefore, comparing individual specifications (for example, the system clock rate) of computer systems can be very misleading.

Main Memory

The main memory is also a very important part of a computer. Main memory is the set of electronic chips that provide a "workspace" for the main processor. That is, it holds the information (program instructions and data) being used by the main processor. As mentioned earlier, this main memory (RAM) is called "Random Access Memory" because it can store and retrieve information independent of the sequential order in which it was originally stored.

The smallest RS/6000 systems come standard with 16 MB (about 16 million bytes) of main memory. The largest systems can have up to 16 GB of main memory. When you have this much main memory in a system, schemes to detect and correct memory defects become necessary to protect the integrity of the information stored in the computer system's main memory. The RS/6000 uses several techniques to protect the integrity of its main memory. The **Error Checking and Correction (ECC)** technique used by members of the RS/6000 family can detect single- and double-bit errors and can correct single-bit errors. This is done by appending seven additional bits (called **ECC bits**) onto every word (32 bits) in main memory. The seven ECC bits are automatically generated by the ECC circuitry based on the value of the associated word and then are stored in main memory alongside that word. New ECC bits are calculated and stored every time a word is written to main memory. Later, when that word is read back from main memory, the value stored in the corresponding ECC bits is checked to make sure that the word didn't somehow get corrupted through some type of main memory failure. The most common type of failure is to have a single bit in the word accidentally get changed to the wrong value. In this case, the ECC circuitry can use the value stored in the ECC bits to actually correct the error on the fly and allow normal operations to continue undisturbed. On rare occasions, a main memory failure will cause two bits in a single word to be changed. In this case, the ECC circuitry can only detect and report the error. In addition to monitoring all read/write activity in main memory, the ECC circuitry periodically scans all of main memory to ensure the integrity of the information. This is called **memory scrubbing**. The RS/6000 main memory employs some other techniques to ensure the integrity of the system: bit scattering, memory bus parity, and bit steering.

Bit scattering means that memory chips used to make up the main memory system are organized in a way that minimizes the impact of a single chip failure. **Memory bus parity** refers to an extra bit appended to the parallel group of wires (called a **bus**) used to transfer information to and from main memory. This extra bit, called a **parity bit**, is used to detect any errors that may occur as the information is transferred along the memory bus. In fact, parity bits are used on chip-to-chip data busses and throughout most internal chip data paths. Finally, **bit steering** is a concept in which extra memory bits designed into the main memory system can be used to replace failing bits, in many cases without disrupting normal operation. The extra bit is "steered" onto the memory bus in place of the failing bit. All of these things help protect the integrity of the information in an RS/6000 system and allow the RS/6000 to recover from errors without disturbing users.

In any computer system, a great deal of information is moving in and out of main memory. For this reason, the design of the main memory can significantly affect overall system performance. There are two major reasons why so much time is spent moving information in and out of the main memory. First, the programming instructions of the active program(s) reside in the main memory. Therefore, every instruction in the program must at some point be retrieved from the main memory. Second, the main memory holds and accepts data used in the program(s) being executed. If the overall information flow to and from main memory (assisted by the instruction cache unit and the data cache unit) cannot keep pace with the main processor, the main processor will be delayed and system performance will suffer. For this reason, the main memory must be designed to keep up with the speeds achievable by the main processor.

The design of the RS/6000 main processor and its main memory are balanced through the use of separate data and instruction caches and the wide path between main memory and the caches, as discussed earlier. To further balance the system, the path or "bus" between the caches and main memory (which can operate at up to 2700 MB/sec) is independent from the Micro Channel bus used for input/output activity such as disk information transfers. This prevents interference between main memory activity and input/output activity, which can decrease the overall performance of the system.

Finally, the RS/6000 main memory design uses a technique called **interleaving**. This is a way of subdividing the memory chips to allow an overlap of multiple transfers to and from main memory; that is, two words of data (64 bits) can be read from a memory card in a single system clock cycle (two-way interleaving). The wider data path of the more powerful RS/6000 models allows the two memory cards to each provide two words per cycle, for a total of four words (128 bits) per cycle (four-way interleaving). Interleaving increases the effective transfer rate between main memory and the caches, ultimately feeding the RS/6000 main processor with the necessary programming instructions and data.

Memory Management

The way in which a computer system utilizes available main memory and disk storage is called the computer's **memory management** scheme and is basic to the capabilities of the computer. Understanding the basics of this memory management will give insight into one of the features of RS/6000 computers. Figure 3.12 shows conceptually what the memory in RS/6000 systems looks like. The main memory is contained inside the computer's **System Unit**. The disk storage may be inside the System Unit or in a separate box cabled to the System Unit.

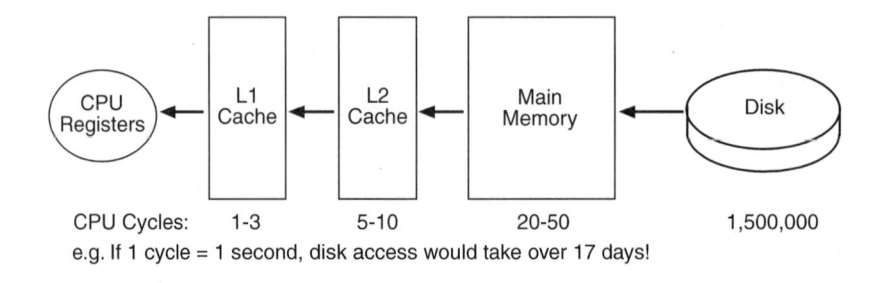

```
CPU          L1        L2       Main
Registers ← Cache  ← Cache  ← Memory  ← Disk

CPU Cycles:  1-3       5-10      20-50       1,500,000
e.g. If 1 cycle = 1 second, disk access would take over 17 days!
```

Figure 3.12. Conceptual view of the RS/6000 main memory and disk storage illustrating the value and speed of large cache and memory over disk storage.

When the RS/6000 computer is first turned on, information vital to an orderly start-up and smooth operation is automatically copied from disk storage to the main memory. Once normal system operation is established, users can begin to do their work. During the course of this work, the user will start various computer programs. As the user starts each program, it is copied from disk storage to main memory and then executed. Based on the work being done by the user, the computer programs manipulate various sets of data that are also loaded from the disk storage to main memory as needed. It doesn't take long to realize that the main memory in a computer can quickly become filled up with programs and data as the system is called upon to do more and more work. In earlier days of computing, the main memory size limited the amount of work a computer could manage at any one time. This limitation capped the size of programs, the number of programs that could be run concurrently, the number of users who could share the system, and so on.

In today's environment, a technique called **virtual memory** alleviates the need to squeeze all active programs and data into main memory. In computers that support virtual memory, the computer basically fakes out the computer programs, making the computer system appear to have much more main memory than it actually has. The largest of today's RS/6000 systems can have 16 GB of main memory. The virtual memory supported by all RS/6000 systems is a whopping 4 TB (terabytes) in size (2 raised to the power 52, or over 4500 trillion bytes). The RS/6000 system's 4 TB of addressing capability is enough to keep track of the information contained on over 2 trillion pages of single-spaced computer output. That's a stack of paper over 200,000 miles high—almost reaching the moon.

Virtual memory therefore allows more programs, data, and users to be simultaneously active on the system than could be supported in real main memory without virtual memory. That is, it allows you to make the most out of whatever size main memory you actually have.

Here's how virtual memory works. Say a user tells the computer to start a word-processing program. The computer would first attempt to load the needed portion of the word-processing program into main memory. If no space is left in main memory, some space will be made available by overwriting an inactive portion of some program or by **swapping** some inactive data to a temporary space in disk storage. The needed portion of the word-processing program can then be loaded into the available space and the user can begin typing. If the program that was overwritten or the data that was swapped out is needed again, it will be reloaded from disk storage to some other available main memory area. So a virtual memory computer system is constantly swapping programs and information between main memory and disk storage (robbing Peter to pay Paul and then vice versa). Virtual memory allows the maximum size program or combination of all programs and data to be limited only by the combined amount of main memory and disk storage rather than by the amount of main memory size alone. The advantage of having this virtual memory hocus pocus built into the RS/6000 hardware and AIX operating system is that neither the programmers nor the users of any RS/6000 system need be concerned with main memory size. To them, the system seems to have as much main memory as they need, and they are never made aware that information is constantly being swapped from main memory to disk storage and back again. The computer hardware and AIX operating system efficiently manage this swapping (also called **paging**) automatically.

Virtual memory is a powerful system feature, but it comes at a price. The paging between disk storage and main memory is processing overhead that can reduce the overall system performance. A little paging will not appreciably hurt performance, but the more paging, the more system performance will be reduced. When the paging performed by a virtual memory system gets excessive, the system is said to be **thrashing,** or spending too much time paging information between disk storage and main memory. Thrashing can be reduced by increasing the amount of main memory in the RS/6000 system through the installation of memory expansion options described in Chapter 2. Increasing the size of the main memory system will provide more room for programs and data, reducing the amount of virtual memory paging.

The virtual memory concept is implemented in most of today's computer systems to some degree. RS/6000 systems implement their virtual memory scheme through a concept called **single-level storage**. This term simply means that in RS/6000 systems, no distinction is made between disk storage and main memory. All storage appears to be one homogeneous sea of main memory that is accessed in exactly the same way. This consistency provides for a simple and efficient virtual memory implementation that is the same for programs, data, temporary holding areas, and so on. Other virtual memory implementations must create and manage separate address spaces, and they often treat programs differently than they do data, for example. The simplicity of the single-level storage design results in a consistent and more complete virtual memory system than that of most other implementations.

Symmetric Multiprocessing

IBM's Symmetric MultiProcessor (SMP) RS/6000 systems use a design that combines the PowerPC microprocessor, AIX operating systems, and IBM's large systems development experience. The basic design of any SMP system (Figure 3.13) involves multiple processors (CPUs) accessing a common, shared set of resources (for example, memory, fixed disk, communication adapters, and operating system). The processors communicate with each other and main memory via a bus.

Each processor in the system will be performing separate jobs or running different programs at any one point in time (for example, database access, terminal interaction, or network communication). Figure 3.13 gives you a look inside a symmetric multiprocessing system at a *single point in time* with several applications running on the system. It is important to say "single point in time" because in the next few ticks of the system clock, these applications, in a true multitasking environment, have an equal chance to be rescheduled

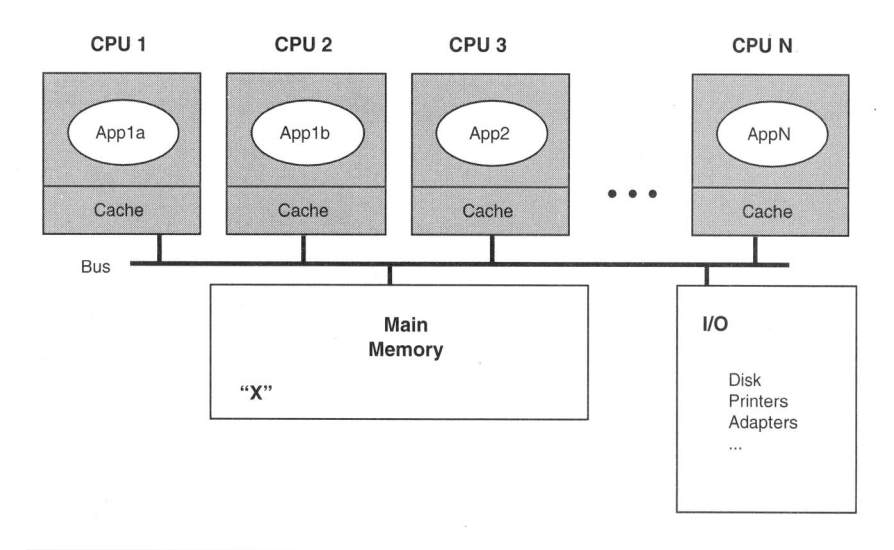

Figure 3.13. Basic design of a typical N-way symmetric multiprocessor.

on the same or other CPUs in the complex. The applications will also be swapped out when they have exhausted their time-slice to let other programs run.

A single application program can be designed and tuned to an SMP architecture such that it will subdivide and run on multiple processors in the SMP system at the same time (App1a and App1b in Figure 3.13). However, this takes special design and coding on the part of the programmers, so today, more often than not, programs will be left to run much as they do on a uniprocessor (App2 and AppN). Not that this is bad (indeed, SMP systems allow many of these independent applications to run at the same time, each scheduled to a single CPU), but in this example, App1 should be able to achieve greater overall throughput than if it had been limited to a single processor. Often this throughput is well worth the coding effort for database developers. If you are purchasing a database, however, the development and tuning work has already been done for you. Often database users will be able to bring forward all of their investment in queries, screens, reports, and so on. They may only require a minor modification or recompilation when moving from the uniprocessor version of the database to the SMP version.

RS/6000 Software

The previous sections closely examined the various models of the RS/6000 family and associated optional equipment. This section will begin our look at how you put that hardware to work, namely, the all-important software. "Software" is a general term for the many programs that execute in computers. It is software that harnesses the RS/6000 system's computational power and allows you to perform many diverse and useful tasks.

Types Of Software—A Conceptual Model

There are different categories of software, diverse in function and purpose. The basic categories of "real software" used in RS/6000 systems can be understood through the simple software model shown in Figure 3.14. There are three basic categories, or software layers, used in RS/6000 systems: the application program layer, the operating system layer, and the device driver layer. Each software layer performs a completely different job, but all three work closely together to perform useful work for the user. Although some special-purpose programs do not fit neatly into any of these three categories, the majority of software does. Let's briefly look at each of the three layers in our software model.

Application Programs

The top software layer in the software model is the application program layer (highlighted in Figure 3.15). The programs in this layer "apply" RS/6000 systems to a specific task (computer-aided design, word processing, accounting, etc.) and thus are called "application" programs. They actually perform the task for which the user purchased the computer while the other two layers play important support roles. A single RS/6000 system might run one application program at a time, or it might run many application programs simultaneously.

The arrows in the figure indicate how users conceptually "see" the computer system. The user usually interacts with the application program layer and (less frequently) the operating system layer. By working closely with the other software layers, the application pro-

IBM RS/6000

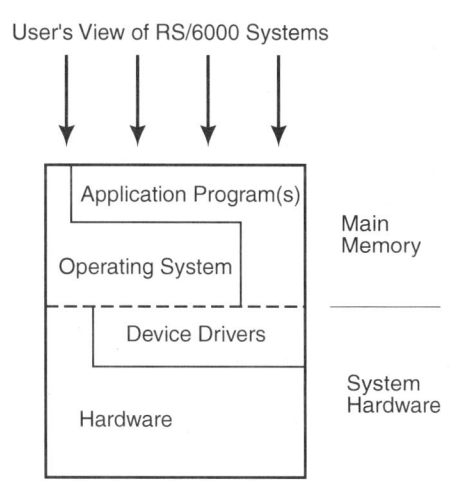

Figure 3.14. The three layers of the RS/6000 system's basic software structure, shown in the conceptual software model above, work together to perform useful work for the user.

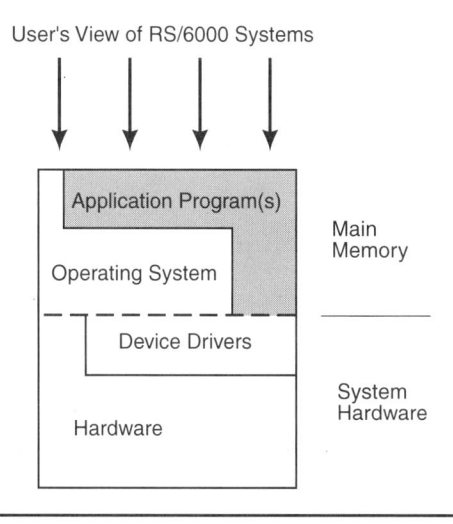

Figure 3.15. The application program software layer, highlighted in the software model above, is the application program that defines the particular task the company is performing for the user.

gram processes the various keystrokes made by the user and responds by displaying information on the computer's display or some other output device.

As we will see later in the chapter, many programs written for other computers that run the UNIX operating system (i.e., open systems) can be migrated to the RS/6000 and the AIX operating system by the software developer. This allows RS/6000 users to capitalize on many application programs originally developed for other open systems. There is an application program to help users with just about anything they wish to do. Want a program that computes the number of eggs needed to completely fill a swimming pool? Softwares as unique as this do abound. Some functions that might be useful to you include accounting, computer-aided design, statistical analysis, financial modeling, word processing, desktop publishing, database management, electronic mail, animated computer graphics, and so on.

Operating Systems

The next layer in our software model is the operating system (highlighted in Figure 3.16). The operating system must manage the hardware resources of the computer system and perform tasks under the control of application program(s) and keyboard/mouse commands issued by the user. The application program can rely on the operating system to perform many of the detailed housekeeping tasks associated with the internal workings of the computer. Thus, the operating system is said to provide the environment in which application programs execute. The operating system layer also accepts commands directly from the user; for instance, it can copy files, change a user's password, and so on.

The base operating system used by RS/6000 systems is AIX. AIX provides an environment that can run one application program at a time or many application programs simultaneously. There are also many extensions to the AIX operating system, such as the graphics program OpenGL, that allow the user to customize the operating system environment. Because of the modular nature of AIX these extensions plug right into and essentially become a part of the operating system.

User's View of RS/6000 Systems

```
          Application Program(s)        Main
                                        Memory
          Operating System
          - - - - - - - - - - - - -
                  Device Drivers
                                        System
          Hardware                      Hardware
```

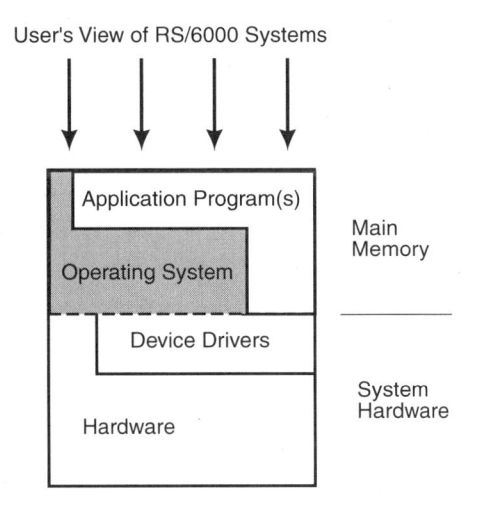

Figure 3.16. The operating system software layer, highlighted in the software model above, provides the environment in which the application programs run.

Device Drivers

The third and final layer of software in our software model is the device driver layer (highlighted in Figure 3.17). **Device driver** is a fancy term for a set of highly specialized programs, usually written by the manufacturer of computer hardware. These specialized programs reside in RS/6000 main memory or in memory provided right on the adapters they control.

Unlike application programs or operating systems, device drivers are only used by other programs. That is, device drivers never interact directly with the users and exist only to help application programs and the operating system perform their tasks. They interact directly with computer hardware elements under the control of the operating system or application program layers. Device drivers also help shield application programs from the hardware specifics of computers, allowing for evolutionary product improvements without sacrificing application program compatibility.

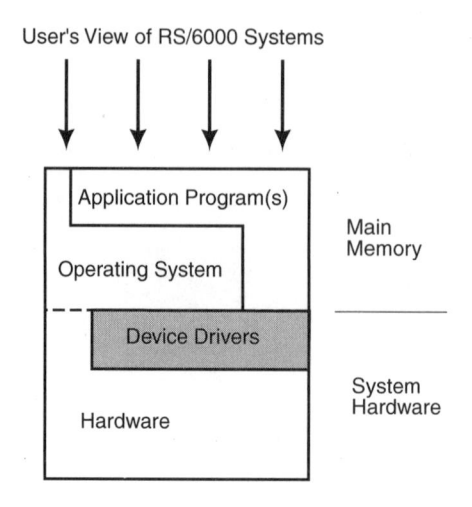

Figure 3.17. The device driver software layer of the software model directly controls the hardware elements of the RS/6000 systems and shields application programs and operating systems from hardware details.

RS/6000 Software Compatibility—Why It Is Important

Computer systems that run the UNIX operating system have been in existence for many years. As a result, a wide variety of application programs have been developed for UNIX. The flexibility afforded by virtue of this large and diverse software base allowed computers running the UNIX operating system to fill many different needs. Of course, this plethora of available application programs did not exist when the original UNIX operating system was first announced. It took the independent efforts of a great many people over many years' time to develop the large number of application programs (called an application program **software base**) that exist today. In order to capitalize on that software base, application software compatibility was a primary objective in the design of the AIX operating system. That is, most application programs written for UNIX operating systems can easily be migrated to the RS/6000 system and the AIX operating system by the software developer.

It is important to understand that of the three software layers in our software model, compatibility with programs in the application programs layer is most important. Why? First of all, application programs typically represent the lion's share of a user's software investment. Further, being forced to abandon an application program due to incompatibilities may also make users throw away whatever data and training or experience they have accumulated with the application program—both of which can be substantial. Some users have developed custom application programs at considerable cost in development time and money. Incompatibility at the application program level would render these programs virtually useless. Finally, and perhaps most important, application layer compatibility allows RS/6000 system users to choose from the thousands of application programs that were originally developed for the UNIX operating system.

What about the operating system and device driver layers? The ability to run earlier UNIX operating system software is important for several reasons. Operating systems typically represent only a small fraction of the user's software investment; they can be upgraded easily without changing the user's view of the computer system. Further, a new operating system is usually necessary to allow users to have access to new features of the computer system not considered by the programmers of the old operating system. Of course, one of the primary purposes of the device driver layer is to allow the computer hardware to change without affecting compatibility with the operating system and application programs. This is done by changing the way a device driver interacts with the hardware without changing the way the device driver interacts with the operating system or application programs. The user is supplied with new device drivers to support RS/6000 hardware.

AIX for the RS/6000

Few areas in information processing create more confusion and apprehension than the operating system. This section will help remove some of the mystery associated with the **Advanced Interactive eXecutive (AIX)** operating system used with all RS/6000 systems. First a note regarding AIX levels: AIX Version 3 was the level introduced with the first RS/6000 back in 1990. It has been through two major releases (3.1 and 3.2), both of which are now unavailable. The current version of AIX, which is version 4, is still available at three different release levels (4.1, 4.2, and 4.3) at the time of this writing. Check the companion Web site cited on page xiv of this book for the latest on AIX.

AIX Overview

Over the years, the UNIX operating system, originally developed by AT&T's Bell Labs, has continually been enhanced by various independent organizations (both academic and business), often in a nonstructured way. These independent efforts have resulted in a very powerful, somewhat cryptic, often awkward, and usually flexible operating system. As we saw at the beginning of this chapter, the UNIX operating system became popular for several reasons. First, AT&T licensed the operating system to many different computer manufacturers who used the UNIX operating system for their computers rather than investing in writing their own operating systems. Second, the UNIX operating system was prevalent in colleges and universities. As students learned the UNIX operating system in these academic environments, it was only natural that they would seek out such systems after entering the nonacademic, business world. Finally, the **C programming language** fostered by the UNIX operating system is a highly popular one, offering very flexible and powerful programming structures.

The UNIX operating system has evolved to be the basis for the open-systems marketplace, where compatibility with industry standards is the hallmark. Compatibility means that programs written for one brand of "open system" can easily be migrated to another brand. The open-system concept is good for application program developers because they can easily offer their products on many different brands of computers. This is also good for users because they have a multitude of software from which to choose no matter which brand of open system they buy. On the down side, open systems discourage vendors from offering programming features unique to their systems, in that compatibility problems can arise as they diverge from industry standards. This tends to hold back some innovative ideas in the name of compatibility and makes product differentiation more difficult.

IBM took the basic UNIX operating system and incorporated many enhancements developed by other organizations (e.g., UC Berkeley), added many enhancements of their own, and came out with their version called the Advanced Interactive eXecutive (AIX). An entire family of AIX operating system products was developed, comprised of AIX operating system versions for the smaller personal computers, RS/6000 computers, and the larger System/370 and System/390 family of mainframe computers. This open-system approach was a departure from IBM's proprietary systems such as that of the AS/400 minicomputer or the MVS operating system for IBM's S/370 and S/390 mainframes. The RS/6000 and the associated version of the AIX operating system represent IBM's second-generation UNIX-based operating system and workstation/server. (The IBM RT System was the first.)

The AIX operating system for the RS/6000 is a multitasking, multiuser operating system adhering to industry standards. The base AIX operating system product itself provides all of the essential functions necessary to make up a complete computer system, but there are several separately purchased **extensions** to the AIX operating system that, when installed, become a part of the operating system, as shown in Figure 3.18. These extensions each add new functions to the AIX operating system. This building-block approach allows each user to select only the functions needed, minimizing software costs and required hardware resources.

The AIX operating system and its extensions perform all housekeeping tasks for the RS/6000 and interact with users to do things such as starting application programs, changing passwords, erasing files, and so on. The base AIX operating system comes with command-driven user interfaces that require the user to type in somewhat cryptic commands. **AIXwindows** is an extension to the AIX operating system that provides an easier-to-use graphical user interface. The graphical user interfaces, along with the **Systems Management Interface Tool (SMIT)** and on-line documentation, provided as standard, make the RS/6000 version of the AIX operating system easier to use than any of its previous versions. The AIX operating system maintains a high level of compatibility with earlier UNIX operating system versions and industry standards to provide compatibility with many application programs written for other open systems.

124 EXPLORING IBM TECHNOLOGY AND PRODUCTS

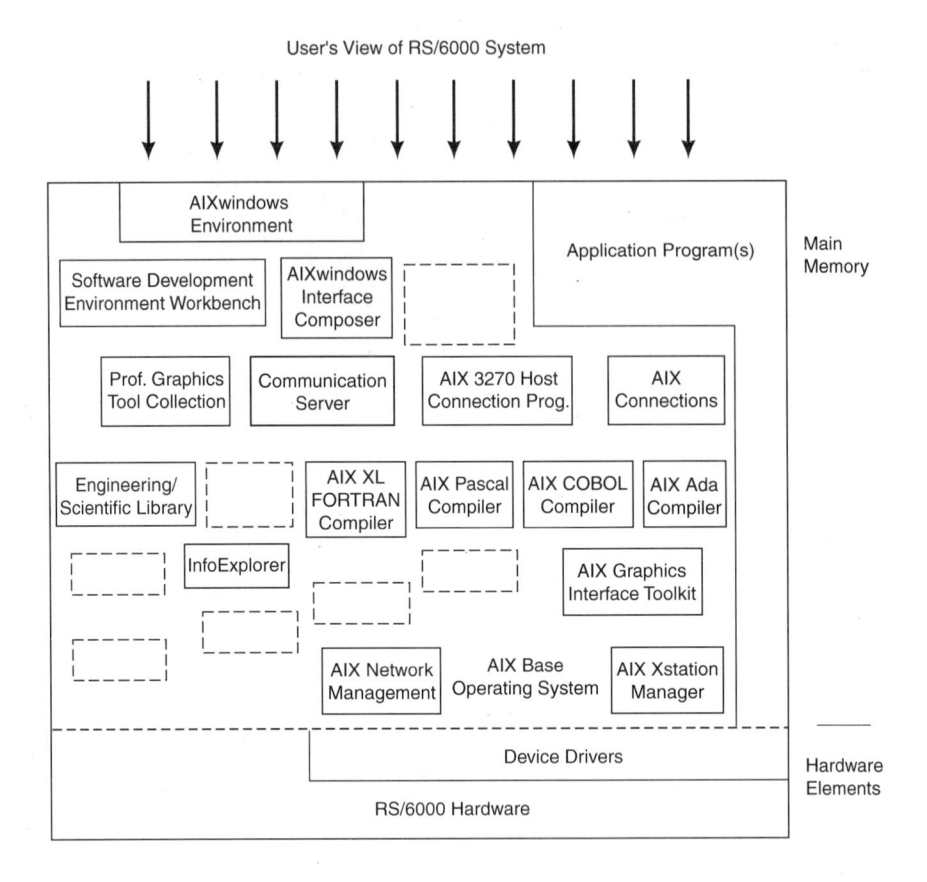

Figure 3.18. The basic functions necessary to provide a complete computer system are provided as standard with AIX. Optional extension products can be added in a buliding block fashion as necessary to add function to AIX.

IBM has also added improvements such as more flexible disk management, improved security, and better data availability. Traditional UNIX development tools (such as the Source Code Control System, subroutine libraries, and the Make command) are addressed as well as some newer tools (e.g., object-oriented programming and computer-aided software engineering products). The AIX operating system communications functions address traditional UNIX operating system communications (e.g., asynchronous ASCII protocol), current industry standards (e.g., TCP/IP and the Network File System), and the IBM System Network Architecture (e.g., 3270 emulation and LU 6.2 protocols). Finally, personal computers can be attached to RS/6000 systems in order to share disks, printers, data, and so forth.

Basically, IBM has started with the UNIX operating system base, incorporated enhancements made by many organizations, and added some new ideas, all without losing compatibility with industry standards (POSIX, SVID2, or Open Group). The AIX operating system with the RS/6000 is an open system, and IBM has stated its intention to evolve the AIX operating system to conform to new industry standards as they emerge. One organization that has a major influence on the development of AIX is the Open Group. The **Open Group** is a nonprofit consortium of computer vendors (including IBM, HP, DEC, and others) formed in 1996 by the merger of X/open and the Open Software Foundation (OSF). The mission of the Open Group is to develop specifications and software for the open-system arena and make the resulting specifications and software available to computer vendors under fair and equitable licensing terms. The Open Group solicits members and nonmembers for submissions of concepts and software to solve a particular problem, then evaluates each submission and selects the best. This submission then becomes the Open Group-endorsed standard for the open-system environment. This process is designed to foster the development of vendor-neutral, open-system standards that many different computer vendors can implement in a compatible fashion. IBM has committed to support Open Group technologies and standards as they emerge in AIX.

4

IBM AS/400 Computers

This chapter will examine IBM's AS/400 computer family. The AS/400 is a very popular mid-range business computer. We will start with a look at the history of the AS/400 and then take a closer look at AS/400 hardware and software.

A Glance Backwards

On July 30, 1969, IBM executives from the entire company joined 1,200 IBMers at their plant site in Rochester, Minnesota, to announce the System/3 computer shown in Figure 4.1. This system was the first computer totally developed at the IBM Rochester, Minnesota, location. Although only of historical interest today, the System/3 represented some significant advances in the technology of its time. For example, it introduced Monolithic Systems Technology, which allowed engineers to package more circuitry in a smaller space, as well as a punch card one-third of normal size that held 20 percent more information. This was the first advancement in punch-card technology in over 40 years!

The Rochester plant, which became a full IBM Division in November of that year, was subsequently tasked to develop a "low-end" computer family. One System/3, fondly named "Old Reliable," ran faithfully until it was shut down in September, 1973. When it was finally retired, its meter showed that it had run for 15,377.97 hours, representing more run time than any other system in existence.

The System/32, shown in Figure 4.2, was the next member of the family. It was announced in January, 1975 and featured direct key-

Figure 4.1. IBM System/3.

Figure 4.2. IBM System/32.

board data entry and a display that could present up to 6 rows of text 40 characters long. The System/32 had up to 32K of memory and up to 13 MB of fixed disk storage.

The System/34 computer, announced in April, 1977, was the first system truly designed to manage multiple (local and remote) workstations (i.e., terminals and printers), each being up to 5,000 feet away from the computer. This allowed it to perform tasks for up to eight local users simultaneously. The System/34, shown in Figure 4.3, provided up to 256K of memory and 13 MB of fixed disk.

Next came the System/38, announced in October, 1978. This represented a divergence from its S/3X predecessors, offering a new architecture optimized for application development productivity. The System/38, shown in Figure 4.4, could support up to 32 MB of memory, 14 GB of disk storage, and 256 local workstations.

Once again, building on the architectural base of the System/34, the first System/36 was announced in May, 1983 (Figure 4.5). It grew to support up to 7 MB of main memory, 1.4 GB of disk storage, and 72 local workstations. Other models of the System/36 varying in processing power and capacity were announced over time. Collectively the System/3, System/32, System/34, System/36, and System/38 are known as the **System/3X** family of computers.

Figure 4.3. IBM System/34.

Figure 4.4. IBM System/38.

Figure 4.5. IBM System/36.

The last S/36 model (the 5363) was enhanced and renamed the **IBM AS/Entry** system. IBM has announced its intentions to provide future enhancements to the AS/Entry products. This means that they are vital to IBM's midrange product strategy, as we will see later in the book.

On June 20, 1988, IBM unveiled the AS/400 family of products. The AS/400 has close architectural ties with System/38 while in most cases providing application program compatibility with both the System/36 and the System/38. Since the original announcement of the AS/400 family, IBM has regularly announced new AS/400 hardware and software products—a trend that shows no signs of slowing.

What Makes Up an AS/400 Computer System?

The IBM Application System/400 (AS/400) family of products represents IBM's latest generation of midsize business computing systems. Like their predecessors, the System/3X family, they are **multiuser** computer systems, meaning a single computer can interact with more than one user at a time. In developing the AS/400 systems, designers drew from the ease-of-use features of the System/36, combined these with the advanced architecture and productivity of the System/38, and then added new functions. In addition to the many application programs developed directly for execution on the AS/400, many of the application programs developed for the System/36 and System/38 computers can be migrated to and used on AS/400 systems by applying the migration tools available.

Many users have no conception of what equipment makes up the computer system they use daily. Fortunately, they do not have to—just as it is not necessary to understand the inner workings of a carburetor to drive a car. However, it is helpful to have a fundamental view of what general elements make up an AS/400. Figure 4.6 shows the components of a very simple AS/400 system configuration. The heart of the system is the system unit, which contains the "brain" that runs the computer programs and controls all activities. People interact with the computer system through terminals (or personal computers acting as terminals) that display computer information and allow for keyboard entry. The terminal shown on the left side of the figure is the **system console**. The system console is a specially

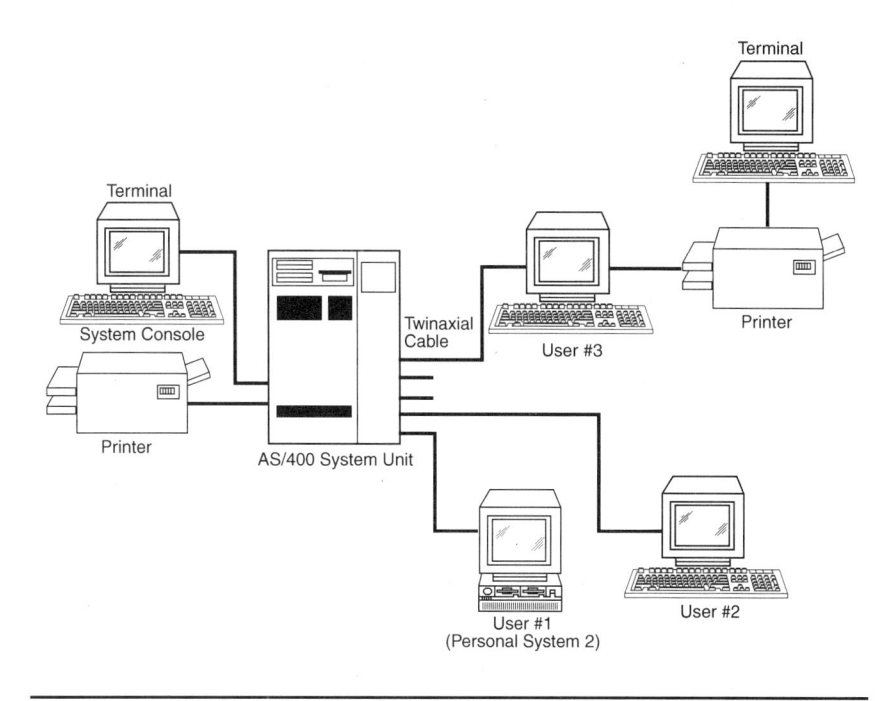

Figure 4.6. Components of a simple AS/400 system.

designated terminal used by the system operator to manage the day-to-day operations of the computer system. The other terminals are for general-purpose use. The printers shown in the figure are used to generate reports, documents, graphs, and the like. A printer can be a workstation used to fill the needs of specific user(s), or it can be shared by all users. Both terminals and printers were initially attached to the system unit via twinaxial cable (or twinax), typically laid in the building's walls or ceiling. In today's environment, the terminals (personal computers) and printers are attached through many other media including radio communications and telephone wiring.

Meet the AS/400 Family

As of this writing, six basic computers form the core of the IBM AS/400 family: the Advanced Entry Model 150e, the Advanced 36, the Advanced System 600e with four processor options, the Advanced System 620e with four processor options, the Advanced System 640e with three processor options, and the Advanced System 650e with two processor options. In addition, there are five server models structured from the core set: the entry Server model 150e, S10e with two processor options, the S20e with four processor options, the S30e with four processor options, and the S40e with a single 12-way processor option. There are also three special server models structured from the S20e, S30e, and S40e. The S20e-ISV and S30e-ISV models provide improved interactive performance running the specific software packages provided by J. D. Edwards and Software Systems Associates. The S40e-SB1 is a main storage, DASD and other I/O device-constrained version of the 12-way processor version of the S40e server, specifically tuned to provide high performance in the compute-intensive environment required by many multi-tiered computing environments. The S40e-SB1 is intended to be used as a SAP R3 application server to a separate second-tier server. (Note: visit the companion Web site cited on page xiv of this book for the latest AS/400 product updates).

Figure 4.7 contains a photograph of the AS/400 Advanced Series family. Let us briefly look at each of these. The "e" in the model names for these systems is intended to signify that the systems are

Figure 4.7. The IBM AS/400 system family, ranging from the Model 400 (furthest left) to the Portable One (furthest right) with an expanded Model 400; Model 500; Model 510 and Model 530, both with disk storage expansion; and Model 50S, Model 40S and Model 150 arranged in between.

capable of supporting the electronic business environment, which means that the user may establish a storefront on the Web and conduct business with the assurance, for both user and customer, that any and all transactions are secure and private.

Inside AS/400 Systems

Many elements provide the functions and performance of IBM AS/400 computers. In this section, we will take a look at some of the things that make AS/400 systems unique.

Hardware Architecture Overview

The underlying arrangement and interconnection of a computer system's electrical components is called its **hardware architecture**. This architecture is the fundamental structure upon which all system functions are built and has the largest effect on how the computer system will behave. A basic understanding of the AS/400 system architecture (depicted in Figure 4.8) makes it possible to compare AS/400 computers with other systems and to understand important aspects of system performance and capacity.

The core of the AS/400 computer (as in all computers) is the **system processor** (shown near the center of the figure). The system processor is the circuitry that actually executes a computer program's instructions and does all the mathematical calculations. To review groupings of data, you will recall that the smallest piece of information (data) in the computer is called a bit. Bits are grouped into bytes (8 bits), half words (16 bits), full words (32 bits), and double words (64 bits) inside the computer. These groupings form the computer's representation of numbers, letters of the alphabet, and instructions in a program. AS/400 system processors move information around one double word (64 bits) at a time. Since much of a computer's time is spend moving information around, the double-word organization helps improve overall system performance.

Other bits inside the system processor are used to uniquely identify or **address** storage and input/output devices (e.g., a disk unit)

134 EXPLORING IBM TECHNOLOGY AND PRODUCTS

```
AS/400 HARDWARE ARCHITECTURE
       (MODELS 200Ð300)
```

- Main Storage
- Control Storage
- SYSTEM PROCESSOR — *Cache
- Service Processor

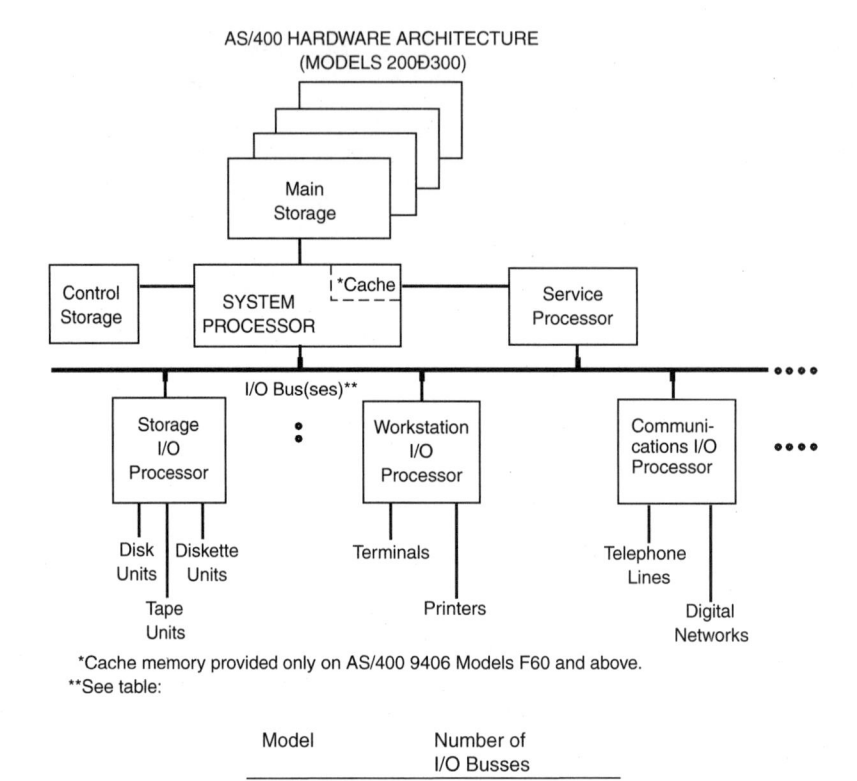

I/O Bus(ses)**

- Storage I/O Processor
  - Disk Units
  - Diskette Units
  - Tape Units
- Workstation I/O Processor
  - Terminals
  - Printers
- Communications I/O Processor
  - Telephone Lines
  - Digital Networks

*Cache memory provided only on AS/400 9406 Models F60 and above.
**See table:

Model	Number of I/O Busses
Model 400/40S	1

Figure 4.8. Block diagram of AS/400 hardware architecture used in all single-processor AS/400 systems (Models 400 and 40S).

within the computer system. AS/400 system processors group 64 bits together to form a unique address. This **64-bit addressing** provides 18,446,744 trillion (2^{6644}) unique addresses, which is more than any other IBM computer system—from PCs to the largest System/390 computers. This is more than enough addresses space for today's mid-size computer environment (and even for the foreseeable future). In fact, the largest AS/400 systems and servers today have not even needed to use *one* trillion of those addresses. This shows the kind of growth inherent in the AS/400 architecture.

The "memory" or **main storage** (shown at the top of the figure) provides a work space for the system processor. Since much of a computer's time is spent moving information to and from main storage, the speed of main storage can be a limiting factor for the overall performance of any computer system. The speed of storage is measured by the time it takes to respond to a request to store or recall information, or the **cycle time**. The main storage cycle time for AS/400 computers varies depending on the model. The shorter the cycle time, the better the system performance. The largest AS/400 computers can have up to 20,480 MB of main storage. The main storage in all AS/400 systems provides **error detection** and **error correction**. These main-storage error functions work to protect the all-important integrity of user information in the computer system.

All AS/400 system processors also use cache memory to help increase the effective cycle time of main storage. A **cache** is a small and very-high-speed memory area that sits between the processor and main storage. The idea is to keep the information most likely to be needed next in cache to avoid the time delay associated with main storage. AS/400 systems have data and instruction caches on the processor to accelerate performance when accessing information/program instructions (respectively).

Another important part of the AS/400 architecture is the **System Licensed Internal Code (SLIC)**. SLIC is a set of extremely simple instructions (never seen by the computer programmer or user) that are directly performed by the electronic circuits within the system processor. All user program instructions are automatically converted into a series of these SLIC instructions, which are then executed by the system processor.

The input/output processors (shown at the bottom of the figure) are responsible for managing any devices attached to the AS/400 system. Each of these specialized processors has independent responsibilities and performs tasks in coordination with the system processor. A computer that has multiple processors working together with the system processor has what is called **multiprocessor architecture**. The advantage of having multiple processors performing work simultaneously is simply that more work can be done in a given period of time. For example, the workstation (I/O) processor manages the detailed processing associated with the multiple terminals and printers attached to the system, allowing the system processor to concentrate on doing more productive work for the user. The same is true of the other specialized I/O processors, such as the storage I/O processor that manages disk, diskette, and tape devices attached to the AS/400 system. The I/O processors communicate with the system processor over an I/O bus (called the **SPD bus**) which is a group of wires that carry information very quickly from one area to another inside the computer system. As indicated in the figure, some AS/400 systems have a single I/O bus, whereas others have multiple I/O busses. Because only one information transfer can occur on any one bus at any one time, systems with multiple busses have the advantage of allowing overlapping transfers between I/O processors and the system processor or main storage. Therefore, multiple busses contribute to the overall system performance of larger AS/400 systems.

Various controllers and adapters plug into physical slots in each of the packages used to provide electrical connections to the bus. In addition to I/O processors, a service processor (shown in the upper-right of the figure) is built into every AS/400. It is responsible for starting the system and constantly monitoring the health of the entire computer. It interacts with the system operator through the control panel and helps with such things as system fault isolation, error detection, and error reporting. It's like having a built-in service technician who watches over things with relentless consistency.

All AS/400 systems employ a **multiprocessor architecture** in that they have a system processor and multiple specialized processors (e.g., workstation and I/O processors) to handle specific tasks. However, larger AS/400 models (e.g. models 620, 640, S20, S30, S40, and 650) employ **multiple-system processors** to cooperatively executing a single copy of the operating system (OS/400), thus appearing to be a single large processor. This multiple-system processor architecture is called the **N-way multiprocessor** architecture (where "N" is replaced by the number of processors), also referred to as the **Symmetric MultiProcessor (SMP)** architecture. Figure 4.9 shows how N-way models are organized (note: all system processors share the same I/O busses, I/O processors, and main storage). Symmetric MultiProcessors process in parallel, sharing a task list. Each processor in a Symmetric MultiProcessor set has its own data and instruction cache, and its own virtual storage view of the system. In the case of a query, each processor in the SMP group will process in parallel against a segment of disk storage to resolve the query.

IBM AS/400 Computers

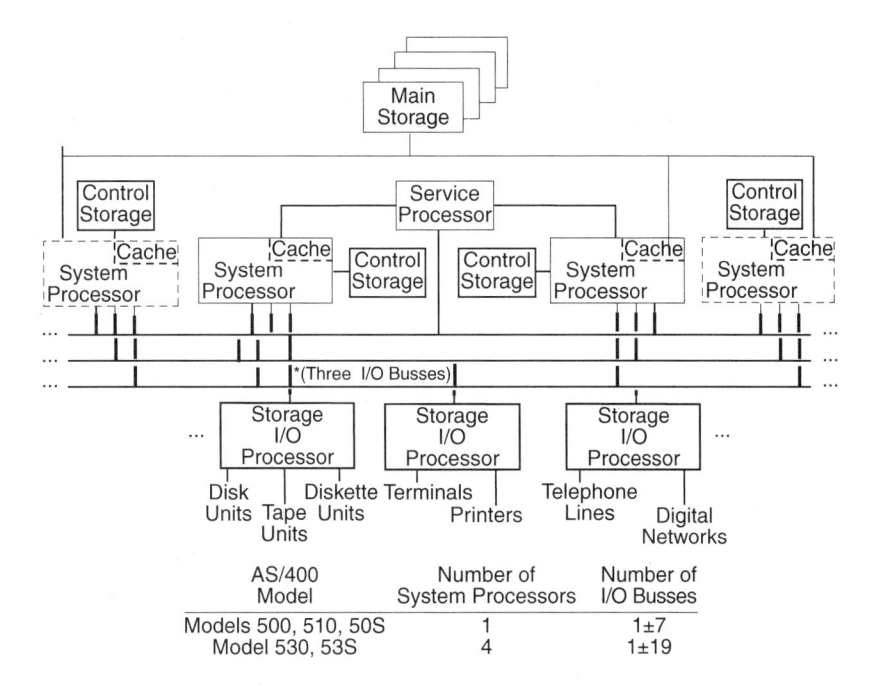

AS/400 Model	Number of System Processors	Number of I/O Busses
Models 500, 510, 50S	1	1±7
Model 530, 53S	4	1±19

Figure 4.9. Block diagram of AS/400 N-way multiprocessor architecture used in Models 500, 510, 50S, 530, and 53S.

The Move from CISC to RISC

As we have seen, the system processor is the circuitry that actually executes a computer program's instructions and does all the mathematical calculations. Prior to 1995, all AS/400 systems processors were based on the **CISC (Complex Instruction Set Computer)** concept.

Although additional improvements could have been achieved with the CISC-based processor, the AS/400 moved to a **RISC (Reduced Instruction Set Computer,** pronounced "risk") base because RISC provides extended future growth, is mainstream and strategic, can be optimized for commercial usage, and offers several advantages at a complete system level—which involves more than chips. RISC also better enables an optimizing compiler as well as simplifying the instruction decode function.

Auxiliary Storage

Auxiliary storage, commonly used to keep data and program information in all computers, is an inexpensive way to retain and later access information. The information kept on auxiliary storage can be easily modified or kept unchanged over long periods of time as an archive. Because all auxiliary storage is nonvolatile, the information stored remains intact whether the computer is turned on or off. The AS/400 systems use four types of auxiliary storage: **diskette, disk, optical libraries,** and **tape**.

Diskette Storage

Diskettes are a portable magnetic storage medium that can be used to record and later retrieve computer information via a diskette unit. The diskettes consist of a flexible disk with a magnetic surface permanently enclosed in a square, protective outer jacket, as shown in Figure 4.10.

One of the primary functions of diskettes is to provide portable storage, allowing for the transfer of programs and data between computers. To this end, all similarly configured AS/400 computer systems can freely exchange programs and data via diskettes. Also, information on System/3X diskettes can be freely exchanged with a properly configured AS/400 computer.

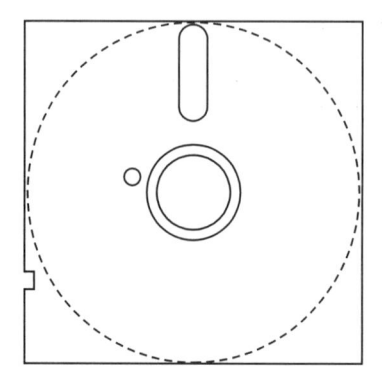

Figure 4.10. Diskette used with Application Systems.

Disk Storage

Earlier in the chapter we introduced another kind of auxiliary storage used with AS/400 systems called disk storage units or **Direct Access Storage Devices (DASDs)**. These are high-capacity magnetic storage devices commonly used in all types of computers from PS/2s to large mainframe computer systems. The basic anatomy of a disk unit is shown in Figure 4.11. Disks consist of a drive mechanism with permanently installed metallic disks often called **platters** (because they are shaped like a dinner plate). These platters have a magnetic surface that can store information. Disk Units were described in great detail in Chapter 2, under "Disk Storage."

Optical Libraries

Optical libraries consist of arrays of optical disks associated with one or more optical disk read/write units. In some cases, the optical storage read/write units also have one or more conventional magnetic disk storage units associated with them to improve the write performance from a system perspective. The optical disks may be CD-ROM, WORM, or WMRM technology, each of which imposes different requirements upon the read/write unit and upon the controller within the system. **CD-ROM** is an abbreviation for **Compact Disk-Read Only Memory,** and the technology presents digital data in a continuous serpentine path across the surface of the optical disk. **WORM** is an

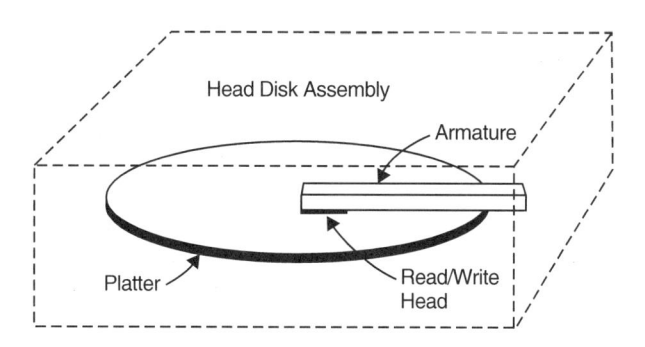

Figure 4.11. The anatomy of a disk unit.

abbreviation for **Write Once, Read Many**. This technology presents data in circumferential paths across the surface of the optical disk. Because the data will only be written once, this technology generally has the header embedded on the raw media, and a sector corresponds to the data content that can fit in the shortest circumferential track. **WMRM**, sometimes referred to as erasable optical disk technology, is an abbreviation for **Write Many, Read Many** and also presents data in circumferential paths across the surface of the optical disk but. But previously written data must be erased before new data may be written to replace it, and it must follow the sectoring, header, trailer, and error-correction rules of magnetic disk technology, including bad track recovery and directory management.

Tape Storage

The last type of auxiliary storage to be covered is magnetic tape or simply "tape." One primary purpose of tape is to provide a backup storage medium for information on the computer's disk storage. The low cost and high recording densities inherent in tape make it ideal for archiving information. Tape is also very useful in distributing programs and transferring information from one computer system to another. Diskettes can be used for these same functions, but the higher storage capacity of tapes is preferred if you are dealing with a large amount of information. Tape storage consists of a long flexible strip coated with magnetic material and rolled onto a reel or into a cartridge.

Storage Management

The methods used within a computer system to manage main storage and disk storage are collectively called the computer's **storage management** and is fundamental to the capabilities of the computer. Understanding the basics of this storage management provides insight into one of the unique features of AS/400 computers as compared with traditional computer systems.

Figure 4.12 shows conceptually what the storage in AS/400 computers looks like. All programs and information currently being used by the computer system must be contained in main storage which

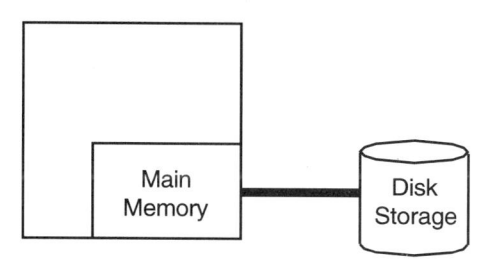

Figure 4.12. AS/400 main storage and fixed disk storage.

resides inside the computer's system unit. Main storage is relatively expensive and responds at very high speeds (compared to disk storage) when called on to provide or store information. Because main storage loses all information when the computer system is turned off, it is called **volatile** storage.

Disk storage is less expensive but cannot provide or store information as quickly as main storage. Disk storage is said to be **nonvolatile** because it does not lose its information when the power is turned off (or lost owing to a power failure). As a result of this nonvolatility and relatively low cost, disk storage is commonly used to hold all information that must be readily available to the computer. The disk storage may reside either inside the system unit or inside a separate box cabled to the system unit (as depicted in the figure).

When the AS/400 computer is first turned on, information vital to an orderly startup and smooth operation is automatically copied from the disk to main storage. Once normal system operation is established, users can begin to do their work. During the course of this work, users will start various computer programs. As each program is started, it is copied from the disk to main storage and then executed. Depending on the work being done, the computer programs manipulate various sets of data that are also loaded from the disk as needed. It does not take long to realize that the main storage in a computer can quickly become filled up with programs and data as the system is called upon to do more and more work.

In earlier days of computing, the main storage size limited the amount of work a computer could manage at any one time. This limitation capped the size of programs, the number of programs that could be run concurrently, the number of users that could share the system, and so on. In today's environment, a technique called **virtual storage** alleviates the need to squeeze all active programs and data into main storage. In computers that support virtual storage, the computer basically "fakes out" the computer programs and users and appears to have much more main storage than it actually has. The AS/400 allows a virtual Storage size of 18 million Terabytes. Virtual storage therefore allows more programs, data, and users to be simultaneously active on the system than could be supported in real main storage without virtual storage.

Although virtual storage is a powerful system feature, the "swapping" between disk and main storage is processing overhead that can reduce the overall system performance. A little swapping does not appreciably hurt performance, but increased swapping does. When the swapping performed by a virtual storage system becomes excessive, the system is said to be **thrashing**, or spending too much time swapping information between disk and main storage. Thrashing can be reduced by increasing the amount of main storage in the AS/400 system through the installation of main-storage expansion options. Increasing the main storage in the system provides more room for programs and data, reducing the amount of virtual storage swapping. Thrashing can also be reduced through system management means such as rescheduling work for off-peak periods.

The virtual storage concept is implemented in many of today's computer systems to one degree or another. AS/400 systems implement their virtual storage scheme through a concept called **single-level storage**. This simply means that in AS/400 systems, no distinction is made between disk storage and main storage. All storage appears to be one homogeneous mass of main storage accessed in exactly the same way. This consistency provides for a simple and efficient virtual storage implementation that is the same for programs, data, temporary holding areas, and so forth. The simplicity of single-level storage results in a consistent and more complete virtual storage system than most other implementations.

Another difference between AS/400 storage management and that of conventional computer systems is its **object-oriented access**. With this concept, all programs, databases, documents, and so on stored in AS/400 computers are stored as independent entities called **objects**. The AS/400's object-oriented access again provides the user and the programmer with a simple and consistent way of managing all programs and information in the system. Users can access an object by simply referring to its name. The AS/400 security system will check to make sure that the user has authorization to use the object and that it is being used properly. This is called **capability-based addressing**. The AS/400 system manages the complexities associated with the physical location and addressing of the information.

AS/400's implementation of single-level storage and capability-based addressing spreads information through various disk units in a way that optimizes storage efficiency. Objects provide consistency in the areas of security, usage, and systems management for all items stored on AS/400 systems. Objects can be organized into groups called libraries. A **library** (which is also an object) is analogous to a drawer in a file cabinet (or a subdirectory, for those familiar with personal computer disk management). A library might contain all programs related to the accounting function of a business to keep things organized. Because access to libraries can be restricted by the AS/400 security system, a payroll database, for example, might be kept in a library separate from other business information for security reasons.

Opticonnect/400 Systems

All AS/400 systems are multiprocessor systems. While some processors are performing the system-level processing function, other processors are performing the I/O functions of the system. Prior to Opticonnect/400, when the performance at the system-level processing function was exhausted, additional processing performance could only be obtained by replacing the existing computer system with a model that executed the system-level processing function faster.

Opticonnect/400 systems allow the interconnection of the existing system with other AS/400 systems at a functioning level just below the main storage interface to share data and processing capability. This interconnection is referred to as **loosely coupled computing** and is similar to the distributed computing environment for the server models, except that the sharing is performed at a much higher level in the individual systems. The higher the level at which sharing is performed, the lower the complexity introduced in the execution of the sharing function.

Each system participating in the sharing function loses one I/O bus to the sharing function. Figure 4.13 shows the sharing function

144 EXPLORING IBM TECHNOLOGY AND PRODUCTS

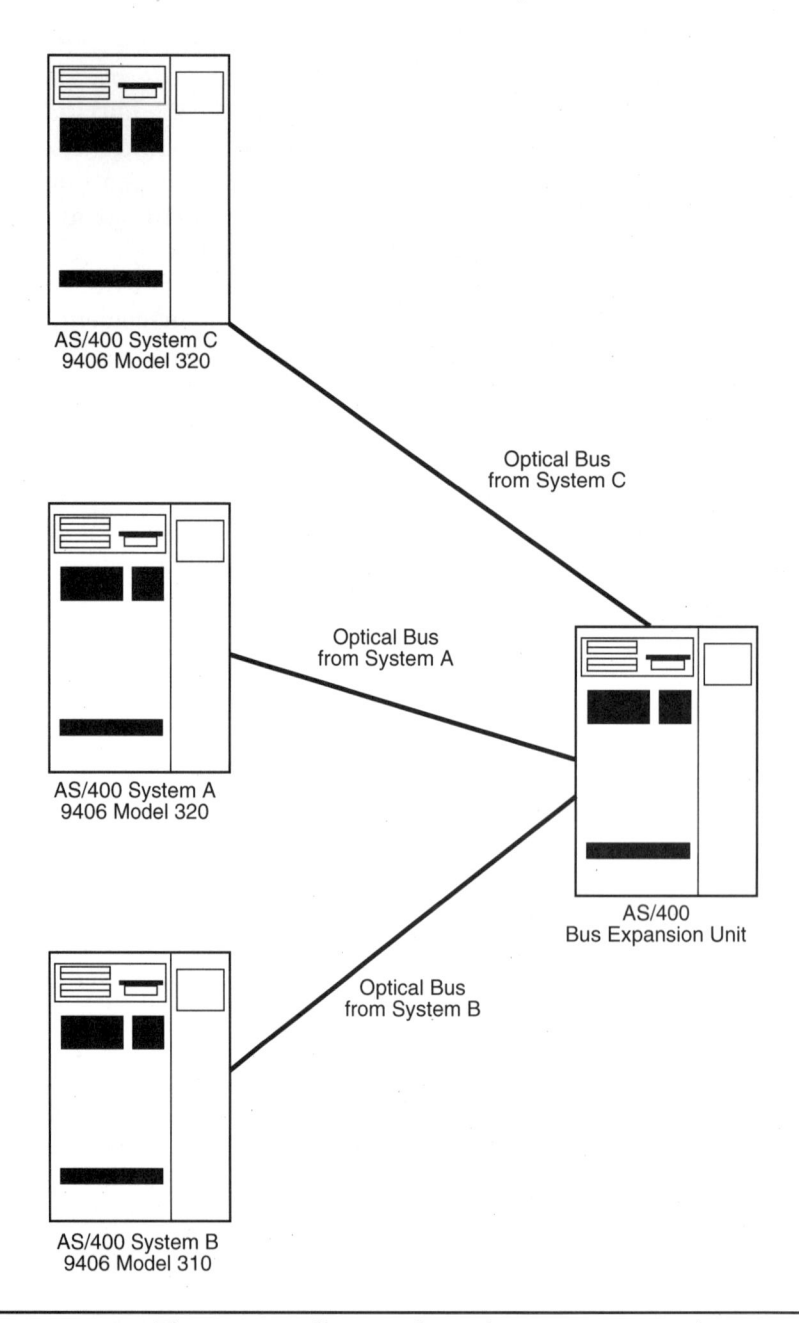

Figure 4.13. Three system cluster with one bus given up in each system to connect to the expansion tower.

for three systems. The clustering is performed including one of the fiber optic buses from each system (Advanced Series 500, 50S, 510, 530, 53S, 620e, 640e, 650e, S20e, S30e, S40e, and S20e-ISV, S30e-ISV, S40e-SB1 systems only) in the system cluster. The fiber optic bus is connected to the other systems by using an Optical Bus Adapter in a Bus Expansion Unit. One Optical Bus Adapter must be used for each system to be included in the system cluster. A maximum of 32 systems can be included in an Opticonnect/400 system. To achieve the maximum 32-system interconnection, 3 fiber optic buses and 3 Bus Expansion Units must be used from at least one system. Data and applications may be shared across Opticonnect/400 systems using the distributed data management facilities of the OS/400 operating system with an overhead of less than 3 ms for data transfers from disk access on other systems. With the availability of the 1063-Mbps fiber optic bus adapter on the Advanced Series 530, 53S, 620e, 640e, 650e, S20e, S30e, S40e, and S20e-ISV, S30e-ISV, S40e-SB1 systems, the latency and performance of this connection is improved by better then seven times.

AS/400 Software

As with other types of computers, AS/400 systems use several different types of software, each diverse in function and purpose. Let's take a look at AS/400 software.

Types of Software—A Model

The basic categories of real software used in AS/400 systems can be understood through the simple software model (Figure 4.14). Three basic software layers are commonly used with Application Systems computers: the **application program** layer, the **operating system** layer, and the **System Licensed Internal Code (SLIC)** layer. Although each software layer performs a completely different job, all three work closely together to perform useful work for the user. Some special-purpose programs don't fit neatly into any of these three categories, but the majority of software commonly used does. Other chapters focus on the application and operating system layers. For now, let us briefly look at each of the three layers in our software model.

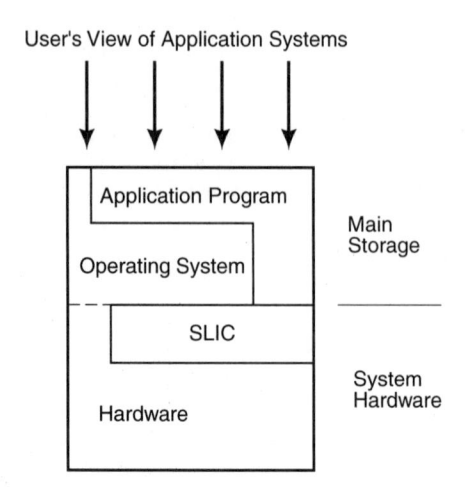

Figure 4.14. Conceptual software model of Application Systems' basic software structure. The three layers of the software model work together to perform useful work for the user.

Application Programs

The top software layer in the software model is the *application program* layer (highlighted in Figure 4.15). The programs in this layer *apply* Application Systems to a specific task (e.g., payroll or accounting) and thus are called application programs. They actually perform the task for which the user purchased the computer, whereas the other two layers play important support roles. The *user's view* arrows in the figure indicate that the user usually interacts with the application program layer and less frequently with the operating system. By working closely with the other software layers, the application program processes the various keystrokes made by the user and responds by displaying information on the computer's display or some other output device.

Programs written for System/3X computers can be either directly executed or migrated to Application Systems. This allows Application Systems users to capitalize on the thousands of application programs available for these popular business systems. There is an application program that can help users with just about anything they wish to do. Some more common functions application programs perform in the business environment are accounting, financial mod-

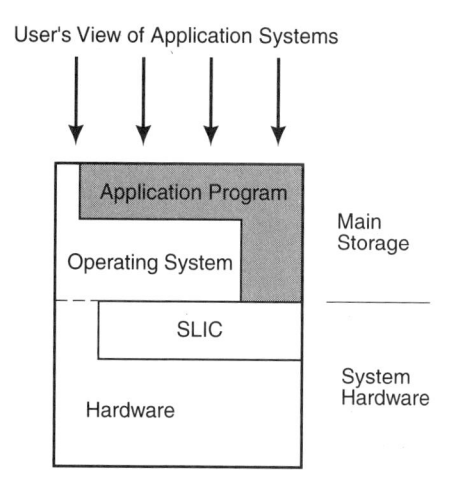

Figure 4.15. The application program software layer of the model, highlighted above, defines the particular tasks the computer is performing for the user.

eling, word processing, database management, electronic mail, and computer graphics.

Operating Systems

The next layer in our software model is called the **operating system** (highlighted in Figure 4.16). The operating system must manage the hardware resources of the computer system and perform tasks under the control of application programs and keyboard commands typed by the user. The application program can rely on the operating system to perform many of the detailed *housekeeping* tasks associated with the internal workings of the computer. Thus, the operating system is said to provide the *environment* in which application programs execute. Operating systems also accept commands directly from the user to do such things as copying files and changing passwords. The operating system must also manage the system variables used for tailoring the major types of objects supported by the system, such as programs, files (databases, print, display, etc.), communications protocols, and provide national language support.

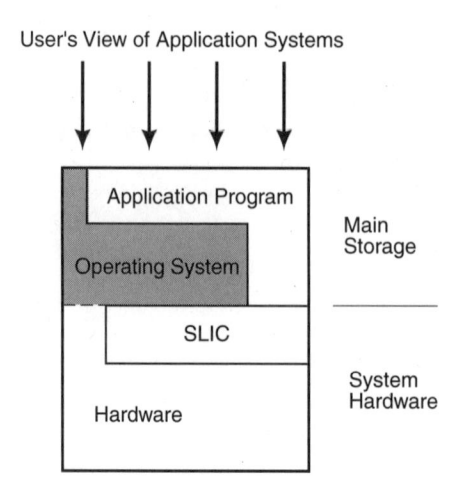

Figure 4.16. The operating system software layer of the model, highlighted above, provides the environment in which the application program(s) run.

SLIC Instructions

The third and final layer of software in our software model is called the System Licensed Internal Code (SLIC) layer (highlighted in Figure 4.17). SLIC (as previously described) is a set of highly specialized programs written by the manufacturer of a computer and never tampered with by the computer operator or users. The set of SLIC instructions in AS/400 computers is embedded deeply within the computer system and is therefore considered to be part of the computing machine itself rather than part of a program running on the machine. Unlike application programs or operating systems, SLIC is used only by other programs. That is, SLIC never interacts directly with the user or the programmer and exists only to help application programs and the operating system perform their tasks. SLIC instructions also help shield application programs from the hardware specifics of computers, allowing for evolutionary product improvements without sacrificing application program compatibility.

It is the particularly rich SLIC layer in AS/400 that helps set its architecture apart from those of more conventional computers. The built-in database, single-level storage, object-oriented architecture, and other AS/400 features are all designed into the SLIC layer of AS/

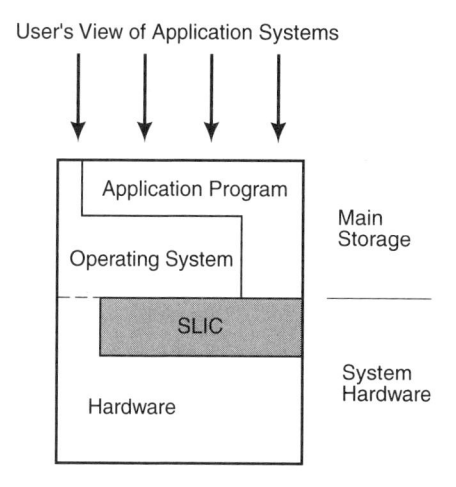

Figure 4.17. The SLIC software layer of the model, highlighted above, directly controls the hardware elements of the Application Systems and shields application programs and the operating system from hardware details.

400, making them part of the machine itself. This results in highly efficient, consistent, and easy-to-use implementations of these functions.

AS/400 Operating Systems

AS/400 Systems use one of two operating systems. The Advanced 36 computers use the IBM **System Support Program** (**SSP**) originally developed for System/36 computers. All other current AS/400 models use OS/400 as their primary operating system (though they can also run SSP to meet special needs. Let's take a quick look at both operating systems.

SSP

The System Support Program, commonly called SSP, was the operating system originally offered for IBM System/36 computers. Because of the popularity of that computer family, SSP has become widely used in the business community. As a result, many application programs were developed for SSP and the System/36 by many different software companies. As the System/36 computers evolved, SSP was revised to support the enhancements in the computer hardware. Although each new version of SSP provided additional functions, compatibility with earlier application programs was maintained. SSP is the operating system used on the Advanced 36 systems and provides full compatibility with earlier System/36 computers. It consists of a set of programs designed to perform many diverse hardware "housekeeping" tasks under the control of either the computer user or an application program. Tasks performed by SSP include managing multiple users, providing security, managing the flow of batch and interactive jobs through the system, sending information to a printer, and so forth. SSP can also be run on any current AS/400 system as a guest operating system under OS/400 in order to provide compatibility for S/36 application programs.

OS/400

Operating System/400, commonly called OS/400, is a multiuser operating system exclusively used with all AS/400 computer systems. It works closely with SLIC instructions in AS/400 systems to implement the database, security, single-level storage, and so on that are basic to AS/400 architecture. Its extensive database and communications support allows AS/400 to manage large amounts of information and participate in many communications configurations. Available application development tools improve the productivity of programmers for those writing their own custom application programs. For current users of System/36 or System/38 systems, the OS/400 System/36 and System/38 modes (along with the migration aids) ease the migration to AS/400 systems.

Although OS/400 offers the user complex and sophisticated features, many things have been done to make OS/400 easier to use. One of the most significant enhancements is the incorporation of the **Operational Assistant**. Based on many of the ease-of-use functions of the System/36, the Operational Assistant is a set of menus and functions for OS/400 that masks many of the OS/400 concepts users have found confusing. The Operational Assistant helps the user do a things such as working with printer output, batch jobs, and electronic messages. Figure 4.18 shows the main menu presented by OS/400's Operational Assistant. To initiate OS/400 tasks, the user can either type in a command or step through a series of menus and prompts. Novice or infrequent users will appreciate the menu structure as it guides them through any OS/400 function. More experienced users will likely use the commands, which provide results more quickly than stepping through the menus. Other OS/400 items that directly address ease of use include automatic configuration of devices and table-driven customization.

Extensive help and online (computer-based) documentation is provided to reduce the need to go to reference manuals when the user needs more information. Online education is built into OS/400, allowing users to learn how to use the system while sitting in front of their terminal.

In addition to performing tasks under the direct control of the user, OS/400 can perform tasks under direct control of an applica-

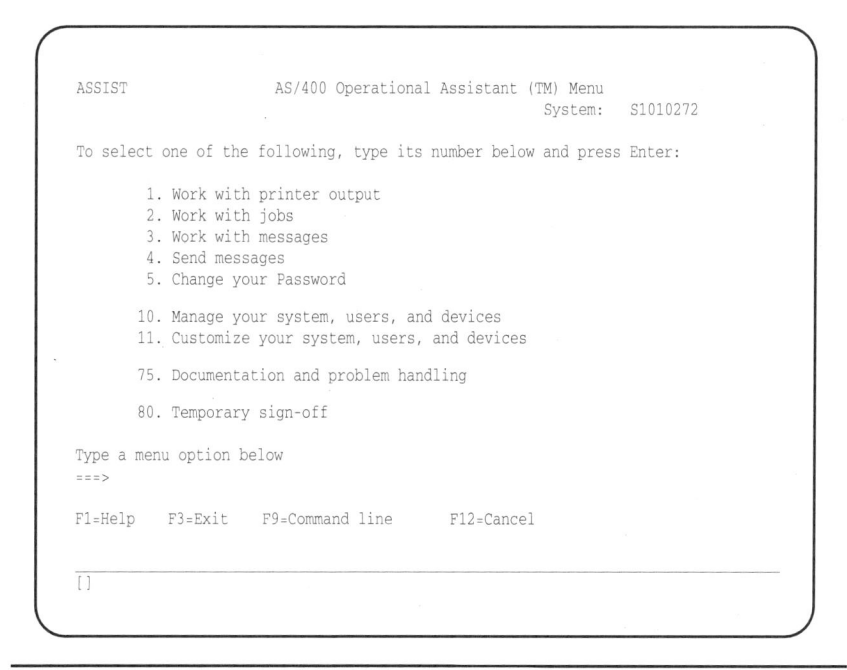

```
ASSIST                AS/400 Operational Assistant (TM) Menu
                                                 System:    S1010272
To select one of the following, type its number below and press Enter:

        1. Work with printer output
        2. Work with jobs
        3. Work with messages
        4. Send messages
        5. Change your Password

       10. Manage your system, users, and devices
       11. Customize your system, users, and devices

       75. Documentation and problem handling

       80. Temporary sign-off

Type a menu option below
===>

F1=Help    F3=Exit    F9=Command line    F12=Cancel


[ ]
```

Figure 4.18. Menu presented by the Operational Assistant component of OS/400.

tion program, which can issue OS/400 commands through the OS/400. There is a defined protocol for passing information directly between the application program and OS/400 with no user interaction required. Often, OS/400 subsequently calls on the routines of the SLIC instructions to effect the desired action.

OS/400 provides multiple application programming interfaces to maintain compatibility with programs written for System/36, System/38, and of course AS/400. The AS/400 application programming interface provides some new capabilities not found in earlier operating systems, such as the structured query language (SQL) method of dealing with databases. OS/400 provides online education facilities and online help to assist users during interaction with the operating system. If a user gets stuck on some operating system screen, pressing the Help key causes some help text to appear on the screen. The particular help text shown depends on where the cursor was on the screen when the Help key was pressed; that is, the text will address the particular item at which the cursor was positioned. This is called **contextual** help.

5

IBM S/390 Computers

This chapter provides an overview of the S/390 family. It also takes a look at the changing role of large computers in the age of network computing.

A Glance Backwards

In the 1950s, IBM helped shape the fledgling computer industry with a line of computers—with names like the 650, the 701, and the 305 RAMAC—based on vacuum tubes (Figure 5.1). (The 305 RAMAC, shown in Figure 5.2, provided the first disk storage in the industry.) During the decade of the 1950s, IBM enhanced these products and continued development of other computer systems—each uniquely designed to address specific applications and to fit within narrow price ranges.

This undisciplined proliferation of unique and incompatible computer systems caused confusion, even within IBM's own marketing, service, and software development organizations. The lack of "compatibility" among these systems also made it difficult for customers to migrate to new generations of IBM computers.

Figure 5.1. Vacuum tube rack used in the Model 701.

Figure 5.2. IBM 305 RAMAC computer system.

In 1961 a corporate task force (code-named "SPREAD" to indicate a wide scope) assembled at a Connecticut motel to define a new family of mutually compatible, general-purpose computers. The task force's final report recommended building a new series of computer systems spanning a wide range of price and performance. IBM's senior management accepted the recommendation just a week later, and a new development project was launched.

The first task undertaken by the development team was to define a set of rules—termed an **architecture**—to which a group of five computers would conform. This architectural definition step was the key to ensuring that all five computer systems would be compatible with one another—a first for IBM. The architecture was completed and documented by the fall of 1962.

After defining the architecture, the development team turned to the task of simultaneously designing the five different models that made up the family. Enhanced core memory and a new **solid logic technology (SLT)** improved performance and reliability. Finally, on April 7, 1964, IBM held a press conference, with over 200 editors and writers in attendance, to announce the IBM **System/360** family of computers (Figure 5.3). The "360" in the name referred to all points of a compass to denote the universal applicability, wide range of performance and price, and the "whole-company" scope of the development effort. A wall-sized compass rose was displayed on the stage backdrop during the press conference.

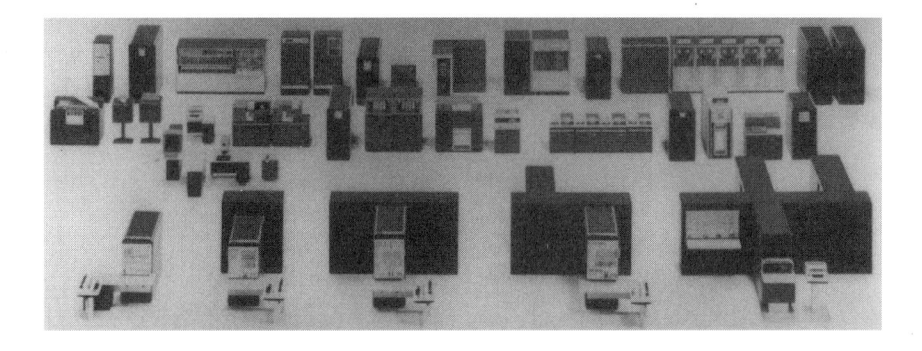

Figure 5.3. The IBM System/360 family of computer systems (mainframes foreground).

Although the System/360 architecture remained unchanged for six years, just six months after its introduction, IBM executives began to plan for systems that would exploit the emerging **monolithic circuit** (**MLC**) technology. By the end of 1965, a draft document defining a new family of computer systems, called "NS" for "new systems," was complete. The new systems were to be based on monolithic circuit technology and an extended System/360 architecture to be called **System/370**.

In June, 1970, IBM announced the System/370 Models 155 and 165. The System/370 architecture preserved **upward compatibility** with application programs written for the System/360 architecture (that is, applications written to run on System/360 could also run on System/370 systems, but those written for System/370 would not execute on the older systems).

During the development of the System/370 family, IBM recognized the need to expand the amount of **main storage** (often referred to as memory or central storage) available to application programs. This need led to the development of a second wave of System/370 computers that implemented a new concept called **virtual memory**. The virtual memory concept used a level of storage **address translation** to increase the amount of storage perceived available by application programs. That is, virtual memory made computer systems seem to have much more main storage than they actually did. Virtual memory was publicly announced in August, 1972, along with the System/370 Models 158 and 168 (Figure 5.4), replacing the original System/370 Models 155 and 165.

The Models 158 and 168 brought the **multiprocessing** configuration to the System/370 family. With multiprocessing, two or more processors housed in a single computer system cooperate to execute available work. Also announced at the same time were virtual memory options for the Models 155/165 and the disclosure that previously announced System/370 Models 135 and 145 had built-in virtual memory capabilities. By the end of 1976, the addition of the Models 125 and 115 brought the number of announced System/370 models to 17.

Prompted by the still growing need of users for main storage fueled by the increase in **interactive processing** (in which users hold a dialog with the computer), the System/370 product line was split into two compatible lines: the 30XX series of large systems and the 43XX series of mid-range systems (Figure 5.5).

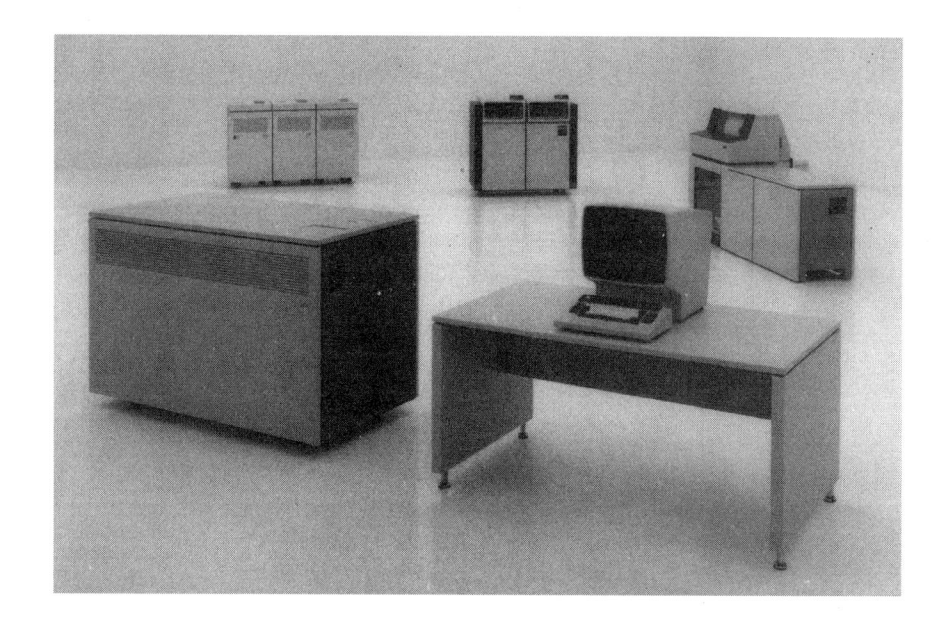

Figure 5.4. IBM System/370 Model 168 computer complex.

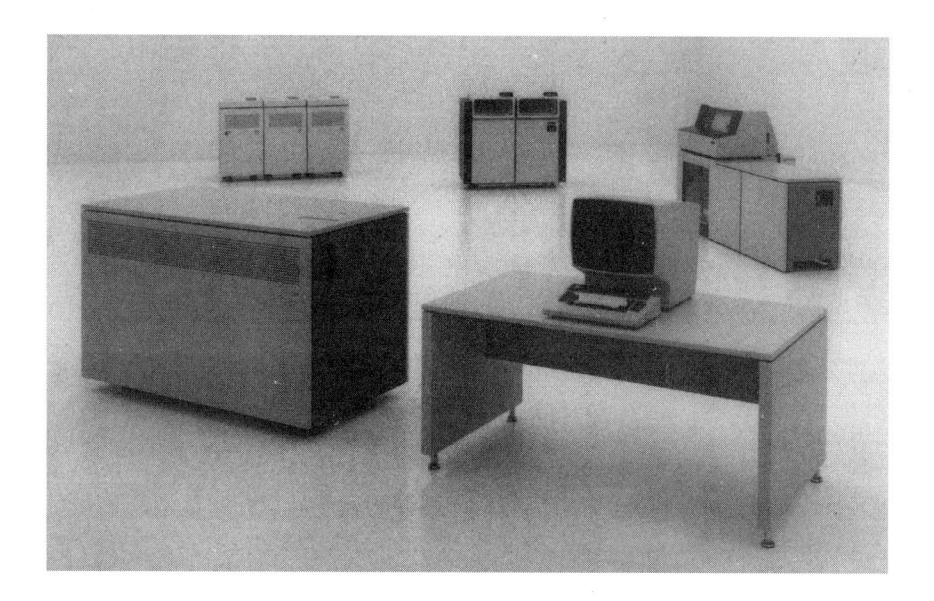

Figure 5.5. IBM 4331 computer complex.

In 1981, the main storage addressability of the 30XX series was quadrupled (up to 64 MB) by exploiting some extra addressing bits available, but not used in the System/370 architecture. Additional main storage support came with the System/370 Extended Architecture (370XA) **System/370 Extended Architecture** (370-XA), announced in 1981 and first shipped in 1983. The 370-XA increased the main storage addressing capability by 128 times by extending the address field from 24 to 31 bits. At the same time, it maintained a 24-bit compatibility mode (upward compatibility), allowing application programs written for systems without this new option to run unchanged.

In February, 1985, IBM extended the 30XX series with the addition of the IBM 3090 (Figure 5.6). This series, originally announced with the Models 200 and 400, extended the performance range of the System/370 architecture beyond that of the preceding members of the 30XX series. The 3090 series was later extended and became IBM's large-system flagship. The 370-XA added **expanded storage** to the 3090. Expanded storage was a new form of processor storage, separate from main storage, used to hold much more information inside the computer. This additional storage resulted in an overall system performance improvement.

Figure 5.6. IBM 3090 Model 200 computer complex.

The true test of any computer architecture is in the marketplace. Only by the life or death of the architecture do computer designers really know whether they hit the mark. The longevity and extendibility of the System/360 and System/370 architectures speak highly of their original designers. In fact, Bob Evans, Fred Brooks, and Erich Block received the National Medal of Technology at a White House ceremony in 1985 for their part in developing the System/360.

In October, 1986, IBM extended downward the range of the System/370 architecture with the introduction of the IBM 9370 series of computers. These rack-mounted systems were designed to work as distributed processors in a network of System/370 computers or as stand-alone computers for smaller businesses or departments.

The next advance in the architecture came in 1988 with the introduction of the Enterprise Systems Architecture/370 (ESA/370). This architecture again improved virtual storage addressing by adding access registers which allowed access to another form of virtual storage called **data spaces**. Data spaces allow more data to reside in main and expanded storage, reducing input/output (I/O) and improving throughput. Other capabilities of the ESA/370 architecture made it easier for information to be shared among the users of the system.

In September, 1990, IBM introduced the **Enterprise System Architecture/390 (ESA/390)** and the **ES/9000** family of computers covering the range of price/performance previously held by the System/370 9370, 43XX, and 3090 computers. The ESA/390 architecture and the 18 original models of the ES/9000 line again maintained application program compatibility all the way back to the first System/360 computers while enhancing performance and increasing functionality. ESA/390 today includes many new features, such as ESCON and parallel sysplex, continuing IBM's evolution of its large business computer architecture.

In 1994 IBM announced extensions to the System/390 (S/390) family including additions to the ES/9000 line and introduced new, scalable System/390 parallel-processing computers in a parallel-sysplex environment. For IBM, two new computing directions were set with this announcement. CMOS (Complementary Metal Oxide Semiconductor) technology was introduced as a building block for very large computers, complementing bipolar technology; and computers targeting specific application environments—rather than the full general-purpose environment—were introduced. Later announcements extended the CMOS technology to low-end, stand-alone servers and then to a broad range of servers providing performance not quite to the top of the older bipolar technology processors. These changes reduced the overall cost of computing for businesses while providing them with greater flexibility. Over time, new System/390 models were announced to replace the ES/9000 models and the evolution of this long popular family continues. The remainder of this chapter will focus on today's S/390 family.

What Makes Up a S/390 Computer System?

Figure 5.7 shows the basic elements that make up a bare-bones S/390 computer system (suitable for testing a system but not for executing a productive workload). The **processor unit** houses the millions of electronic circuits that form the heart of the computer. Within the processor unit there are one or more (up to 10) **central processors** (CPs)—the elements that actually execute the computer programs. Systems that utilize a single CP are called **uniprocessors**. Those that utilize multiple central processors to achieve higher performance levels are called **multiprocessor** models. These are designed to operate as a single image (dyadic or triadic models for example) or to be physically partitionable into two separate processors.

Even when a single computer system employs multiple central processors, it appears to the system operator and users to be a single system (it presents a single-system image). Conversely, any S/390 computer, regardless of the number of central processors, can be divided logically into parts so that it gives the appearance of multiple computers to the users and to the system operator. This is called **logical partitioning**, and it is facilitated by the Processor Resource/Systems Manager (PR/SM) logical partitioning—a standard feature on all S/390 computers. With PR/SM, a single S/390 computer can be divided into as many as 10 logical partitions (**LPAR**s), and some multiprocessor models can be divided into as many as 20 logical partitions.

The processor storage (often called central storage or main memory) holds the programs and data upon which the central processor(s) acts. It is made up of two different regions of memory: central storage and expanded storage. **Central storage** is the traditional type of memory found in most computers, from the smallest personal computers to supercomputers. It is a high-speed storage area

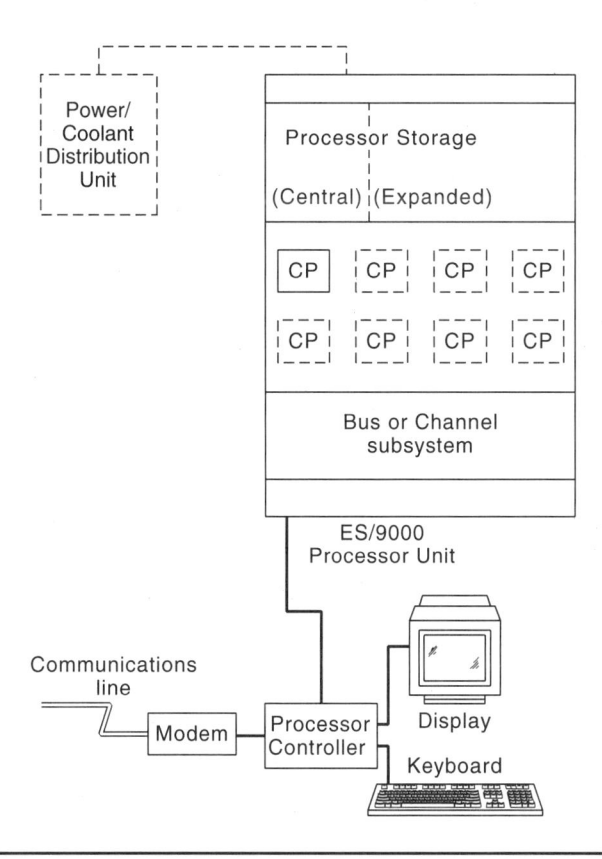

Figure 5.7. ES/9000 processor unit, power/coolant distribution unit, and processor controller.

used to hold information currently needed by the processor unit. This information is addressed a single byte at a time.

Expanded storage, though still residing within the processor unit, is usually a little slower and less expensive to use than central storage. Expanded storage holds information beyond the immediately pertinent information being used in central storage. This information is addressed only in increments of 4,000 bytes (4 KB), referred to as a **page**. Staging information in expanded storage avoids the need to retrieve this information from even slower external storage devices (such as a disk drive). Thus, expanded storage provides a relatively low-cost method of increasing the amount of information held in the processor unit, typically resulting in an overall increase in the performance of the computer system.

Support for attaching I/O subsystems is also housed in the processor unit. This is a **bus subsystem** and/or a **channel subsystem**. The bus subsystem, used only on the rack-mounted ES/9000 9221 processors, provides a way to add optional **integrated I/O adapter cards** to the system. These adapters provide support for selected input/output function and devices (such as a communications line interface or a control unit for tape/DASD). A channel subsystem, available on all S/390 computers, provides a more versatile way to attach optional devices (such as a 3745 Communications Controller or a 3990 Storage Control) to S/390 computers. It is necessary to attach external devices to an S/390 computer in order to make a complete computer system, but the choice depends on the user's needs.

Also shown in Figure 5.7 is the **processor controller**. This device starts up, configures, and maintains the S/390 computer. It is the "cockpit" of the computer system and is used exclusively by the personnel who support the system, not by the business application users of the computer system. The processor controller consists of a small computer (actually, in some S/390 computers, it is a derivative of an IBM Personal Computer), a display, and a keyboard.

Attached to the processor controller is a **modem**. The modem enables the processor controller, if authorized, to send and receive information over a telephone line; that is, the modem has the circuitry necessary to convert information encoded in the computer (**digital** information) to signals suitable for transmission over telephone lines (**analog** information) and vice versa. This modem link allows the S/390 computer, for example, to automatically call an IBM Remote Support Facility and electronically report any problems detected with the system.

Finally, the water-cooled S/390 computers come with a separate **power/coolant distribution unit**, which provides electrical power in the form needed by the S/390 computer and circulates coolant to keep the operating temperature of the system within permissible limits.

Although the S/390 computer shown in Figure 5.7 could be set up and tested, it lacks devices required to perform useful work. Figure 5.8 adds the devices necessary to make a functional computer system. A **direct access storage device (DASD)** subsystem is added to provide disk storage for the system. Whereas the processor storage holds programs and data currently being acted upon by the central processor(s), disk storage holds programs and data not currently being used but that may be needed at any instant.

A **tape subsystem** is used to store data that is less frequently processed than data on disks (for example, large sequential files), to hold archival data, and to provide a level of backup in the event of system failure. Frequently, information stored on the DASDs is backed up to magnetic tape either to use DASD space more efficiently or to ensure a backup copy if the DASD should fail. The tape subsystem also provides a way to load program products (which are often distributed on tape) into the system and to exchange programs and data with other computer systems.

To allow people to interact with the S/390 computer, **workstations** are attached to it. A workstation is either a simple device with a display and keyboard or a complete computer system, such as a personal computer, in its own right. In either case, the workstations are attached to a local **workstation control unit**, which manages the traffic flow between the workstations and the channel subsystem within the S/390 computer. Since this workstation control unit is directly attached to the channel subsystem of S/390 computers, it is called a **local** workstation control unit. One of the workstations is used by the system operator to monitor, manage, and perform the housekeeping associated with the S/390 computer. (Note: Although a local workstation is shown in Figure 5.8, a remote workstation can be used by a system operator, enabling the support staff to be located elsewhere.) The other workstations are for business users who perform the work for which the computer system was installed.

Meet the Family

There has been a major shift in the S/390 processing family over the last few years. Gone are the days where the S/390 processor complex occupies floors of computing space. Today the S/390 processors are compact, air-cooled processors, that can occupy significantly less floor space and require a fraction of the energy that was required with the processors used earlier in the 1990s, while providing many times the

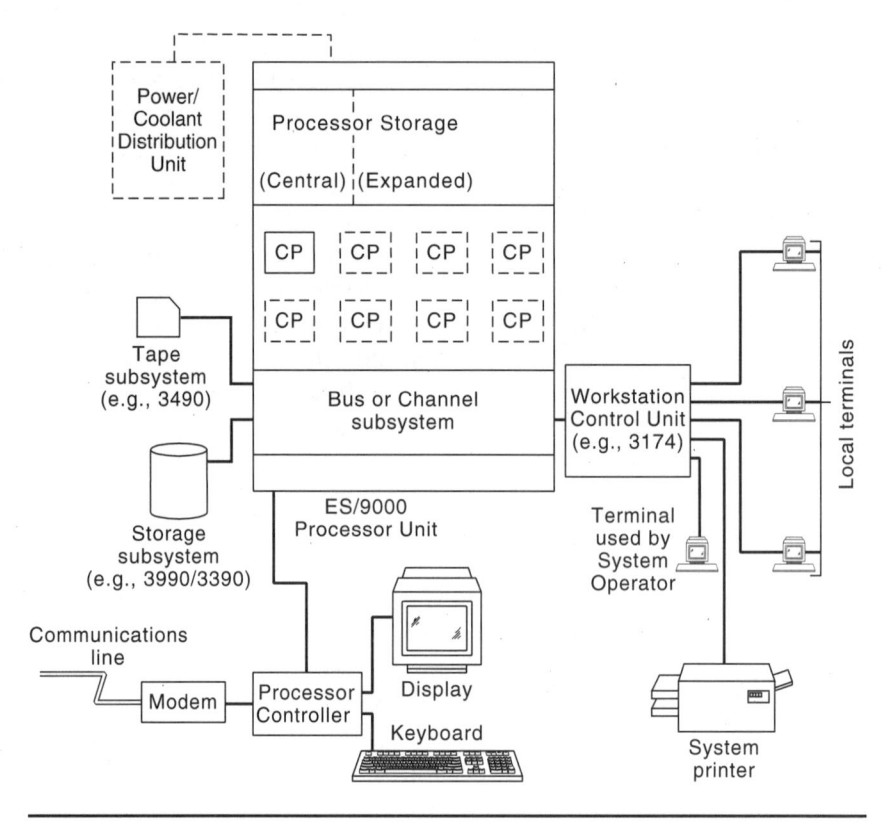

Figure 5.8. A DASD subsystem, tape subsystem, workstations, and printers must be attached to the ES/9000 to make a complete computer system.

processing power of their predecessors. Computer rooms that once were filled with IBM S/390 processing power, now appear empty – not because the mainframe has been replaced, but simply because of the reduced space that the S/390 processing complex requires. The S/390 physically smaller processors have improved in processing power to the point where they can replace much larger bipolar processors.

In 1994, IBM began a major shift to new technology for its microprocessors used within the S/390. The new technology, known as Complementary Metal Oxide Semiconductors (CMOS), replaced the earlier technology which was known as bipolar processors. A fundamental difference between the two technologies enabled a shift from the water-cooled processor requiring significant environmental investment to a simplified air-cooled processor requiring reduced infrastructure costs. The improvements that CMOS made possible are nearly unbelievable. While a state of the art machine in the early 1990s weighed over 31,000 pounds, the new G4 CMOS-based server weighs in at only 2100 pounds. The number of parts required dropped from over 6000 parts in the ES9000 to only 92 parts in the newer G4. That's quite an improvement.

The S/390 family covers a wide range of performance for PC Servers to the high end S/390 Parallel Enterprise Servers. The S/390 Parallel Enterprise Servers exploit technology known as parallel sysplex. Parallel sysplex enables two or more OS/390 images to be combined for full operating redundancy. Parallel Sysplex enables nearly continuous application availability when combined with many of the new functions of OS/390, eliminating the impact of planned and unplanned outages to S/390 users.

The S/390 Parallel Enterprise Servers consists of the Generation-3 (G3) and Generation-4 (G4) S/390 servers. Availability of the application to the enterprise customers is probably the most important deliverable of any processing platform. The S/390 G3 and G4 Enterprise Server processors deliver extremely high industry availability in a single footprint. High availability is provided by the S/390 G3/G4 Enterprise Servers through very high component reliability and design features that provide fault tolerance and concurrent repair of many subsystems. CP/SAP sparing and recovery, an internal battery feature providing backup power, enhanced LPAR dynamic storage reconfiguration, partial memory restart and dynamic memory sparing are examples of built-in functions that help to eliminate planned and unplanned outages.

Inside S/390

Many components and structures work together to comprise a System/390 computer system. In this section, we will take a quick look inside S/390.

Storage Hierarchy—Making Data Available

As defined earlier, central processors actually manipulate the data as necessary to do work for the user. The rest of the computer system basically feeds information (programs and data) to the central processor or accepts information from it. If the rest of the computer system cannot keep pace with the central processors, the system is constrained and overall system performance is reduced. Thus, the rest of the computer system must be carefully balanced with the central processor(s) for maximum efficiency. To achieve balanced performance in a cost-effective manner, most computer systems (including the S/390 family) employ several types of information storage devices with varying performance levels. In other words, they have a storage hierarchy. (Figure 5.9 illustrates the storage hierarchy used in the S/390 family.)

The whole purpose of the storage hierarchy in S/390 computers is to respond as quickly as possible to the central processor's relentless requests for the retrieval and storage of information. To achieve this, the system constantly adjusts and moves information among the different levels of the storage hierarchy, placing the information most likely to be needed next as high in the hierarchy as possible. The movement of information among the top four layers of the storage pyramid is primarily managed by the central processors and central storage circuitry.

The computer system's full performance potential is realized only when information is kept as high in the storage hierarchy as possible. For this reason, each S/390 computer is configured (or tuned) to provide the correct amount of each storage type for the environment in which it is used—something not always easy to predict. As the environment changes, it may become necessary to expand various types of storage to keep the system running at its best.

Processor Storage

At the top of the storage pyramid are the **registers**, which are very fast circuits inside the central processor that hold only the programming instructions and data on which the execution units (also within the central processor) are acting. Whereas general-purpose registers hold 32 bits of information, floating point registers hold 64 bits of

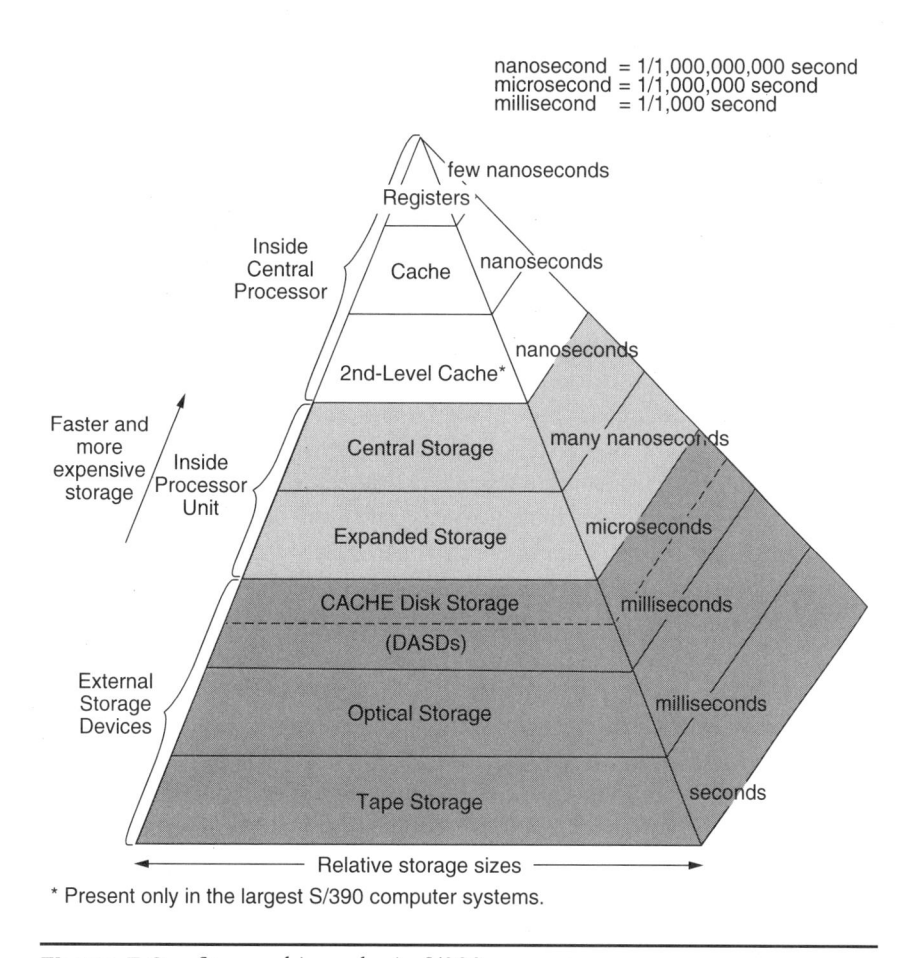

Figure 5.9. Storage hierarchy in S/390 computers.

information. Since they are in the central processor and are extremely high-speed circuits (which switch in a few nanoseconds), they are very efficient at meeting the immediate storage needs of the central processor's execution units.

Next in the storage pyramid is the **cache storage,** an array of very high-speed electronic memory circuits that are also found in each central processor. The cache storage contains the next instruction to be fed to the central processor's execution units.

The **second-level buffer,** next in the storage pyramid, resides outside the central processor. It automatically collects information from the next pyramid layer (central storage) and stages that information for the cache. The whole purpose of the second-level buffer is to provide information to the cache more quickly than could the central storage. Like the cache storage, the second-level buffer consists of an array of very high-speed electronic memory circuits.

Central storage, housed inside the processor unit, is the pivot point of the storage hierarchy. All information to be acted upon by any central processor or I/O channel must reside, at some point, in central storage. It is much larger than the pyramid layers above it, but it still provides information to the central processor(s) very quickly. Central storage is known also as memory, main storage, and random access memory (RAM). It is made up of a large array of high-speed electronic circuits that reside inside the processor unit.

The next layer in the storage pyramid is **expanded storage,** a cost-effective way to augment central storage without sacrificing too much in performance. It consists of a very large array of electronic memory circuits that act as an overflow area for central storage. In some S/390 computers, expanded storage is a region of central storage that behaves like expanded storage. This allows those S/390 computers to comply with the requirement defined in the ESA/390 architecture to have expanded storage. In the larger S/390 computers, expanded storage actually is electronic circuits set apart from the central storage circuitry. Information that is still likely to be needed but cannot quite fit into central storage is moved automatically to expanded storage. All of the information stored in expanded storage, however, must be moved back to central storage before it can be accessed by the central processors. This transfer is managed by the S/390 computer hardware and operating system, which relieve the programmer from having to deal with the different memory subsystems. In fact, the central processors do not know that expanded storage exists. Together, central storage and expanded storage are referred to as **processor storage.**

External Storage

The next layer in the storage pyramid is **disk storage,** provided by direct access storage devices (DASDs), which are subdivided into DASDs with a high-speed cache for performance and DASDs without cache. DASDs are the first type of storage covered so far that physically resides outside the processor unit. They exist as I/O devices attached through one or more S/390 I/O channels or system buses. DASDs are also the first storage covered so far that is able to retain information even when the power is turned off. Thus, disk storage is said to be permanent storage.

Issues related to external storage are no longer "peripheral." The speed with which organizations create new data and information, new applications that require a "data warehouse," the growing amounts of business-critical information on workstations, and the development of open system architectures all drive changes to the way data is managed. Capacity is no longer the primary issue. Rather, data availability, performance of the access method, data security and integrity, and data storage costs are driving rapid changes to computing environments. Nevertheless, the basic interactions between external storage and internal storage remain the same.

Like expanded storage, information stored on **DASDs** must be moved to central storage before it is available to a central processor. There is generally a delay (in the computer's time reference) from the time the central processor requests the information until the time that it is available inside the central processor. This delay results from the fact that DASDs are electromechanical devices, which are slower than electrical devices because they are constrained by mechanical motion. Further, since the DASDs are located outside the processor unit, the information is brought in through an I/O operation, which involves additional subsystems (I/O channel or system bus and a control unit) and the delays associated with them. If, however, DASD with cache is used and the data is within the cache, the mechanical motion and the reading from disk is eliminated. Data is transferred directly from the cache in response to the I/O operation. With a **write-through cache**, a write operation does not need to wait for the data to be written to disk before freeing the channel. When the data reaches the cache, the channel is freed for other operations, and the write then occurs synchronously from cache to disk.

The basic anatomy of a DASD is shown in Figure 5.10. It consists of a drive mechanism with permanently installed metallic disks, often called platters because their shape is like that of a dinner plate. These platters have a magnetic surface that can store information. A single DASD usually has multiple platters in order to store more information. The platters spin constantly at very high speeds while a built-in read/write head records or recalls information on the platter's

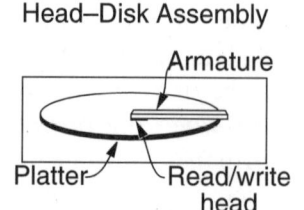

Figure 5.10. The anatomy of a direct access storage device (DASD).

surface. The arm that positions the read/write head is called the actuator. Although read/write heads in DASDs never actually touch the platter's magnetic surface, they are positioned extremely close to that surface. Together, the read/write heads and the platters compose a **head–disk assembly (HDA)**. The disk storage provided by DASDs acts as an extension to expanded storage in that both are used as an overflow area for information unable to reside in central storage.

S/390 computers support DASDs that store information in two formats: **Count-Key-Data (CKD)** or **fixed-block architecture (FBA)**. In either case, information is stored as small groups of data called blocks. With the CKD format, the byte count is stored in the first part of the block and defines the length of that block, so the size of a block matches exactly the amount of information that needs to be stored. With DASDs that use the FBA format, information written to the DASD is stored in blocks of fixed length. In this format, even if only 1 byte needs to be stored, a full block of DASD is consumed. Although wasteful of DASD space, the FBA format lends itself to higher performance than the CKD format.

Newer DASD technologies introduced to the System/390 family include RAMAC devices and RAID. **RAMAC**, a name chosen by IBM to recall the earliest storage system, storage subsystems require far less physical resources (space and cooling, for example) while maintaining very high data densities, up to 180 GB in a single configuration. **RAID**, standing for **redundant array of independent disks**, assures the availability of data to the user by providing several techniques for mirroring and rebuilding data should a storage device become unavailable to the system.

The next layer of the storage pyramid is **optical storage**. Rather than using magnetism as with DASDs, optical storage systems use optical techniques to achieve their extremely high recording density. Current optical storage technology, however, is significantly slower than DASDs and, therefore, cannot replace the need for DASDs. Optical storage provides the capacity, random access, and volumetric efficiency needed to justify on-line access to the many documents that an enterprise now files on paper, microfiche, or microfilm. This is especially true of infrequently referenced information, where business value is gained from the speed and efficiency of on-line accessibility. Another advantage is the cost-effective retention of current on-line data for longer periods of time.

There are two types of optical storage technology: write-once and rewriteable. Each uses a 5.25-inch optical cartridge. For permanent records, the **write-once technology** uses an ablative process (removing a portion of the surface) to record data permanently on the cartridge. Once data is written, it cannot be erased. A specialized microcoded file system allows the medium to appear as rewritable; however, previously recorded data remains on the disk, creating a permanent audit trail. For other storage uses, **rewritable technology** uses a reversible magneto-optic process. This recording technology is useful where stored data rapidly becomes obsolete and information archiving is not required. When the stored information is no longer needed, it is erased and the cartridge is reused.

Finally, the lowest level of the storage pyramid is **tape storage**. Tape consists of a long, flexible strip coated with magnetic material and rolled onto a reel or into a cartridge. A tape drive reads and writes information on the tape much as a cassette recorder records and plays music on audio cassette tapes. The tape drive runs the tape across the read/write head. S/360 tapes had contact with the read/write head, but today's tape drives do not; the tape rides over the head on a cushion of air. Electrical impulses in the read/write head transfer information to and from the tape's surface. One primary purpose of tape storage is to provide a backup storage medium for information in the computer's disk storage. Tape is also commonly used in distributing programs and transferring information from one computer system to another. For general-purpose information archival and disk storage backup, tape is often used over optical storage due to its lower cost. Tape continues to be the frequently chosen medium for sequential processing applications because of its high data transfer rate over ESCON channels.

Parallel Sysplex

A **parallel sysplex** is a group of two or more S/390 computer systems operating as one computer system. The purpose of a parallel sysplex is to allow users to combine the processing power of more than one System/390 while having them appear (to the system operators and users) to be one large computer system—called a **single-system image**. It enables them to cooperate as a single, logical computing facility by synchronizing their time references and enabling them to share data at the record level while preserving data integrity. While doing this, it keeps its underlying structure transparent to users, networks, applications, and operations management. Benefits of a parallel sysplex include synergy with existing applications, continuous availability, single-image operations, dynamic workload balancing, and data sharing and integrity across multiple processors.

In a single system, growth is limited by the size of the system. Managing the system, however, is relatively easy because all of the resources are under the control of one copy of the operating system. Taking a large workload application (such as transaction processing) and permitting it to run on a large number of separate systems adds capacity for growth but significantly complicates managing the workload, which includes distributing the workload effectively across all of the systems. The parallel sysplex solves this problem by providing the flexibility of multiple S/390 systems with the simplicity of a single-system image. Transaction-processing workloads are dynamically balanced across processors, and, with the introduction of high-performance coupling technology, data is also dynamically shared at a fine level of granularity with read and write access and full data integrity (Figure 5.11). The shared data model simplifies planning for new business applications; dynamic workload balancing manages changing patterns of use; and the parallel sysplex participates as an element of an open, network computing environment.

S/390 Software

The previous sections of this chapter introduced the processor units and associated hardware options used to configure S/390 computers.

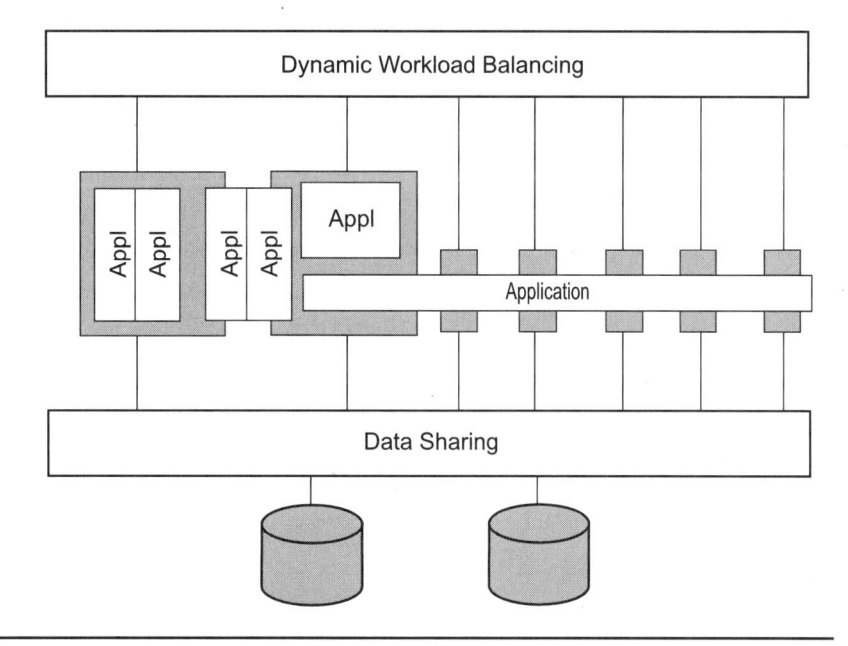

Figure 5.11. Interrelationship of parallel sysplex features.

This section introduces the element that puts the hardware to work—namely, software.

Types of Software—A Model

The previous sections of this chapter introduced the processor units and associated hardware options used to configure S/390 computers. This section introduces the element that puts the hardware to work—namely, software. Software (a general term for the many programs that execute in computers) harnesses the S/390 computer's computational power and allows users to perform many diverse and useful tasks.

The software used in S/390 computers is depicted in the simple software model shown in Figure 5.12. Three basic categories (or software layers) of software are used with S/390 computers: application program, operating system, and licensed internal code (LIC). Each

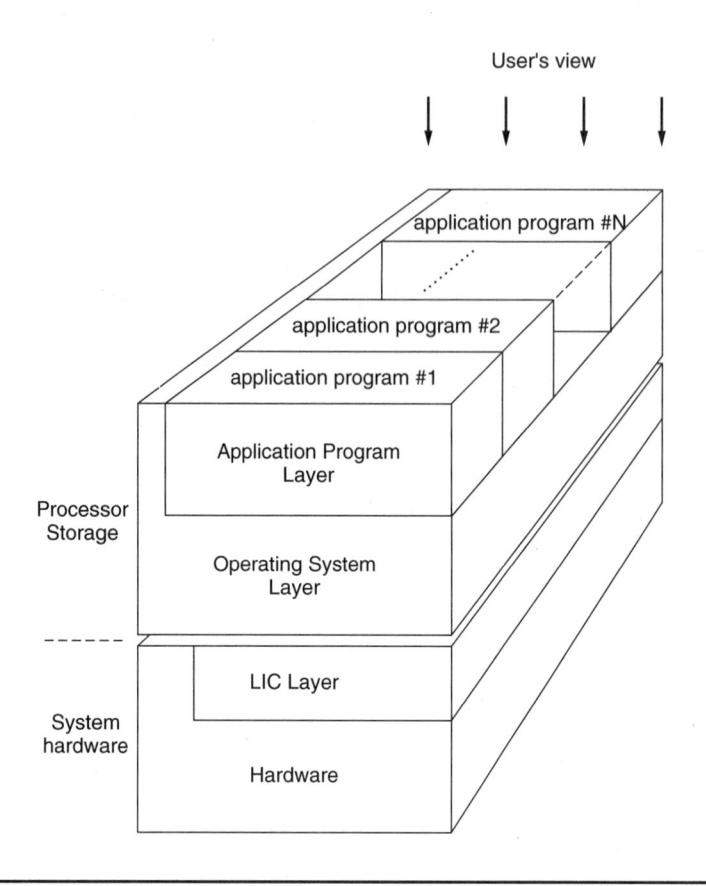

Figure 5.12. Software model of System/390's basic software structure.

software layer performs a completely different job, but all three work closely together to perform useful work for the users.

Application Programs

The top software layer in the software model is the **application program** layer (the top layer in Figure 5.12). Application programs perform the tasks (word processing or accounting, for example) for which the computer was purchased, but the other two layers play essential support roles. The "user's view" arrows in the figure indicate that the user most often interacts with an application program and less frequently with the operating system. Working closely with the other software layers, the application program processes the various keystrokes made by the user and responds by displaying information on the computer's display or other output devices.

Programs written for System/370 computers can usually be executed directly on S/390 computers. This compatibility allows S/390 users to bring forward their investment in application program development, database design, and user training when upgrading their hardware. Frequently, application programs in the business environment are used for such tasks as accounting, financial modeling, word processing, database management, electronic mail (E-mail), and computer graphics. Application programs interact directly with the operating system to perform different tasks (such as reading and writing disk storage or sending information over a communications network). The interaction between the operating system and application programs takes place through the **application programming interface (API)** presented by the operating system. Program products, called **application enablers,** extend the API presented by the operating system. Application enablers add function to the API, thus offering more services to application programs (Figure 5.13). As the figure shows, application enablers reside between the operating system and the application program layers of our software model, and they actively communicate with both layers.

By adding services to the API, application enablers make the job of application program development easier. This enables software development companies to develop prewritten application programs more easily, providing S/390 users with more prewritten application programs from which to choose. In the same way, the productivity of developing custom application programs is improved, since the application enablers provide many functions that would otherwise have to be written from scratch by the developer during the custom application development project. IBM's DB2 is an example of a database application enabler family of products. IBM's CICS products are examples of a transaction-processing application enablers.

Operating System

The next layer in our software model is the **operating system.** The operating system manages the hardware resources of the computer

176 EXPLORING IBM TECHNOLOGY AND PRODUCTS

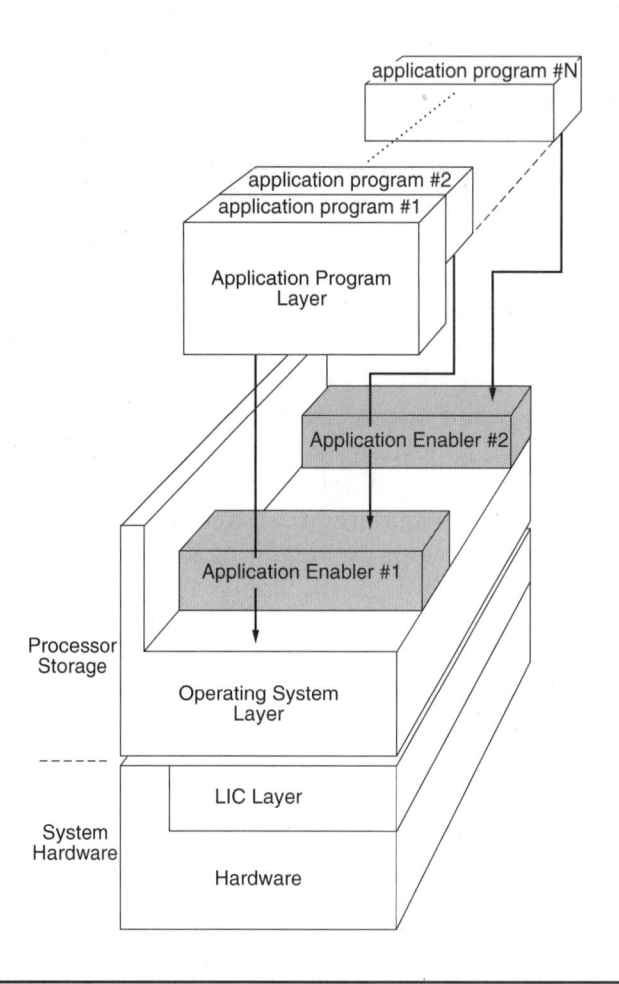

Figure 5.13. Application enablers build on the API of the operating system, offering additional services to application programs.

system and performs tasks under the control of application programs and keyboard commands typed by the users. Because the application program can rely on the operating system to perform many of the detailed housekeeping tasks associated with the internal workings of the computer, the operating system is said to provide the operating system **environment** in which application programs execute. Since the application program interacts directly with the operating system, application programs are generally designed to work under a specific operating system. Operating systems also accept commands directly from the users to copy files, change passwords, and perform various other tasks.

LIC

The third and final layer of software in our model is the **licensed internal code (LIC)**. LIC is a set of highly specialized programs written by the manufacturer of a computer and rarely modified by either system operators or users. The set of LIC in S/390 computers is embedded deeply within the computer system and is therefore considered to be part of the computing machine itself rather than part of a program running on the machine. Unlike application programs or the operating system, LIC is used only by other programs; that is, LIC never interacts directly with the user or the programmer. LIC exists only to help the S/390 hardware perform the more complex instructions in the ESA/390 architecture. The LIC includes the programming executed by the many different microprocessors in an S/390 computer. For example, some LIC is executed by the microprocessors used to implement the I/O channels in an S/390 computer.

The LIC approach helps shield the hardware details of the processor unit from the software's view of the processor unit. That is, it preserves compliance with ESA/390 architecture, and thus compatibility with operating systems and application programs, in the face of evolutionary hardware improvements.

When data is sent to a computer from an external source, such as a workstation, the software layers of our model come into play. First, the I/O channels and associated LIC verify that all went well in receiving the data; then the LIC notifies the operating system that the data is correct, ready, and waiting for use. The operating system makes the data available to the application program and then reactivates the application program, which was dormant waiting for the next keystroke(s). The application program processes the data as necessary and instructs the operating system to wait for the next keystrokes, and the whole cycle starts all over again.

Computers easily perform these steps in small fractions of a second. Similar but more complicated cooperation among the three software layers occurs for most functions performed by the computer such as reading or writing a file on a DASD and communicating with other computers.

Operating Systems

Operating systems help manage the internal workings of a computer system and provide services to users and other programs. S/390 computers can use one of several different operating systems. In fact, they often use multiple operating systems. Now let's take a quick look at the most popular S/390 operating systems.

OS/390

OS/390 is a popular S/390 operating system based on the long-popular MVS operating system. While OS/390 Releases 1 and 2 were primarily repackaging efforts (combining the popular MVS operating system with other required software), later releases have contained substantial new function. OS/390 represents a broad base of functionality, probably richer than any other computing environment. OS/390 allows S/390 systems to run traditional S/390 applications, UNIX applications, and object-oriented applications. It also provides distributed computing and LAN services functions.

OS/390 features include:

- Exploitation of object technology across systems and networks

- Use of the Java, write once, run anywhere technology to build business applications

- Support for data mining operations

- Web serving capability with integrated web server

- Integrated firewall function

OS/390 provides the Lotus Go Webserver for OS/390 as a integrated function, NetQuestion, a powerful search engine, and IBM's Book Server for OS/390. OS/390 includes integrated communications functions through the eNetwork Communications Server for OS/390 which provides SNA and TCP/IP communications protocols. OS/390 supports access to the S/390 through any Java-enabled web browser that supports IBM's eNetwork Host on Demand software. It also supports the IBM Network Station and the IBM network computer.

OS/390 fully supports the S/390 parallel sysplex environment for both SNA and TCP environments through exploitation of the Work Load Manager (WLM) function which enables computing tasks within the S/390 to be balanced based across the multiple processors within the S/390.

VM

The **Virtual Machine** or **VM** operating system gets its name from the fact that it uses the virtual-storage concept to subdivide a single computer system into multiple, virtual computer systems, each with its own processor storage, disk storage, tape storage, and other I/O devices. That is, VM/ESA uses software techniques to make a single S/390 computer appear to be multiple computer systems. Each of these simulated computers (called **virtual machines**) acts as an independent and complete computer system. In some cases, a virtual machine is like an S/390-compatible "personal computer" with a single-user operating system serving the needs of a single user (or application program). A group of single-user virtual machines can be linked together to create all **virtual local area network** of S/390 computers within a single system all simulated by software (Figure 5.14).

Alternatively, a single virtual machine can run a multi-user operating system (for example, OS/390) and serve the needs of many users. VM's unique approach to resource management (that is, subdividing a single computer system into multiple, virtual computer systems each with its own resources) makes it especially useful for **interactive computing, client/server computing,** and running multiple operating systems. Interactive computing provides for flexible dialog between users and application programs allowing users to perform ad hoc queries to databases, to write memos, or to perform mechanical design. Today, VM's large-scale interactive computing capabilities include support for thousands of office users, data analysis and decision support, advanced database processing, application development, and ad-hoc problem solving.

Client/server computing is facilitated by allowing a virtual machine to be dedicated to running a program that provides services

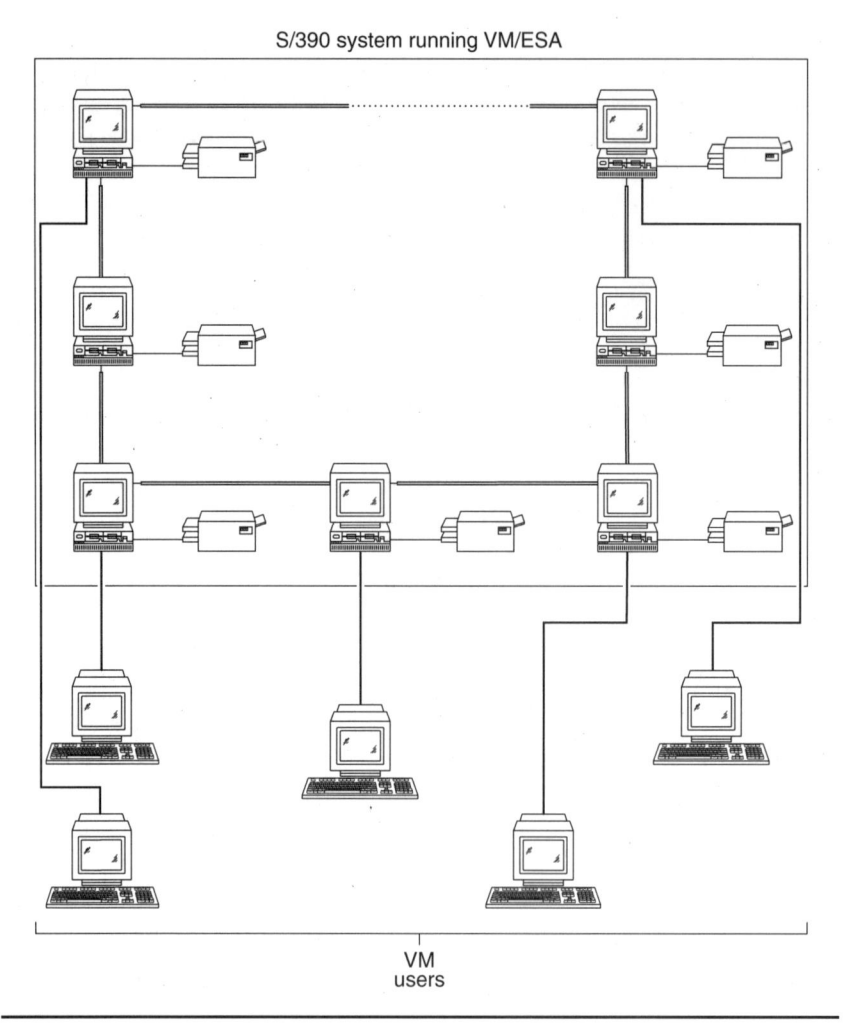

Figure 5.14. Conceptually, VM creates a local area network of single-user computers within an S/390 system.

(thus called a **server**) to the users of other virtual machines (called **clients**); programs designed to run in their own virtual machine and to provide services to virtual machine users are called **service virtual machines**. VM capabilities enable businesses to integrate mainframe strengths with VM-unique server capabilities, and LAN and workstation technologies. The VM and mainframe strengths include very fast access to large volumes of data, access to high bandwidth communications and high capacity devices, and efficient and secure administration of large numbers of users and applications.

Finally, each virtual machine runs one of several different operating systems in addition to (or on top of) VM itself. This frees each user to run the operating system (for example, CMS, VSE, or OS/390) that is required or best suited to the application program. Other operating systems running under VM in a virtual machine are called **guest operating systems**. The efficiencies generated through VM acting as a **Hypervisor** or "host" system, in which resources are shared among multiple different systems on a single processor, make it practical to use VM to create, test, and run applications from any S/390 operating environment. This simplifies migration and experimentation with new platforms and functions. The VM operating system spans the entire range of S/390 processors. As of this writing, there are more than 17,000 VM installations worldwide with over 5,000 running the latest version. As many as 9 million people are estimated to use VM every day.

VSE

The **Virtual Storage Extended** or **VSE** operating system is used primarily in small to midsized S/390 computers. The easiest way to understand the environment that VSE/ESA creates within S/390 computers is to review its history. VSE/ESA is the descendant of the Disk Operating System (DOS) introduced in 1965 for use with the smaller models of the System/360 mainframe computer family. Figure 5.15 shows how DOS organized the central storage of a System/360 computer into four regions called **partitions**. DOS itself was loaded from disk storage into the first partition. The next partition, labeled "Batch #1" in the figure, was used to execute a single batch application program. **Batch jobs** in the System/360 days were typically submitted to the computer by placing a stack of computer punch cards into a card reader, which would transfer the information (that is, the batch job instructions) into the computer. System/360 batch application programs usually presented their results in the form of a printed report.

How the actual hardware
installed in System/360
was organized by DOS

```
Installed      ┌─────────────┐
Storage *      │  Batch #3   │
 (max)         ├─────────────┤
               │  Batch #2   │
               ├─────────────┤
               │  Batch #1   │
               ├─────────────┤
               │    DOS      │
  0 MB         └─────────────┘
               Central Storage
```

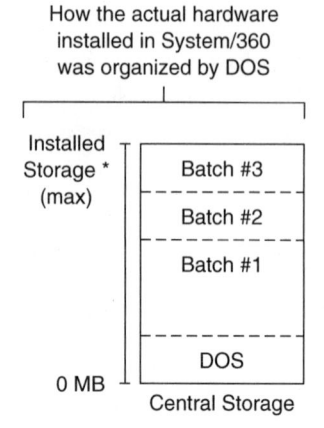

* Maximum central storage varied based on the expansion capabilities of the particular System/360 processor unit model of interest.

Figure 5.15. DOS divided the central storage of System/360 computers into four partitions.

The next evolutionary step after DOS was the **Disk Operating System/Virtual Storage (DOS/VS)** operating system, introduced in 1972. A major enhancement made in DOS/VS was the introduction of virtual storage—a feature in the operating system that makes a computer system seem to have more central storage than it actually does.

In the DOS environment, computer programmers and users had to concern themselves with the physical amount of central storage available on the computer system that they were using. Once all of the installed central storage was in use, the computer system simply could not start any additional activities (batch or interactive). The virtual storage technique introduced with DOS/VS provided a means for the operating system to manage the storage hierarchy so that central storage seemed "larger than life," relieving users of this concern. Figure 5.16 shows how DOS/VS managed a System/370 processor's central storage. DOS/VS could manage up to 8 MB of central storage physically installed in the System/370 processor (even though no System/370 models were yet available to provide that much). DOS/VS took whatever central storage was installed and, using the central storage technique, "stretched it" to appear to be 16 MB in size. The

16 MB of central storage was then divided into independent partitions like those of the DOS environment. However, DOS/VS could support up to five simultaneously active partitions, each of which could be used to run either a batch or an interactive application program for the users. (One partition could be used to execute an interactive application program that would simultaneously serve the needs of multiple users.)

The next evolutionary step after DOS/VSE came in 1983 with the introduction of **Virtual Storage Extended/System Package (VSE/SP)**. Even though the letters "DOS" were dropped from the name, VSE/SP was an enhanced version of DOS/VSE. Figure 5.16 shows how VSE/SP (Version 3.2) handled System/370 central storage. The **Virtual Addressability Extensions (VAE)** feature introduced with VSE/SP al-

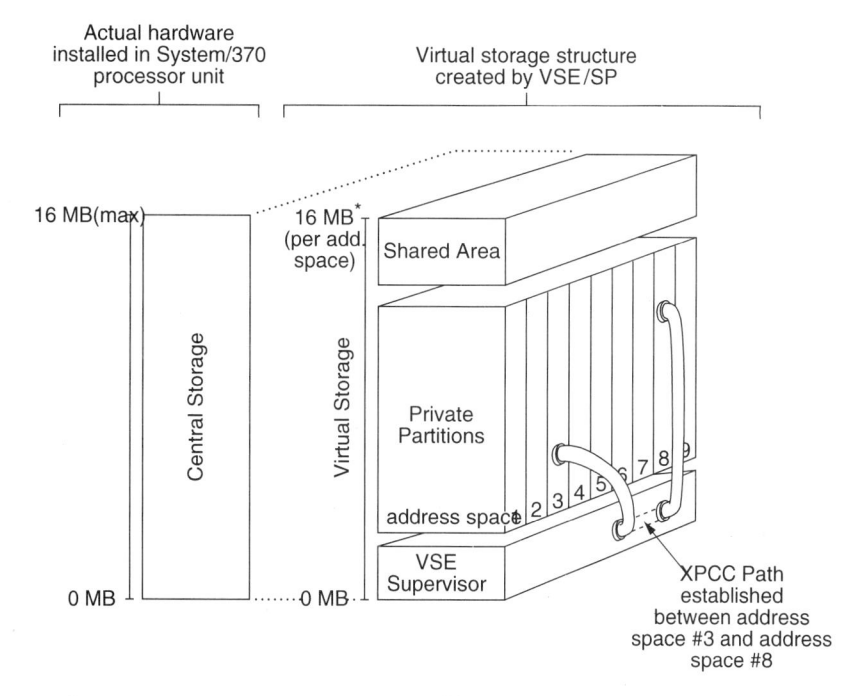

* Maximum central storage is limited to 2^{24} = 16 MB.
† Maximum virtual address range per address space is 2^{24} = 16 MB. Total virtual storage (all address spaces) supported is 128 MB.

Figure 5.16. VSE/SP created multiple virtual address spaces.

lowed users to define multiple 16 MB virtual address spaces each identical to the single 16 MB virtual address space provided by DOS/VSE (Figure 5.16). Having multiple address spaces provided a much-needed expansion of central storage without losing compatibility with existing application programs. More central storage meant the VSE/SP system could handle more and larger batch and interactive jobs. The shared area allowed for inter-program communications.

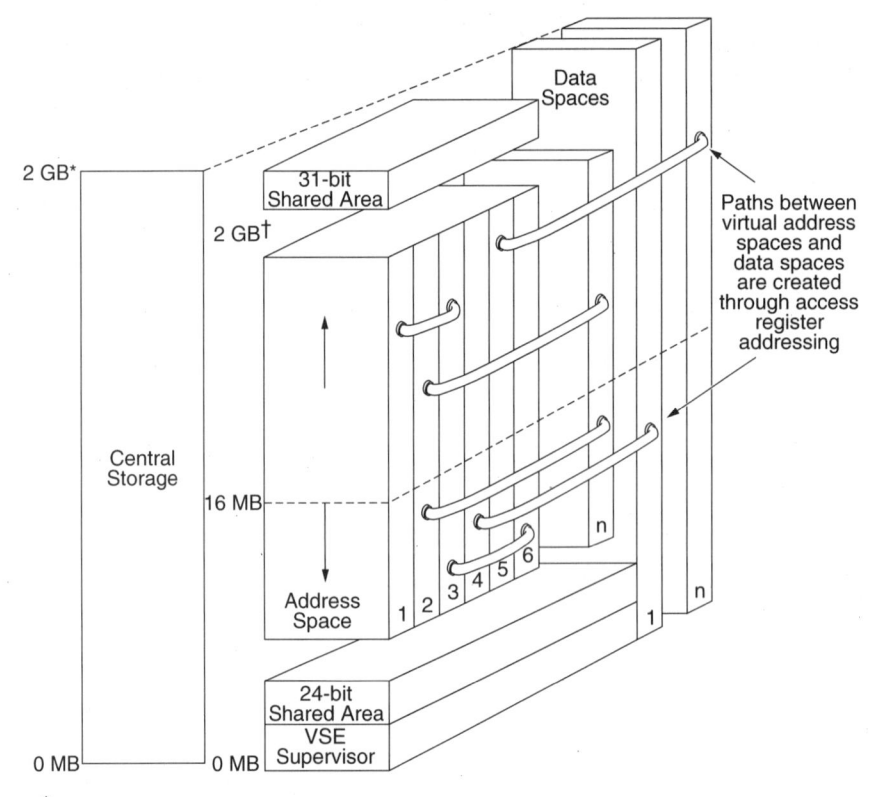

*Maximum central storage is architecturally limited to 2 GB. VSE/ESA design limit is 2 GB; but central storage supported is the lesser of processor central storage or 2 GB.

†Maximum virtual address range for an address space or a data space.

Figure 5.17. VSE/ESA Version 1, Release 3 supports 31-bit addressing and ESA/390 data spaces.

Figure 5.17 shows the way contemporary VSE versions handle central storage. Enhancements provide for expanded storage sizes, better communications between programs (e.g. register addressing) and better facilities for handling large amounts of data (e.g. data spaces). VSE is still a popular operating system with many smaller S/390 users.

6

Computer Networks

Chapter 1 explained IBM's vision of network computing. In this chapter, we will examine the underlying concepts that provide the foundation for the most popular computer communications environments.

The Need to Communicate—An Introduction

Just as a woodworker cherishes a solid block of mahogany, business people cherish accurate, timely, and manageable information. If one activity is most crucial to a business of any size, it is the act of communicating this information to the proper decision maker. Based on the information available to the decision maker, important choices are made that can have far-reaching effects on the success of the business. Improve communications in a business, and you are likely to improve productivity and profitability. Ironically, as a business grows, it becomes both more important and more difficult to maintain efficient, accurate communications—the very thing that facilitated business growth in the first place. Communications difficulties grow geometrically with the size of the business.

Today's businesses are quickly finding that computers are a communications tool unequaled in significance since Bell invented the telephone. Computers are already commonplace in the business environment, and now there is an increasing emphasis on computer communication. This communication can occur between two computers or among a group of computers in a communications network and allows business information to move at electronic speeds. Furthermore, communication allows users at remote locations access to vital business information on a distant computer. All of IBM's computer families are designed to participate in a wide range of communications environments.

IBM'S Overall Networking Blueprint

The **IBM Networking Blueprint** (see Figure 6.1), introduced in March, 1992, is a guide to IBM's networking commitments. The blueprint lays out the framework for integrating into a single network multiple separate networks and their applications that use different communications protocols, different hardware components, different bandwidths, and different network management techniques. The Blueprint incorporates existing and anticipated industry standards and open systems standards. It complements the Systems Application Architecture (SAA) specifications, which embody the SNA communications standards as well as the Open Software Foundation's **Distributed Computing Environment** (DCE) and ISO communications specifications, but it does not replace them.

The IBM Networking Blueprint framework provides the freedom to choose network elements to meet application and business needs, rather than force-fitting those requirements to inappropriate networking solutions. The Blueprint allows a mixture of international standards, industry standards, and architectures. As standards evolve, the Blueprint will change to keep pace. The Blueprint is divided into four layers, representing the elements necessary to make up a network.

Applications Layer

The IBM Networking Blueprint provides all major interfaces for distributed computing. The first layer, starting from the top of the Blueprint, is the **applications layer**, which represents the full range of

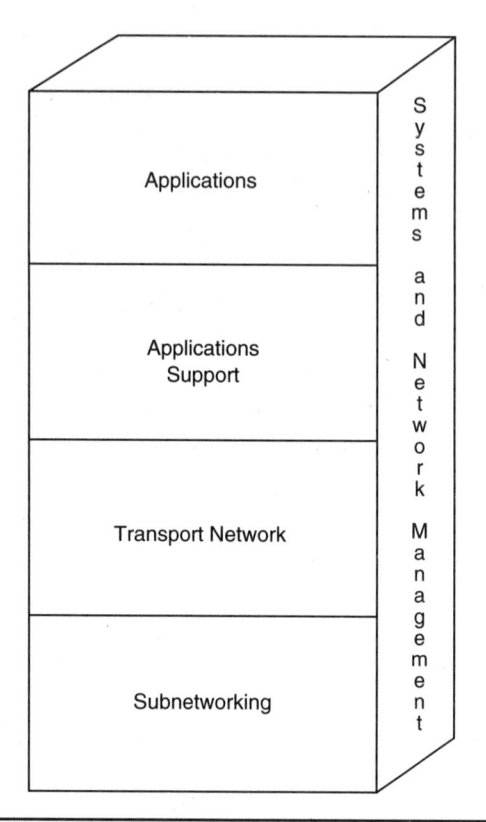

Figure 6.1. IBM's Networking Blueprint Structure.

applications and application enablers (e.g., high-level languages and program generators) that support an organization's business. The applications and enablers make use of the underlying capabilities of the network.

Application Support Layer

The second layer, the **application support layer** (see Figure 6.1), represents multivendor application interfaces and services. There are three primary interfaces (see Figure 6.2): **Common Programming Interface for Communications (CPI-C), Remote Procedure Call (RPC),** and the **Messaging and Queuing Interface (MQI).**

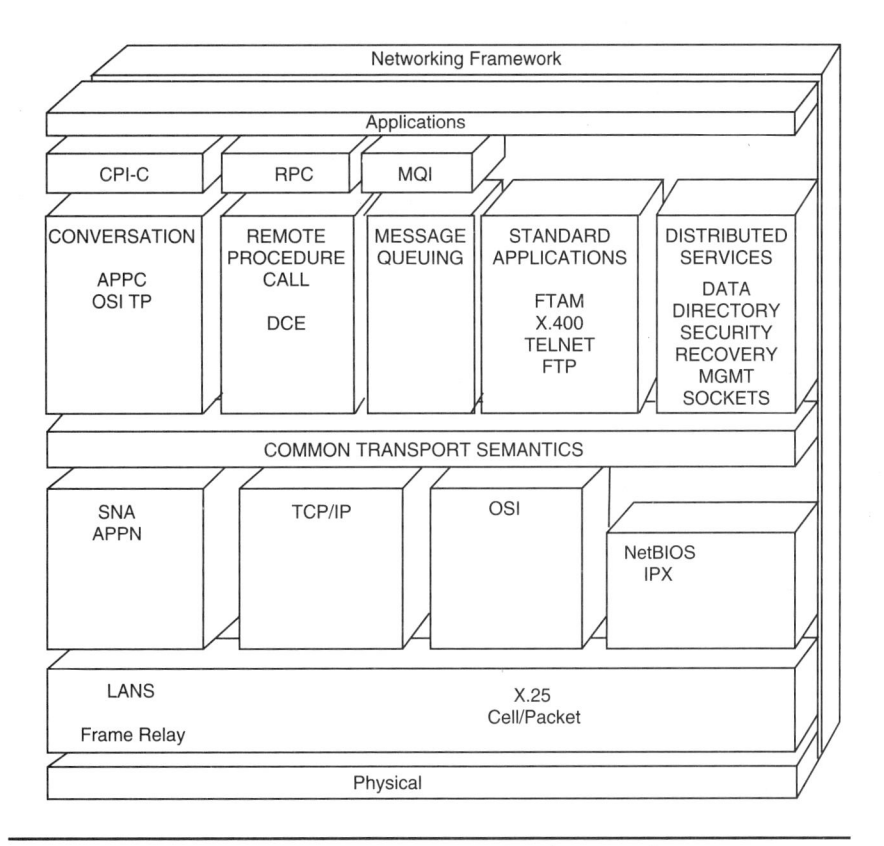

Figure 6.2. EAS/400 MPTN Networking Blueprint interfaces.

Transport Network Layer: SNA-TCP/IP-MPTN

The **third** layer, the **transport network layer** (see Figure 6.1), is the layer for integrating multivendor network protocols into one efficient network. Networking protocols are used for sending and receiving information throughout the network. Typically, applications and application services are bound to a specific networking protocol. CPI-C applications use SNA networking; RPC applications use TCP/IP; X.400 applications use Open System Interconnection (OSI); other applications use NetBIOS, Internet Packet Exchange (IPX), DECnet, or other protocols, but within this layer, the **Common Transport Semantics framework** (see Figure 6.2) provides a structure for supporting multiprotocol networking capability.

Subnetworking Layer

The **fourth** layer, the **subnetworking layer,** represents a piece of a larger network, a connection to local area networks (LANs), wide area networks (WANs), host channels, or other high-speed transmission services. The IBM Networking Blueprint provides a framework for integrating LAN and WAN networks, providing management services, efficient link utilization, high availability, and predictable response time. A key component of the Blueprint-systems and network management applies to all four Blueprint layers. It encompasses all management disciplines and supports multiprotocol and multivendor environments through industry standards such as SNA management services, the TCP/IP Simple Network Management Protocol (SNMP), and the OSI Common Management Information Protocol (CMIP).

SystemView is the framework for providing enterprise-wide systems and network management, planning, coordination, and operations. It enables both centralized management and distributed management. The proposed OSF Distributed Management Environment (OSF/DME) fits with the SystemView structure. Two SystemView-conforming products, NetView and NetView/400, help manage applications in an MPTN environment, where the applications use transport protocols different from the ones for which they were originally designed.

Local Area Networks

Just as there is a need for office personnel at any one location to talk frequently with each other, there is value to allowing the computers at a given location to communicate with each other efficiently and easily. We've seen some hardware and software configurations that allow various computers to communicate through terminal emulation. Local area networks (LANs) are another way of attaching computer systems together for the purposes of communication. LANs allow the user to electrically attach a group of local computers that might be found in a department, building, or campus. Each computer attached to the LAN is called a network node and can share information, programs, and computer equipment with other computers in the network. Some common types of LANs include Ethernet and Token-Ring Network.

Wide Area Networks

When the need to share information and programs spans long distances (beyond a building or campus), wide area networks (WANs) are used. WANs can connect computer systems (thus their users) together across town or around the globe. WANs can be public networks like the Internet or private networks maintained by businesses or other institutions. WANs can be built using various communications standards and protocols. IBM's system network architecture is one example of a popular type of WAN.

What Is Client/Server Computing?

In a services business, such as law or accounting, a "client" is someone who requests assistance from a specialized services provider. Lawyers provide legal services to their clients; they do not provide accounting services. Mechanics fix your car; they do not wash your windows. When you request help from a service provider, you find the right kind of provider, or "server" to meet your needs. Often, providers have knowledge you lack or can perform tasks more efficiently because they specialize. Finally, when you tell your accountant and your mechanic what you need done, you must understand at least a little of what they can do. Otherwise, they may not understand your needs properly.

Computing is no different. The key idea is this: The terms **client** and **server** refer to software, not to hardware. A software client is a computer program that doesn't know how to do everything. It therefore requests help from other software, the server software. Server software is specialized to perform specific tasks effectively. A software server that understands printing probably would not be able to help a client that needs help retrieving a stock quote. Software clients are also like service business clients because software clients must interact with servers using a common language.

The Internet's popular World Wide Web is an example of client/server computing. The client is the Web browser program, and the server is the Web server who provides you with the web pages you see. There are many other examples and implementations of client/server computing.

What Makes Up a Client/Server Computing System?

Figure 6.3 shows how the parts of a software client and a server relate. A software client usually consists of two pieces. The first piece is the client application software; the second is what we'll call "client-enabling software." They talk using a carefully specified common language, called an **Application Programming Interface (API)**. Because computer programs must be specified precisely, the API de-

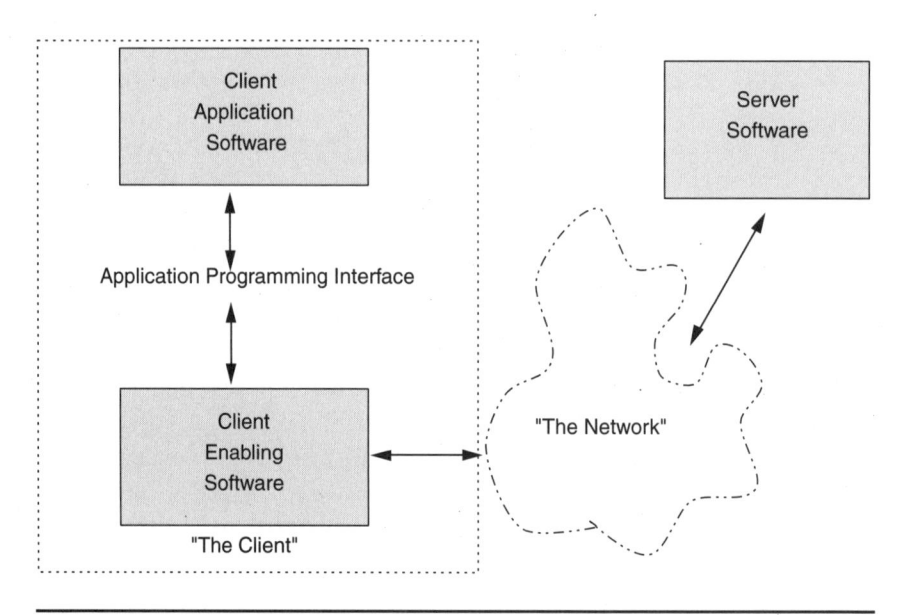

Figure 6.3. Client/server concept.

termines exactly what interactions are possible between the client application software and the rest of the client/server system.

The client-enabling software takes any request the client application software makes via the API and verifies it for correctness. It then decodes the request and forwards it to one or more servers for action. Usually, the servers reside somewhere else on a network, so the client-enabling software also creates "links" or "sessions" over the network to the servers. When the servers are done, they send the results back to the client-enabling software. The client-enabling software then interprets these results and gives them back to the client application software via the API.

Client-enabling software and server software generally talk using a binary language; that is, it is made up of only zeros and ones. Humans cannot easily read a binary language, but computers interpret it efficiently. A network, usually a LAN, carries the interactions between client-enabling software and the servers. The server software can usually accept requests from dozens, hundreds, or even thousands of clients concurrently. Clients may request services from one server or from many servers, depending on the application's needs.

To make another analogy, a client application is like a customer in a restaurant, client-enabling software is like a waiter, and the server software is like the chef that prepares the meal. A customer can only order from the menu and passes instructions to the waiter. This interaction works like the API between client application software and client-enabling software. The waiter verifies these requests and writes them down, often in a shorthand language, then passes these requests to the chef. Upon completing the meal, the chef notifies the waiter, who delivers the food to the customer.

Client/server computing environments usually encompass personal computers working hand in hand with larger, shared computers. The larger machines may store and retrieve shared data, provide large memories and greater processing power, or provide shared access to costly or specialized I/O devices. Using larger machines can also reduce operational costs.

Users of client/server computing software might work within the same building, using a LAN to communicate, or they might use client/server software using a Wide Area Network (WAN), which links computer systems across global distances. client/server computing can take place within an organization or between organizational or enterprise boundaries to support a business process.

Common Approaches to Client/Server Computing

There are many different ways to use the client/server computing model. Here, we will discuss six examples:

- Sharing Resources in Workgroups: The Resource Sharing Model
- Automating Process Flows: The Process-Driven Model
- Giving Applications Face Lifts: The Front-End Model
- Pointing and Clicking Over the Network: The Remote Presentation Model
- Dividing and Conquering: The Distributed Logic Model
- Keeping Replicas of Data Close at Hand: The Data Staging Model

Sharing Resources in Workgroups: The Resource Sharing Model

The first model, the **Resource Sharing Model** (called the "resource-centric reference design" by the IBM Systems Journal), extends PC users' access to files, devices, and databases residing elsewhere in the network. It works well for workgroups, and can also extend beyond the workgroup. Figure 6.4 shows parts of the Resource Sharing Model.

This model covers most of the client/server marketplace today. File servers, printer servers, client/server database software, fax servers, and similar products all fall into this model. Here, client/server software makes remote devices and data appear local to personal computer applications and users. For example, by using a file server, data stored in files on a server look to the user like data stored in files on a local hard disk. This would be true even if each system used different data storage methods. The file server and its corresponding client-enabling software would provide a way of "translating" any differences in formats between the client and the server.

In the Resource Sharing Model, the application software resides on the system closest to the user, which is usually a personal com-

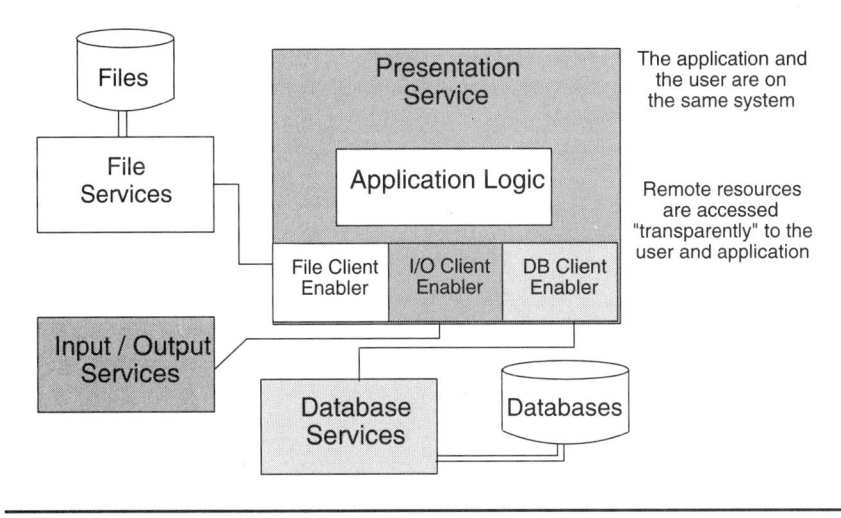

Figure 6.4. The Resource Sharing Model.

puter. This software is usually not aware that the served resources reside elsewhere on the network. The client-enabling software resides on the personal computer as well.

The clearest examples of the model are disk servers and file servers. A computer running PC-DOS usually has one or more long-term storage devices, called hard disks or hard drives. PC-DOS called the first such hard disk the C drive, and the term stuck. IBM's **Operating System/2 (OS/2)** also calls the first hard disk the C drive. When a machine has multiple hard disk drives, the second is the D drive, the third the E drive, and so forth. When the disk server's client-enabling software is loaded, usually when the computer is first started, information on the server is "mapped" to local drive letters. For example, if a client's machine has only one hard drive, the C drive may be local, whereas the D, E, and F drives reside on the file server. Some call the drives residing on the file server "served drives."

All access to data on the served drives occurs as if the drives were local to the user's PC. No changes in commands, applications, or other software need occur. Reading and writing data to the served drives may be slower than using a local drive, but everything else works as it does on a single machine. This is an important plus and at the same time a potential problem of using applications with a file server.

Consider, for example, software designed for a personal computer. Since a PC has only one user, many applications do not include logic to prevent simultaneous changes to data. If you need concurrent access to a record, using such software will likely cause corrupted data. Unfortunately, many workgroups use file servers without knowing that their software does not prevent uncoordinated, concurrent access to data. To them, it looks "the same," but it isn't.

Also, consider performance. If the application reads or writes data only a few bytes at a time, the client-enabling software must repeatedly transfer small amounts of information over the network. In a stand-alone PC, this isn't a problem, but in a shared, networked system, it is. Many such requests will visibly decrease software responsiveness by clogging the network and by making the client and the server do more work. This is especially true when the network includes WAN links, which are slower than LANs anyway.

For many workgroups, though, the Resource Sharing Model provides important advantages. Because everything "looks the same," users need little additional training. Existing procedures and support processes may still work. Many more people understand this model compared to other client/server computing models. Finally, some software, especially database software, provides logic to avoid corrupted data. If you choose your software carefully, the Resource Sharing Model can help you provide good service to your PC users at a reasonable cost.

Automating Process Flows: The Process-Driven Model

The second model for client/server computing is the **Process-Driven Model**. With it, you may build systems using either grassroots or corporate approaches, perhaps as part of a business process redesign. It fits well with the notion of "business process reengineering," both in a department and throughout a company. However, most of the applications to date are smaller applications, so we encounter this model most often in a grassroots approach.

The Process-Driven Model stems from the idea that a large process can be broken down into smaller processes, with data and status passing between them. A main process path may have several exception paths. Several points may exist where work can enter or exit the process, although a well-designed process tries to reduce these. When work enters the process, it needs to be "told where to go" based upon the business practices the policy supports. A **workflow manager** coordinates the system's activities, shepherding each work item along the correct path. The workflow manager dictates this path, but decisions taken in individual steps of the process can cause the workflow manager to change the path. Figure 6.5 shows this model.

The Process-Driven Model is a good emulation of how people conduct business. For example, in a capital-spending justification process, a committee might decide to suspend approval of a request pending further analysis. Someone then goes off and gets the information the committee needs. When the analysis is done, the committee makes a decision. The Process-Driven Model works the same way. It allows people and machines to make decisions based upon the work entering the process. Then, the workflow manager takes the results of these decisions and guides the work item to the next step of the process for that work item.

In this approach, software designers keep the data and the processing for each step together. This differs from the other models. Here, the step itself defines how to distribute functions across computers. Steps 1 through 3 might reside on machine A, while step 4

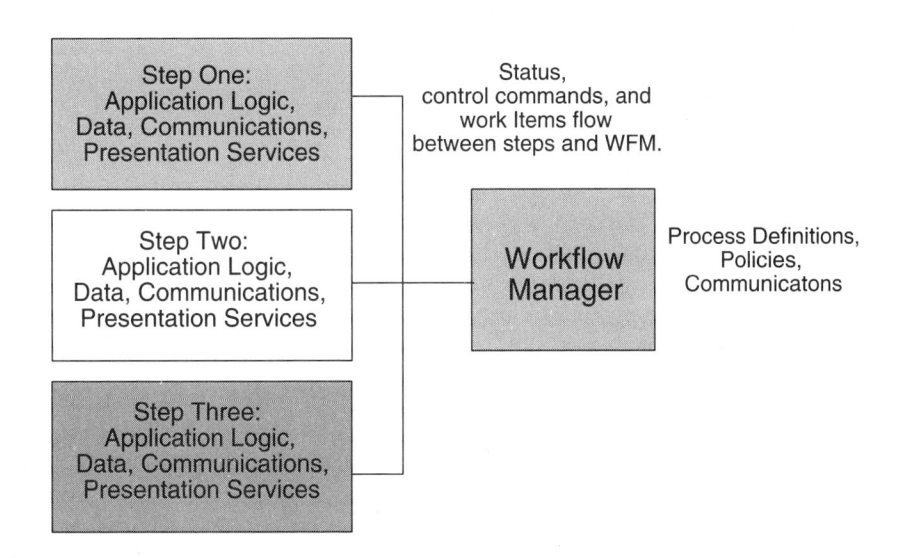

Figure 6.5. The Process-Driven Model.

runs on machine B, and steps 5 through 7 use machine C. The workflow manager also might reside on one or more machines.

Message passing is usually used to communicate between steps, allowing work to flow through the system "at its own pace." Messages inform the workflow manager of changes in status, send data between process steps, and send constraining information to process steps. The system can send messages immediately or, if it detects a failure, put messages into queues for later retransmission. The workflow manager may thus send messages reliably, even if immediate delivery is impossible. This approach provides flexibility in updating pieces of the system at a time. It also allows for downtime on individual computers for needs such as preventive maintenance and software changes. Programmers, though, can find message passing harder to understand at first than with other communications techniques, possibly increasing development costs.

A step within the Process-Driven Model may choose to use other client/server techniques, such as resource sharing. For example, a step to approve expense statements might use a database server to find the approving manager's employee number and electronic mail address. Here, the step avoids keeping track of redundant information. However, if a step uses or changes data local to another step, this breaks with the spirit of the model.

Giving Applications Face Lifts: The Front-End Model

Figure 6.6 shows the next model, the **Front-End Model**. This approach provides a graphical **front end** for existing applications. Some call it the "face lift" approach, because the looks improve while everything else remains the same. Because this approach requires no changes to the existing application, it can be done in a grassroots manner. However, the client application software depends upon consistent screens from the existing application. So, it helps to cooperate with the application's owner where possible.

GUIs, like Microsoft's Windows or IBM's OS/2 Presentation Manager, have become popular as personal computers have become a ubiquitous business tool. Because it presents a visual (versus text) screen, a **GUI (graphical user interface)** simplifies how a user relates to an application. So, using software with a GUI can decrease training time and costs, and can sometimes provide better performance.

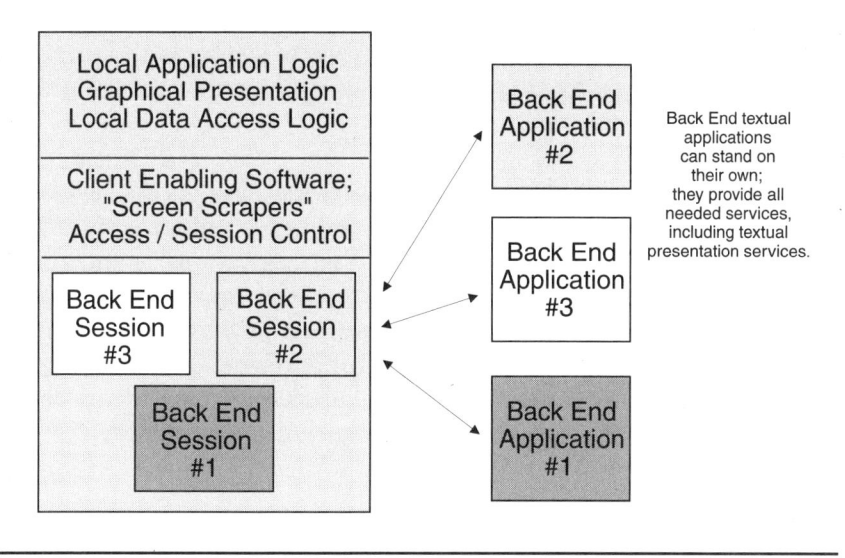

Figure 6.6. Front-End Model.

The Front-End Model increases user productivity and reduces training costs without changing the original software. A front end can also provide an integration point between multiple existing applications by providing "cut and paste" functions between them. For example, the textual output of a transaction could be "massaged" by the front end's application software, turning it into input to another program on a different computer.

In the diagram, we show three sessions to three different existing applications. Three is convenient for us; it could be one or more. The user's machine, usually a machine running OS/2, Windows, or Apple's Macintosh operating system, **MacOS System 7**, is on the left. It may contain some local program logic, and it may use local data along with data from the existing applications. The software uses these applications via a network, although we do not show the network in the diagram.

Graphical front-end enabling software (along with networking software) starts, maintains, and ends sessions with target applications or subsystems. Front ends also intercept or "scrape" data from these sessions and divert it to the local application program. There, the local program can interact with the user or manipulate the data somehow. Once this is done, the local program "pastes" the resultant information back into the session to the back-end application and sends it over the network. Sometimes, writers and programmers call the client-enabling software "**screen scrapers.**"

The back-end applications usually work with terminals, not PCs. They are complete; they may provide data access services, transaction services, locking services, and other similar services. The applications already know how to present data to users and accept textual data from users. They format streams of data, most often block mode screens, for output, and they interpret keystrokes as input. Other users may use the same back-end applications using block mode or character mode terminals, while PC users concurrently use the graphical front end. Either way, the application doesn't know that the data is coming from another program rather than a user typing on a keyboard.

This approach explicitly ties the front-end software to the back-end application. If the back-end application changes the way it sends data to a screen, for example, the front end must adapt to the new format. Let's assume an additional input field is added to one screen of a back-end application designed to interact with a block mode terminal. The positions of the existing fields also change to adapt to the new field. When the new version of the back-end application goes into production, the front end will probably function incorrectly until it also reflects the new field positions.

A second consequence of this approach is more fundamental: It doesn't change the way you do business unless you combine it with other changes. As a result, building a front end is sometimes the start of a longer journey to redesigning business processes and their supporting software. Some people might say, "Where's the server?" in this model. Well, you can look at the existing applications as the server. The protocol between the client-enabling software and the server is the data stream the application thinks is going to a terminal. The client simply interprets this data stream differently, giving the application's user a better interface.

Pointing and Clicking Over the Network: The Remote Presentation Model

The **Remote Presentation Model** is conceptually simple. First, visual output generated by an application on one system gets displayed on another. Next, the system that displays the output also takes the user's actions and turns them into input for the application. Several examples of the Remote Presentation Model exist, but two approaches dominate today: the X-Windows System and Web Browsers.

The X-Windows System

The model's first common application is the **X-Windows** windowing system. The X-Windows consortium has defined five releases of their software, sometimes called X11 or simply X. They call the current release X11 Release 5 (X11R5). The Massachusetts Institute of Technology (MIT) first developed the X-Windows system, with funding from IBM and other computer vendors, and has since licensed X-Windows to many vendors. Software that uses X11 can thus be more portable than software that uses a different way to interact with users.

X11 defines a graphical interface server that runs on the user's machine. This is different from most client/server enablers, where the client is closest to the user. UNIX-based application software commonly uses X-Windows, but many other operating systems support X11 as well.

In X-Windows, as shown in Figure 6.7, the application processing is done on the client machines. In the diagram, three client applications have three windows open on the server system; the user interacts with one of these windows (and therefore with one application) at a time. A program may have more than one window open at a time, but we show a one-to-one correspondence between windows and applications to simplify the drawing. The server provides a graphical output device for these client applications. It also takes the user's mouse movements, keystrokes, and menu choices and sends them on to the correct application. Here, the client application doesn't know how to display graphical output or grab mouse movements, so it asks for help from the server. The server and the client-enabling software are bound together by a series of events and messages both must understand; these events and messages encode the user's actions and the application's output requirements. Sometimes, writers call the protocol that defines these events and messages **X-Wire**.

The last component of X-Windows is the window manager. It defines how the windows "look and feel." It also dispatches events,

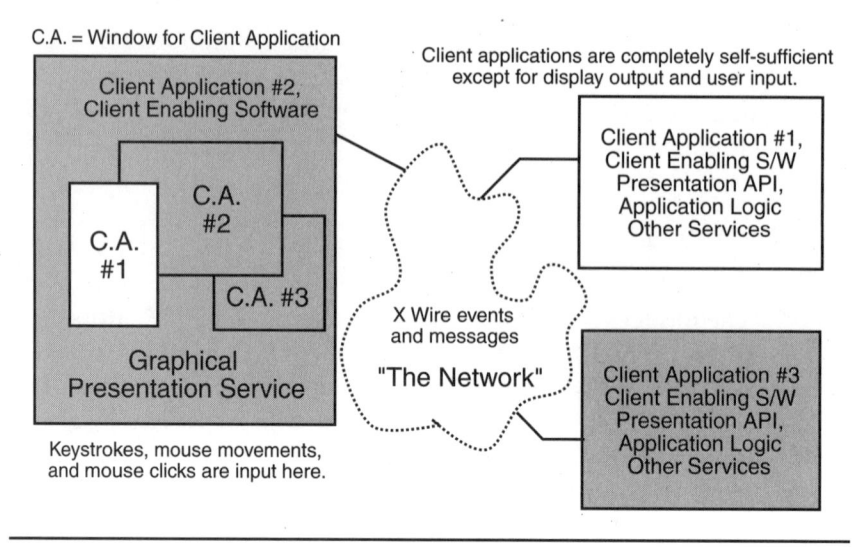

Figure 6.7. The Remote Presentation Model.

making sure all the mouse clicks and other user actions end up being sent to the correct client application. The Open Software Foundation's Motif is the most commonly used window manager.

X11 contains only openly specified protocols. So, vendors have developed several very different devices that act as X-Windows servers. On some fast, graphical workstations, such as an IBM RISC System/6000, the client application, the client enabler, and the server software can exist on the same system. IBM, among other vendors, also makes low cost devices optimized to run an X-server. These **X-terminals** have a smaller processor and a graphical, PC-like display. IBM calls its device an **X-Station**. If an X-Station user wants to run a client application, X-Windows can direct that program's I/O from the RISC System/6000 to the X-server on the X-Station. The application isn't aware that the user has a different kind of hardware; it only knows that whatever X-server it works with understands the X-Windows system.

Similarly, if an X-server from, say, Hewlett-Packard, uses Motif, then X-Windows and Motif could easily direct the application's output to the HP server. Here, an application, without change, can use the X-Windows system to display output and gather input on vastly different hardware devices.

Surfing the World Wide Web

Another common Remote Presentation application is the **World Wide Web (WWW)**. "The Web," as it is most commonly referred to, is a way of interacting with data stored on machines attached to the Internet. People use software, called a **browser**, to look around the Internet and to retrieve data, including text, images, and video, from servers located throughout the Internet.

Information developers encode data on a Web server, using a language called **HyperText Markup Language (HTML)**, into **pages**. Figure 6.8 shows a sample page (in this case, IBM's main, or "home" page). A home page usually functions like a table of contents for a firm's information. Each page almost always contains text, and pointers to other pages, especially the firm's home page. Optionally, pages can also contain images, sounds, or video clips.

Web pages are becoming increasingly useful. Some firms use pages on the Web as a product catalog. Some vendors use them to describe simple fixes to common problems, avoiding excessive telephone and warranty costs. Newer versions of the software let people using a Web page type in text. As the industry defines a way to keep financial information such as credit card numbers truly secure on the Internet,

Figure 6.8. IBM's home page on the World Wide Web.

vast new marketing possibilities are opening up. For example, someone browsing through your product catalog can place an order for a particular product.

Browsers use the pointers on a page, called **hypertext links**, to move transparently from one page to another. These pages might be on the same server or on different servers. You can also use hypertext links as buttons, to initiate actions. If, for example, you wanted to distribute software updates via the Internet, one way might be to maintain pages that describe the updates. If users wanted to get a particular updated package, a click on a button would transfer the files to their computers.

Linking these pages is important: Servers don't contain any logic to verify that a link continues to be valid. Let's say I maintained a Web page that had a hypertext link to someone else's system, A. If system A's owner moved the page to system B, but didn't tell me, my link would continue to look for system A. In that case, if a user clicked on my pointer, the reference would fail, and the user's browser would display an error message.

The linking concept can be quite powerful, as long as the links stay up to date. Without needing any centralized catalog, users can peruse matters of interest to them to any level of depth. You can go off on to tangent after tangent. On the other hand, without a centralized catalog or searching facility, the Web can be frustrating if you don't know where to look.

Firms also use Web technology for internal purposes. For example, IBM uses the World Wide Web for internal communications. The problems of severed links are also less of a problem when a Web site has a single master.

Dividing and Conquering: The Distributed Logic Model

Our next model, the **Distributed Logic Model**, does what the database vendors did years ago to develop client/server database products. In this approach, neither part of the application can stand on its own. Using the Distributed Logic Model commits a business to using PCs, cash registers, machine tools, and other programmable devices instead of ordinary terminals. This model also maintains its data centrally. This makes it suitable for critical applications and data. It also allows a firm to use distributed TP monitors to safeguard the integrity of business transactions. Figure 6.9 depicts this model's main parts.

Keeping Replicas of Data Close at Hand: The Data Staging Model

Sometimes, sending all the data needed from a central site using the Resource Sharing Model is too costly or time-consuming. Replicating the data to each PC, though, is also unwieldy in some cases. It might be useful to duplicate the data at several sites, however, if little of the data changes regularly. When these conditions fit, the **Data Staging Model** is a good choice.

Various ways exist to duplicate data to or from a central site. Duplicating data regionally might make sense if headquarters needs to use all data, but one regional office sometimes doesn't need to use another office's data. Another method "clears" all changes to data through a central site and then distributes regular data updates throughout the organization. This approach works well with a TP monitor; the TP monitor changes the data, then these changes are regularly sent to the other systems. Other policies for distributing duplicated data could be appropriate under other conditions.

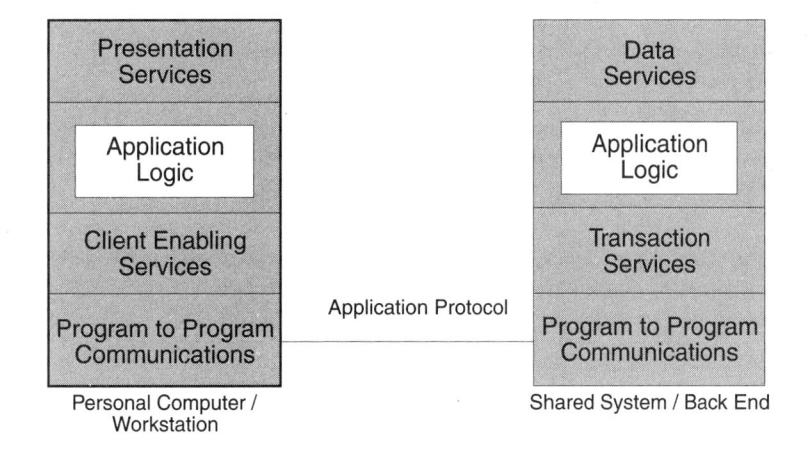

Figure 6.9. The Distributed Logic Model.

Figure 6.10 outlines a Data Staging environment. It shows updates being propagated to one or more intermediate systems. Part of the diagram might look like the Resource Sharing Model, because these models can work together well. The Resource Sharing part is optional, since the data could be staged to a shared system. To keep the distributed data up to date, a program, a schedule, or both regularly send data changes to and from the main computer. This program or schedule operates between the middle box in the diagram and the box on the right.

It is fair to say this approach optimizes the costs and performance of a centralized data storage and retrieval design. It retains the elements of centralized control over the data, but it allows access to the data quickly. This makes it suitable for use, given the right conditions, for workgroups and for critical data. Using this approach, a local facility could probably survive a limited central machine or communications failure, since the data resides locally as well.

Architectures for Client/Server Applications

An **application architecture** is a blueprint you use when you build or buy application software for use in your business. Such an architec-

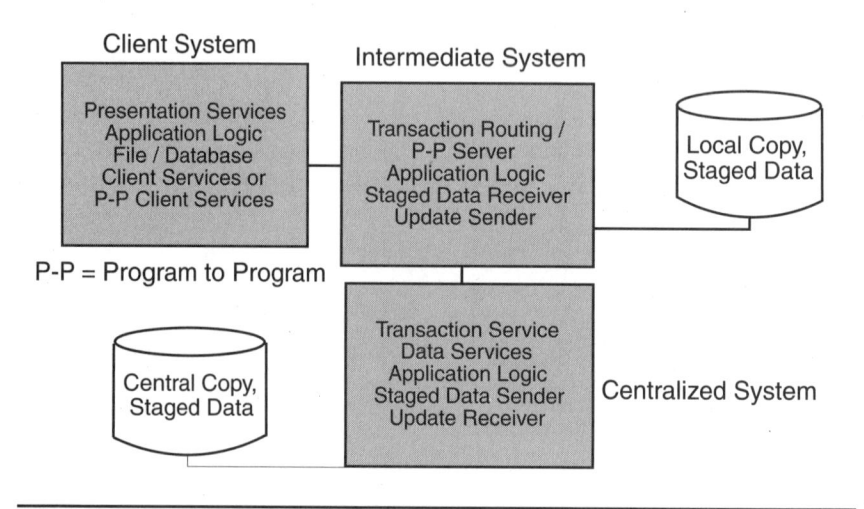

Figure 6.10. The Data Staging Model.

ture defines the relationships between the various functions within the applications you use. It can also specify relationships between applications, and it can define how the applications software used will relate to specific business functions. Loggers have felled forests of trees to supply the paper for books that discuss various architectural techniques. Much of the existing literature applies to client/server and monolithic approaches to building applications. We will only make a few observations specific to client/server computing.

Two-Tiered Client/Server Applications

A two-tiered application architecture is the easiest way to design a client/server application. Someone defines the processing to be done and then decides if each work item is best done on the server or the client. For example, a business application might include several services, such as user interface, data access, transaction management, security, or communications. A firm might buy or build services such as these to include in an application. Most often, companies would buy packages that provide these services. You would want the rules and policies that run your business to be different from other firms, however. That's where your business provides unique value for your customers.

It is simple to imagine allocating each needed service to a client or a server system. Depending upon your staff's sophistication and the demands the software puts on the hardware and the network, you'd assign where components fit best. You can easily buy or build systems designed (some say "architected," a horrid word) in two tiers. This application architecture is shown in Figure 6.11.

Most client/server computing products today fit this application architecture. In a typical Resource Sharing Model workgroup, for example, members share hardware and data without regard to the way the business itself runs. The business rules usually reside in the client application, as if the software stood alone. Two-tiered approaches are good for problems that aren't complex and where the interaction doesn't change often. Some call the two-tiered approach **"first-generation client/server computing."**

However, if you were to build and use software that defines and automates your "methods of business," where would you put those rules? Let's say you decide to place them on the client and you want

```
┌─────────────────────┐              ┌─────────────────────────┐
│      Client:        │              │        Server:          │
│   User Interface,   │              │  Database Management,   │
│  Database Access,   │              │ Transaction Management, │
│ Remote Procedure Calls │           │    Security Control,    │
│                     │              │       Accounting        │
└─────────────────────┘              └─────────────────────────┘
```

"The Network"

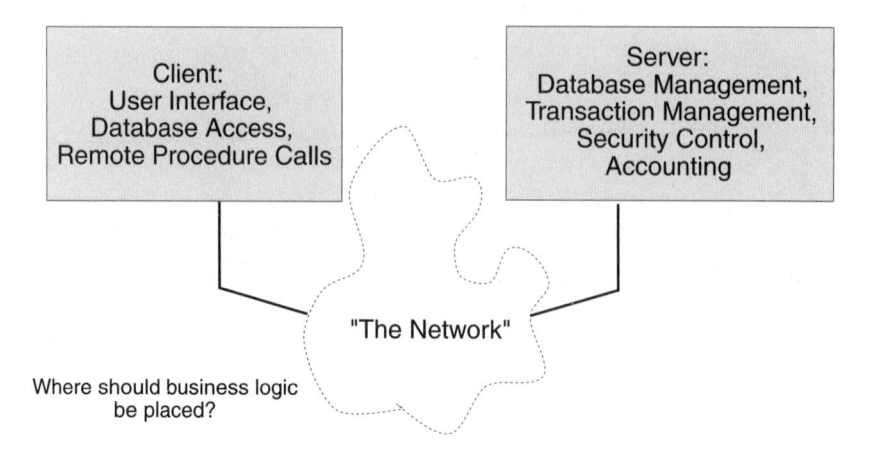

Where should business logic be placed?

Figure 6.11. A sample two-tiered architecture.

to change your accounts receivable practices: Instead of providing 15-day terms, you want to use five-day terms with electronic payments. If you put the logic for this business rule on the client, you will have to change the software on all your clients when you want to change policy. This will be much more difficult than changing your business rules on a few server systems.

On the other hand, **centralizing** the data and logic that embody the rules can intertwine them with other services, such as transaction management and data access. This may make it harder for an organization to respond flexibly to local needs. If the business logic intertwines with other services, the application could become nearly monolithic, with all the rigidity this implies. Then, client/server computing would become a more complex version of existing programs on shared systems. Also, two-tiered designs use client hardware intensively and they use more network capacity. For LAN-based applications, two-tiered approaches might work, but for applications that use WAN lines, a three-tiered design can work better.

Three-Tiered Client/Server Applications

Unlike two-tiered designs, the three-tiered approach directly recognizes the importance of your rules of business. It defines these layers:

the **user interface layer,** the **business logic layer,** sometimes called the **functional layer,** and the **data access layer.** In this view of building applications, all other services or components, such as a transaction manager or communications services, exist to make these three main components more effective. In building applications like this, you should keep the three main components separate, even if you might eventually run two of them on a single machine. Some refer to the three-tiered model as **second-generation client/server computing.** Figure 6.12 shows this approach.

```
┌─────────────────────┐              ┌─────────────────────────┐
│      Client:        │              │        Server:          │
│   User Interface,   │              │  Database Management,   │
│      Remote         │              │ Transaction Management, │
│  Procedure Calls    │              │    Security Control,    │
│                     │              │       Accounting        │
└─────────────────────┘              └─────────────────────────┘

              "The Network"          ┌─────────────────────────┐
                                     │      Middle Tier:       │
                                     │     Business Logic,     │
                                     │ Transaction Management, │
                                     │        Policies,        │
                                     │     Database Access     │
                                     └─────────────────────────┘
```

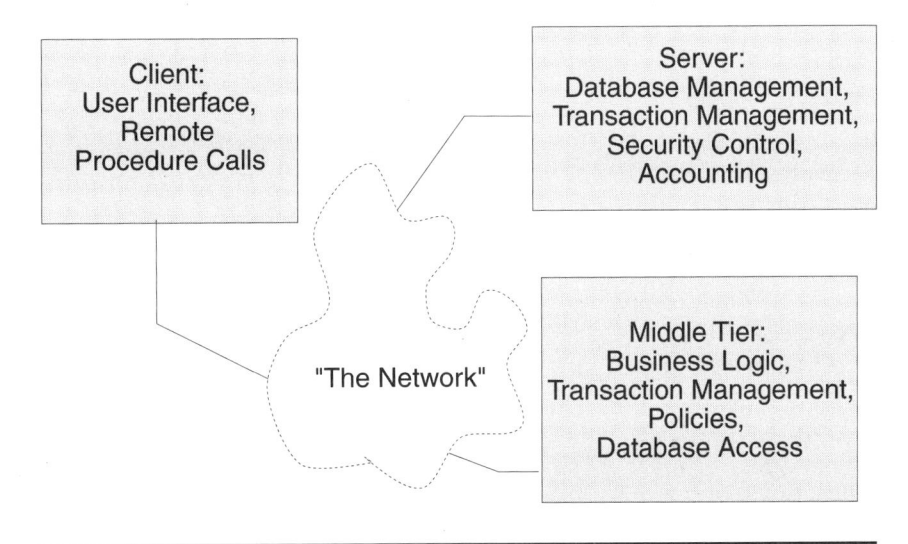

Figure 6.12. A sample three-tiered architecture.

Index

A
activity light, 63
address translation, 156
addressing storage, 133-134
AIX (Advanced Interactive eXecutive).
     See IBM's personal computers;
     RS/6000 computers
AIXwindows, 123
ALU (Arithmetic Logic Unit), 58
analog information, 162
API (application programming interface), 175, 192-193
applications software. See *the various IBM computer series*
architecture, 155
ARPANET, 2-3
AS/400 computers, 126-152
    a look at the history, 126-130
    AS/400 family, 131-133
    components, 130-131
    hardware architecture, 133-137
    CISC to RISC, 137
       overview, 133-136
    Opticonnect/400 systems, 143-145
    software, 145-149
      a software model, 145
      application programs, 146-147
      operating systems, 147
      SLIC instructions, 148-149
    software, operating systems, 147, 149-152
      OS/400, 150-152
      SSP (System Support Program), 149-150
    storage, 138-140
      disk, 139
      diskette, 138
      optical libraries, 139-140
      tape storage, 140
    storage management, 140-143
asymmetric processing, 58
AT&T development of UNIX, 84-85
authoring and publishing, 27-28

B
batch jobs, 181
BIOS, 67-68
bit, 60
bit scattering, 110
bit steering, 110
Bourne shell, 82-83
branch instructions, 106
brands, 52. *See also* naming conventions

bus, 110
bus subsystem, 162
business examples. *See also* case studies
    Knight Ridder SourceOne, 15
    Mason and Hanger, 15
    list of various businesses' uses of the Internet, 6-8
    Olympic Games business example, 23
    selling music on the Internet, 46-48
business logic layer, 209
byte, 60
byte codes, 40

C
C programming language, 122
C Shell, 83
cache, 106
    cache hit, 106
    cache miss, 106
    cache storage, 167
    data cache unit, 107-108
    ICU (Instruction Cache Unit), 106
    write-through cache, 169
capability-based addressing, 143
case studies, 43-48. *See also* business examples
    small business, Ned Connolly's Auto Parts, 44-45
    medium business, Blue Sky Musical Instruments, 45-46
    large business, Stonefield Audio/Video, 46-48
CD-ROM (Compact Disk-Read Only Memory), 139
central processor (CP), 160
centralization, 12-13, 81, 208
channel subsystem, 162
CISC (Complex Instruction Set Computing), 103, 137
client, 12, 180, 191. *See also* client/server computing
    client systems, 54
    IBM's network computing framework, 38
client/server computing, 179-209
    a basic introduction, 192-193
    approaches to client/server computing, 194-207
        Data Staging Model, 205-207
        Distributed Logic Model, 205
        Front-End Model, 198-200
        Process-Driven Model, 196-198
        Remote Presentation Model, 200-204
        Resource Sharing Model, 194-196
    architectures for client/server applications, 207-209
        two-tiered (first-generation) applications, 207-209
        three-tiered (second-generation) applications, 209
clock. *See* system clock
CMOS (complementary metal oxide semiconductor memory), 60-61
collaboration, 28-29
Common Transport Semantics framework, 189
communications protocols, standard, 3-5, 38
compatibility, upward, 156
compiling, 40
compound documents, 30
condition register, 106
connectors, 39
content
    content management, 30-34
    content on the Internet, 5
controller
    integrated, 63
    processor, 162
cost savings of network computing, 12-13
Count-Key-Date (CKD), 170
CPI-C (Common Programming Interface for Communications), 188

CPU (Central Processing Unit), 103
CPU (central processing unit), 57-58
customer services, IBM's strategy regarding, 22
cycle time, 135

D
DASD (Direct Access Storage Device), 139, 162-163, 168-171
data, percent of world's data on IBM, 13
data access layer, 209
databases
    DB2 Universal Database, 33-34
    shared document database, 27
digital information, 162
disk. *See* memory storage
diskette, 61, 63
Distributed Computing Environment (DCE), 187
DMA (Direct Memory Access), 108
domain, 81
Domino.Broadcast, use in case study example, 45-46
Domino.Merchant, use in case study example, 44-45
DOS (Disk Operating System). *See also* IBM's personal computers
    DOS extender, 72
    DOS/VS (Disk Operating System/Virtual Storage), 182
double word, 60

E
e-business as a concept, 13. *See also* IBM's e-business strategy
e-mail, 26-27
    IBM's e-business model of, 26
    influence on development of Internet, 6, 24
early adopter companies' advantage, 12
electronic commerce. *See also* Net.Commerce
    growth in commerce expected by year 2000, 19
    IBM's strategy regarding, 19-23
electronic publishing, 27-28
EMS (expanded memory specification), 71
encryption, 16. *See also* security
enhanced mode, 71
environment, 147, 176
EPROM (flash erasable programmable read only memory), 60-61
error checking and correcting (ECC), 60, 109
extensions, 123
extranets, 15. *See also* intranets

F
FAT (File Allocation Table), 81
firewalls, 16, 27. *See also* security
first-generation client/server computing, 208
fixed disk. *See* memory storage
fixed-block architecture (FBA), 170
fixed-point processor, 107
floating-point processor, 107
folders, 73
frames, 100
functional layer, 209

G
graphics, rich text, 29-30
groupware, 14, 29, 39
guest operating systems, 181
GUI (Graphical User Interface), 71, 198

H
HAL (Hardware Abstraction Layer), 80
head-disk assembly (HDA), 170
help, contextual, 152
high nodes, 100
housekeeping tasks, 147

HPFS (High Performance File System), 81
HTML (HyperText Markup Language), 203
hypertext links, 204
Hypervisor, 181

I
I/O (Input/Output)
   I/O unit, 108
   integrated I/O adapter cards, 162
   programmed I/O, 108
IBM's e-business strategy, 17-34, 36-43
   a basic introduction, 17-19
   concept of *leveraging* to help businesses, 18, 31
   content management, 30-34
      business extension, 33
      business process transformation, 33-34
      legacy system enablement, 32-33
   e-business as a concept, 13
   emphasis on environments, 18
   implementation of the e-business strategy, 36-43
      IBM Global Network, 42
      Java, 39-41
      network computing framework (software and standards), 37-39
      security, 42-43
      server hardware, 41-42
   Internet commerce, 19-23
      customer services, 22
      marketing, 20-21
      Net.Commerce, 23
      sales, 21
   intranets/extranets, 23-30
      authoring and publishing, 27-28
      collaboration, 28-29
      Lotus Notes/Domino, 29-30
      messaging and information sharing, 26

IBM's Global Services, world's largest consultancy, 13-14
IBM's Network Computing Vision, 10-17
   CEO Louis V. Gerstner, Jr., 10, 14
   creation of Internet Division, 14
   how IBM views the Internet, 10-15
   IBM/Lotus 1996 gain of new e-mail users, 14
   network computing, 10
   positioning in the business world, 13-14
   purchase of Lotus Development Corporation, 14
   recruitment of companies with Internet Specialty Program, 14-15
   research on *revolutionary* vs. *evolutionary* change, 16-17
   survey of most important business issues (Fortune 1000), 11
IBM's Networking Blueprint, 187-190. *See also* client/server computing
   applications layer, 187-188
   applications support layer, 188
   subnetworking layer, 190
   transport network layer: SNA-TCP/IP-MPTN, 189
IBM's personal computers, 49-83
   a look at the history, 49-52
      creation of the Entry Systems Division (ESD), 50-52
      Estridge, Philip (Don), 49
      XT, AT, and other early models, 50-52
   hardware, disk storage, 61-64
      CD-ROM drives, 63-64
      diskettes, 62-63
      fixed disks, 63
   hardware, microprocessors and memory, 57-61
      Intel microprocessors, 59-60

memory, 60-61
microprocessor basics, 57-58
multiprocessing, 58-59
PC family (the various models), 52-56
   IBM's Industrial Computer, 56
   IBM's Network Station, 55-56
   IBM Aptiva, 53-54
   IBM IntelliStation, 52-53, 55
   IBM Personal Computer (PC) Server, 54-55
   IBM Personal Computer (PC), 54
   IBM ThinkPad, 55
software, advanced operating systems, 70-83
   AIX (Advanced Interactive eXecutive), 82-83
   DOS Extended with Windows, 70-72
   Operating System/2 Warp, 74-77
   OS/2 LAN Server, 77
   Windows 95, 72-74
   Windows NT Server, 81-82
   Windows NT Workstation, 77-81
software, overview, 64-69
   a software model, 64
   application programs, 65-66
   BIOS, 67-68
   DOS (Disk Operating System), 69
   operating systems, 66, 68-69
IBM. *See* AS/400 computers; IBM's e-business strategy; IBM's Network Computing Vision; IBM's personal computers; RS/6000 computers; S/390 computers
Intel microprocessors, 59-60
interactive capability, 5
interactive computing, 179
interactive processing, 156
interleaving, 111
Internet InterORB Protocol (IIOP), 39

Internet. *See also* web (World Wide Web, WWW)
   a basic introduction, 1-2
   businesses on the Internet, 9-10, 15, 23, 46-48
   businesses on the Internet (list of), and various uses, 6-8
   content on the Internet, 5
   directories, 45
   evolution of the Internet, 2-5
   growth in commerce expected by year 2000, 19
   growth in services and solutions, 14
   growth of the Internet (chart), 4
   Internet publicist's role, 45
   1996 Internet World, 43
   online services, 5-6
   search engines, 45
   Strategic Internet Marketing (Tom Vassos), 25-26, 34-36
intranets, 10, 15-17. *See also* extranets
   business examples, 15
   Fortune 1000 companies with intranets, 15
   Fortune 200 companies with strategies, 10
intranets/extranets
   IBM's e-business model, 23-30
ISA (Industry Standard Architecture), 54. *See also* RS/6000 computers
ISP (Internet Service Provider), 1
IT (Information Technology), 11

J
Java, 13
   as threat to dominance of Microsoft and Intel, 13
   Center for Java Technology, 41
   HotJava, 41
   IBM's network computing framework, 38-39

Index

IBM licensing of, 41
Java technology, 39-41
JavaBeans, 38-39, 41
JavaOS, 41
servlets, 39
joint authoring, 27-28

L
LAN (local area network), 190-191
LAN consolidation, 102
legacy systems, 32-33
legacy systems, 32-33. *See also* IBM's e-business strategy
leveraging, 18, 31. *See also* IBM's e-business strategy
library, 143
LIC (Licensed Internal Code), 177
logical partition (LPAR), 160
loosely coupled computing, 143
Lotus
    Lotus Notes/Domino, IBM's e-business model, 29-30
    purchase of Lotus Development Corporation by IBM, 14

M
MacOS System 7, 199
marketing
    IBM's strategy regarding, 20-21
    Strategic Internet Marketing (Tom Vassos), 25-26, 34-36
megahertz (Mhz), 58
    system megahertz, 109
memory, 57, 60
    memory bus parity, 110
    memory failure, 60
    memory management, 111
    memory scrubbing, 110
    virtual memory, 112
memory storage
    central storage, 160-161, 168
    DASD (Direct Access Storage Device), 139, 162-163, 168-171
    disk storage, 61-64, 168
        CD-ROM drive, 63-64
        diskette, 61-63
        fixed disk (or disk), 61, 63
    expanded storage, 158, 161, 168
    main storage, 135
    optical technology, 139-140, 170-171
    processor storage, 168
    RAID (Redundant Array of Independent Disks), 82, 170
    single-level storage, 114, 142
    storage management, 140-143
    tape storage, 140, 171
    virtual storage, 142
    volatile vs. nonvolatile storage, 61, 141
microprocessors
    Intel microprocessors, 59-60
    microprocessor basics, 57-58
    multiprocessing, 58-59
Microsoft Network, 74
MIS (Management Information System), 12
modem, 162
modes, 69, 71
monolithic circuit (MLC) technology, 156
MPP (Massively Parallel Processing), 100
MQI (Messaging and Queuing Interface), 188
multi-application support, 71
multiple-system processors, 136
multiprocessing, 156
multiprocessor, 58-59, 160
multiprocessor architecture, 135-136

N

N-way multiprocessor architecture, 136
naming conventions, 89
   brands, 52
   product numbers, 54
Net.Commerce
   use in case study example, 46-48
   virtual storefronts with Net.Commerce, 23
Net.Commerce Payment, use in case study example, 46-48
network computing, 186-187. *See also* IBM's Networking Blueprint; Internet; intranets; extranets
nodes, 100
Non-Programmable Terminal (NPT), 55-56
NSFNet (National Science Foundation Network), 11-12
NTFS (NT File System), 81

O

objects and object-oriented access, 142
OLTP (online transaction processing), 98
online services, 5-6
Open Group, 125
open standards, 24
open systems, 88
operating systems software. See *the various IBM computer series*
Operational Assistant (OS/400), 150
optical technology, 139-140, 170-171
OS/2, 195. *See also* IBM's personal computers
   MacOS System 7, 199

P

page, 161
page, web, 203
paging, 113
parity bit, 110
partitions, 181
PC's (personal computers). *See* IBM's personal computers
PCI (Peripheral Component Interconnect), 54, 89. *See also* RS/6000 computers
performance gain, 59
platters, 139
Plug and Play features, 74
portability, 80
POSIX, 79
POWER (Performance Optimized With Enhanced RISC), 87
power/coolant distribution unit, 162
Power2 Super Chip (P2SC), 93
processor card, 57
processor unit, 160
protocols, standard communications, 3-5, 38
push and pull models of information distribution, 28

R

RAID (Redundant Array of Inexpensive Disks), 82, 170
RAM (random access memory), 57
RAMAC devices, 170
rapid application development, 30
RAS (Remote Access Services), 82
real mode, 69, 71
register, 58, 166
rewritable technology, 171
rich text, 29-30
RISC (Reduced Instruction Set Computing), 85, 137
ROM (read only memory), 60-61
RPC (Remote Procedure Call), 188
RS/6000 computers, 84-125
   a look at the history, 84-87
   hardware architecture, 102-115
      main memory, 109-111
      main processor, 103-109
      memory management, 111-114

symmetric multiprocessing, 114-115
RS/6000 family, 87-88
RS/6000 models, 89-92
   Micro Channel systems, 92-96
   PCI/ISA systems, 96-99
   POWERparallel SP, 99-102
software, 116-121
   a software model, 116
   application programs, 116-118
   device drivers, 119
   operating systems, overview, 118
   software compatibility, 120-121
software, AIX operating system, 118, 121-125
evolution of, 85-86, 88

S
S/390 computers, 153-185
   a look at the history, 153-160
   components, 160-163
   parallel sysplex, 172
   S/390 family, 163-165
   software, operating systems, 175-177, 178-185
      OS/390, 178-179
      VM (Virtual Machine), 179-181
      VSE (Virtual Storage Extended), 181-185
   software, overview, 172-177
      a software model, 173-174
      application programs, 174-175
      LIC (Licensed Internal Code), 177
      operating systems, 175-177
   storage, 166-172
      external storage, 168-171
      processor storage, 166-168
sales, IBM's strategy regarding, 21
schools, Internet directory of, 6
screen scrapers, 200
second-generation client/server computing, 209
second-level buffer, 167-168

security. *See also* Net.Commerce
   as the final obstacle, 11
   encryption, 16
   firewalls, 16, 27
   IBM's e-business strategy, 42-43
   Secure Electronic Transaction (SET), 23
   Secure Socket Layer (SSL), 23
   SecureWay for online businesses, 43
server, 12, 180, 191-192. *See also* client/server computing
   IBM's network computing framework, 38
   server hardware, 41-42
service virtual machines, 180
servlets, 39. *See also* Java
set associativity, 108
shared document database, 27
shared nothing environment, 100
Single System Image (SSI), 101, 172
640 KB memory limit, 70
SLIC (System Licensed Internal Code), 135, 145, 148-149
SMIT (Systems Management Interface Tool), 123
SMP (Symmetric MultiProcessing), 55, 136
software. *See the various IBM computer series*
software base, 120
solid logic technology (SLT), 155
SP Switch (SPS), 100
SPD bus, 136
speed of communications, online services, 6
standard linking, 39
standard mode, 71
storage. *See* memory storage
superscalar, 107
swapping, 113
symmetric processing, 58
system board, 57
system console, 130-131

system processor, 133
system unit, 111
sytem clock, 108-109
system clock rate, 58, 109

T
tape storage, 140, 171
TCP/IP (Transmission Control Protocol/Internet Protocol), 3-5
terabyte (TB), 93
thin nodes, 100
thrashing, 113-114, 142

U
U. S. Department of Defense, 2-3
uniprocessors, 160
UNIX operating system, 84-86, 122-125
    scientific vs. commercial users, 86-87
user interface layer, 209
user shell, 82-83

V
VAE (Virtual Addressability Extensions), 183-184
Vassos' 17 Stages (of web site development), 25-26, 34-36
VDM (virtual DOS machine), 80
virtual local area network, 179
virtual machine, 179
virtual memory, 112
    virtual storage, 142
VSE/SP (Virtual Storage Extended/System Package), 183

W
WAN (wide area network), 191
web (World Wide Web, WWW). *See also* Internet
web enablement, 34
web site development (Vassos's 17 Stages), 25-26, 34-36
web surfing, 203-205
Web browsers, 13
    as threat to dominance of Microsoft and Intel, 13
    Java-enablement, 40-41
wide nodes, 100
windows, 71
Windows. *See also* IBM's personal computers
    AIXwindows, 123
    WOW (Windows on Win32), 79
    X-Station, 202
    X-terminals, 202
    X-Windows System 201-202
    X-Wire, 201
Wizards, 74
WMRM (Write Many, Read Many), 140
word, 60
workflow, 29
    workflow manager, 197
workstation, 163. *See also* IBM's personal computers
    Control Workstation (CWS), 100-101
    workstation control unit, 163
WORM (Write Once, Read Many), 139-140
WOW (Windows on Win32), 79
write-once technology, 171

X
X-Windows System, 201-202
    X-Station, 202
    X-terminals, 202
    X-Wire, 201

Reader Feedback Sheet

Your comments and suggestions are very important in shaping future publications. Please email us at *moreinfo@maxpress.com* or photocopy this page, jot down your thoughts, and fax it to (904) 934-9981 or mail it to:

Maximum Press
Attn: Jim Hoskins
605 Silverthorn Road
Gulf Breeze, FL 32561

Exploring IBM's Bold Internet Strategy
by Jim Hoskins and Vince Lupiano
$34.95
ISBN: 1-885068-16-6

Building Intranets with Lotus Notes & Domino
by Steve Krantz
$29.95
ISBN: 1-885068-10-7

Exploring IBM Client/Server Computing
by David Bolthouse
475 pages, illustrations
$32.95
ISBN: 1-885068-04-2

Exploring IBM's New Age Mainframes
by John L. Young
512 pages, illustrations
$34.95
ISBN: 1-885068-05-0

Marketing on the Internet, Second Edition
by Mike Mathiesen
445 pages, illustrations
$34.95
ISBN: 1-885068-09-3

Exploring the IBM PC Power Series
by Jim Hoskins and David Bradley, Ph.D.
300 pages, illustrations
$29.95
ISBN: 0-9633214-5-5

Exploring IBM RS/6000 Computers, Seventh Edition
by Jim Hoskins and Dave Pinkerton
423 pages, illustrations
$34.95
ISBN: 1-885068-14-x

Exploring IBM AS/400 Computers, Seventh Edition
by Jim Hoskins and Roger Dimmick
515 pages, illustrations
$34.95
ISBN: 1-885068-13-1

To purchase a Maximum Press book, visit your local bookstore or call 1-800-989-6733 (US/Canada) or 1-609-769-8008 (International) or visit our homepage: *www.maxpress.com*

What About ProductManager?
by David Curtis
200 pages, illustrations
$34.95
ISBN: 0-9633214-4-7

What About MAPICS/DB?
by Ken Blackshaw
221 pages, illustrations
$29.95
ISBN: 0-9633214-2-0

Dr. Livingstone's On-line Shopping Safari Guidebook
by Frank Fiore
501 pages, illustrations
$24.95
ISBN: 1-885068-07-7

Exploring the IBM AS/400 Advanced 36, Second Edition
by Jim Hoskins and Roger Dimmick
105 pages, illustrations
$29.95
ISBN: 1-885068-11-5

Exploring the PowerPC Revolution! Second Edition
by Jim Hoskins and Jack Blackledge
165 pages, illustrations
$22.95
ISBN: 1-885068-02-6

Exploring IBM Personal Computers, A Business, Ninth Edition
by Jim Hoskins and Bill Wilson,
360 pages, illustrations
$34.95
ISBN: 1-885068-12-3

Real World Client/Server
by Steve Krantz
344 pages, illustrations
$29.95
ISBN: 0-9633214-7-1

Exploring IBM Print on Demand Technology
by Jim Wallace
122 pages, illustrations
$22.95
ISBN: 1-885068-06-9

To purchase a Maximum Press book, visit your local bookstore or call 1-800-989-6733 (US/Canada) or 1-609-769-8008 (International) or visit our homepage: *www.maxpress.com*